ARTHUR SCHNITZLER

THREE LATE PLAYS

STUDIES IN AUSTRIAN LITERATURE, CULTURE AND THOUGHT

TRANSLATION SERIES

ARTHUR SCHNITZLER

THREE LATE PLAYS

The Sisters, or Casanova in Spa

Seduction Comedy

The Way to the Pond

Translated and with an Afterword

by

G. J. Weinberger

ARIADNE PRESS

Library of Congress Cataloging-in-Publication Data

Schnitzler, Arthur, 1862-1931.
  [Selections. English. 1992]
  Three late plays / Arthur Schnitzler : translated with an
afterword by G.J. Weinberger.
     p.   cm.--(Studies in Austrian literature, culture, and
thought. Translation series)
     Contents: The sisters, or Casanova in Spa -- Seduction comedy --
The way to the pond.
  ISBN 0-929497-52-X
  1. Schnitzler, Arthur, 1862-1931--Translations, English.
I. Weinberger, G.J. II. Title. III. Series.
PT2638.N5A28 1992
832'.8--dc20
                                    91-40667
                                    CIP

Cover: Art Director: George McGinnis; Designer: David Hubble

Copyright ©1992 by Ariadne Press
270 Goins Court
Riverside, California 92507

In Memory
of
PAUL KNIGHT
(1916-1990)
Father-in-law, Friend

CONTENTS

ACKNOWLEDGMENTS

I completed these translations and the research for the Afterword with the support of Faculty Development and Connecticut State University-AAUP grants I received from Central Connecticut State University. I also enjoyed considerable help in the form of a reduced teaching load courtesy of Dr. George Clarke, Dean of the College of Liberal Arts and Sciences, and Mr. Ross Baiera, Chair of the English Department at CCSU.

I also wish to acknowledge the help and advice I received from a number of individuals both in this country and abroad: Mr. Ray Shinn and Mr. Norman Asbridge, colleagues at Central, Professor Herbert Lederer, of the University of Connecticut, and Dr. Jeffrey Berlin, of the Philadelphia College of Textiles and Science, who made his vast collection of dissertations on Schnitzler available to me; also Mr. Peter Michael Braunwirth, of the Österreichische Akademie der Wissenschaften in Vienna, Mr. Hartmut Cellbrot, of the Schnitzler Archive at the Albert-Ludwigs Universität in Freiburg, West Germany, and the staff at the German National Library in Marbach.

Finally, I am, as always, grateful to my wife, Jill, for her continuous support, encouragement, and critical reading of my manuscripts. Had unhappy circumstances not intervened, this volume, like my first, would also have been dedicated to her, with the epigraph, "Wo du nicht bist, kann ich nicht sein."

New Britain, Connecticut
May, 1991

iii

THE SISTERS

or

CASANOVA IN SPA

A Comedy in Verse. Three Acts in One.

CHARACTERS

ANDREA BASSI, *a well-to-do young man from Ferrara (23 years old)*

ANINA, *a young woman from the same city who has eloped with Andrea (17 years old)*

THE SUPPOSED BARON SANTIS *(40 years old)*

FLAMINIA, *the Baroness (24 years old)*

HERR VON GUDAR, *a retired Dutch officer (over 60 years old)*

CASANOVA *(32 years old)*

TERESA, *a famous dancer from Naples*

TITO, *the waiter (15 years old)*

A LORD

A WIDOW *from Amsterdam*

A LADY *from Lyon*

HER DAUGHTER

OTHER GUESTS

The action takes place in Spa, on a summer day in the middle of the eighteenth century, in a beautiful, almost magnificent bedroom of a fashionable hotel.

A door at the front right opening to the hall, another one left into the next room. A large window in the back with a view out to the park. To the right a table with writing materials. A large armoire on the left, a secretary on the right. Near the armoire a suitcase. Alcoves to the right, blocked off by a curtain.

I

ANINA   *alone. She glances out into the park and shivers*
slightly, then moves from the window to the table and begins
to write. She stops, reads over what she has written, and
continues writing, more quickly. She hears steps, hides the
letter in her bosom, and steps to the window.

GUDAR   *who was about to pass in front of the window, stops,*
offers his greeting
Lovely morning, dear lady.

ANINA   Still morning?
I thought it was already noon!

GUDAR   The sun
Says so, but no one heeds it hereabouts.
I'll bet Herr Bassi, too, is still asleep.

ANINA   I think not. That is—he's gone out already—
in response to Gudar's apparent surprise
Well, yes, like you, Herr von Gudar, who surely
Woke up at break of day just as he did.

GUDAR   Old men like me have little use for sleep.
It would be all too silly, every night
To make down payments to usurious death,
Who will soon collect our debts for living
In one lump sum.

ANINA *smiling*   I guess you had bad luck
At the card table last night?

GUDAR   It's been years
Now since I have allowed that sort of thing
To disturb my spirits. Losing does not
Concern me, and winning only barely.

ANINA   What does concern you?

GUDAR   The fall of the cards.

ANINA   Even if you don't care how they fall for you?

GUDAR   I didn't say that. I'm always drawn anew
To do combat with the forces of fate.

ANINA   Such big words for such a trifling matter.

GUDAR   Why trifling?   Whether I question the cards
   Or someone ambushes me in the tumult
   Of battle, or whether, as I dare say
   Happened in bygone days, the sparkling eyes
   Behind a mask summoned me from the dance
   To a garden's riddling dusk—neither fear
   Nor joy ever exhilarated me,
   Neither hatred nor love coursed through my blood—
   But always this: What do you want, enemy
   In the dark?—Fate, what is your plan for me?—
   So too when I'm gambling. It's all I have left
   To me now. Hence, it means a lot to me.
ANINA   And so—who was the big winner last night?
GUDAR   You don't know?
ANINA   How should I—
GUDAR   Didn't your husband—?
ANINA *quickly*   I was asleep when he came home. I hardly
   Heard him—and this morning his departure
   Didn't wake me. And yet, I certainly feel
   As if—it's still echoing in my ear—
   As if lots of gold had run through my sleep.
   And rolled one piece at a time into—there.
   *Goes to the desk and opens it, revealing a large quantity of
   gold pieces.*
GUDAR   Such quiet sleep and so noisy a husband.
ANINA *pointing to the gold*   Your gold, Herr von Gudar?
GUDAR   It still was last night.
   Today, Herr Andrea's gold.
ANINA   Oh, perhaps, if you—
   She busies herself with the gold.
   I have no doubt—Andrea will—
   with some embarrassment   how much—?
GUDAR *interrupting her*   I haven't lost anything, dear lady.
   Only Herr Bassi won.
ANINA   But who lost, then?
GUDAR   Herr Casanova. But since his ready cash
   Melted away to nothing very soon,
   It so happened that in the back and forth
   Of the game, all my gold accumulated

In front of your Herr Andrea Bassi.
ANINA   And Casanova—?
GUDAR   Owes me everything
   He lost. Another time—perhaps this evening
   Already—perhaps not until next year—
   In Homburg or wherever it may be,
   He'll repay what I was glad to lend him.
ANINA *as if asking*   An honorable man.
GUDAR   At first sight, as I am.
   One grows into one again from one day
   To the next; and, meantime, should some doubt stir,
   A thrust of the sword silences it at once.
ANINA   You mean you didn't just meet him last evening?
GUDAR *laughs*   Casanova? In Venice, long before
   He paid for his freethinking and his lighter
   Transgressions under the famous lead roof—
   He, a fop still, but handsome and insolent
   As today; I, warmed by the sun's last gleams—
   We matched our powers back then already,
   And not at the gaming table alone.
   Ten years ago! And now his star is still
   On the rise while mine has long since grown pale.
ANINA   You don't love him very much?
GUDAR   But no less
   Than I would have to love my youthful semblance
   Were we suddenly to meet in light of day.
   You didn't know him yet?
ANINA   Only by name.
GUDAR   Did Herr Bassi ever mention his name?
   Husbands in general do not like it.
ANINA   Andrea Bassi is not my husband.
GUDAR   Not yet. Maybe so. But I know people,
   As I should after a sixty-year passage
   In this world, and I think that Herr Bassi's
   Bourgeois propriety could do without
   The favor of his beloved relatives
   As little as your piety, lovely
   Frau Anina, could do without the church's
   Sacred rite and nuptial benediction.

And once adventure's delight and transport
Are scattered by raw foreign winds, causing
Children to dream of being at safe hearths,
You'll be glad to return to where, long since,
In the protective circle of a mild home,
Forgiveness awaits with wide-open arms.

ANINA I find the air here sufficiently mild,
The area charming, the company cheerful,
And we're both as comfortable as could be.

GUDAR But you could hardly have foreseen, a few
Weeks ago, that you'd be with such people—

ANINA With such people?

GUDAR   Like me and the likes of me,
Dining with them, living next door to them,
And taking part in their pleasure-seeking.

ANINA I am not that refined. And nobody,
Neither man nor woman, has violated
My sense of civility or decency
With so much as a word. Baron von Santis,
If noisy when drunk, is always gallant.
Flaminia, though I've noticed her to be
Loose of tongue, has a good heart nonetheless.
faltering somewhat
And Casanova—is a nobleman—

GUDAR Just as Santis is a baron, or I
A prince, or Flaminia perhaps a nun—

ANINA And Casanova?—

GUDAR   Well, where he's concerned,
There where one finds him is where he belongs.
And were I to run into him next year
As an official in Spain;—on the Strand
In London in a den of thieves among
Other rowdies;—as a lace merchant in Paris;—
As the author of a pastoral play
In a Breton castle;—as a police
Agent—as a millionaire, a beggar,
Or even as a common citizen,—
It would not surprise me at all, nor him.
And even if he lost last night—it's still

Possible that he played with a marked deck—
Just as he often lies with truthful words.
This is Herr Casanova. No swindler
Was ever more sincere than he, and never
Did I so little trust a man of honor.
And if I add to this that no woman
He desired ever refused her favors,
Then you will know as much as all the world.

ANINA   Truly, I wish I'd known you in your youth.

GUDAR   Me?

ANINA   Yes, because you spoke of none other.

GUDAR   Only of Casanova. Who, of course
Sprang into being like other young people
And will, one day, I think, end like they do—

ANINA *smiling* Just as wise, you mean—?

GUDAR   No, as long-winded!—
He bows to her and exits.

ANINA   *remains lost in thought briefly, then brings out her letter again, continues writing, folds it and puts it in an envelope, addresses it, picks up the small bell that is standing on the table, but does not ring it; she reflects a moment, then opens the door to the right, carefully looks out into the hall left and right, waves; TITO, a waiter, young, very handsome, still a boy almost, 15 years old, enters.*

TITO   Madame? How may I be of service?

ANINA   Tell me—the gentleman who arrived here
At noon yesterday—
she falters

TITO   Which gentleman? Several gentlemen arrived. . . .

ANINA *quickly* Herr Casanova,
Isn't he staying here—in this hotel?

TITO   Herr Casanova has taken lodgings at "The Golden Lion." We had no more vacancies. That's what "The Golden Lion" lives from. What shall I tell Herr Casanova, Madame?

ANINA *gives him a gold piece* Tell him. . . nothing. Take this letter to him.

TITO   Right away.
About to go.

ANINA   Just a moment. It's a bet, understand?

So, everything depends on its remaining
A secret. Therefore, conceal the letter.

TITO   Oh, Madame can rest completely easy. And shall I
bring the answer back here?

ANINA   No, no answer. You are to leave at once.

TITO   And if Herr Casanova should not be at home, may I
leave the letter with his servant?

ANINA   Yes, you will leave it there in any case.

TITO   I would only ask Madame to consider that the servant
may be a young woman in disguise.

ANINA   You think?

TITO   I don't think anything. I don't even know if Herr
Casanova arrived with a servant.

ANINA   Well then?

TITO   But there could also be someone hidden in his room.
In the closet—in the bed—

ANINA   And why do you suspect that?

TITO   I suspect nothing at all. I'm only offering all the possibilities for Madame's consideration.

ANINA   You're very bright. . . so you can be trusted.
She gives him another gold piece.

TITO   Madame will win her bet. And if Madame should have
any further wishes?

ANINA   No, nothing else.

TITO   I only mean that. . .

ANINA *impatiently*   What is it you want, then?

TITO   We have other rooms here in the hotel. With invisible
doors. One can walk past them without noticing a thing.
They catch in their locks inaudibly. Our loveliest rooms. . .
with the widest beds. And mirrors everywhere, even on the
ceiling.

ANINA   Did I ask you about that?—We are quite
Satisfied here, I and Herr Bassi too.

TITO   Well, if it depended on the husbands—

ANINA   Will you get out finally? Here—
She gives him another gold piece.

TITO   If instead of this last gold piece, I could ask for a
kiss. . .

ANINA   You're mad.

TITO   That may very well be, Madame,—and really, it's no
   wonder.
ANINA *kisses him quickly*   There.
TITO   I fly. *Exits.*
ANINA *alone*   What will become of me? What has?
   A knock at the door to the left   Who's there?
FLAMINIA *in the next room*   It's me, Flaminia.
ANINA   Yes, I'll be right
   there.
   She opens the door to the left, which had been locked.

ANINA, FLAMINIA

FLAMINIA   You're   dressed   already—? Good   morning,
   dearest—
   So early? I'm still half naked. You see?
   She lifts her dress
   Was it immodest for me simply to knock?
   But since we're neighbors—
   looks around   I stayed in this room
   Once, too. I recognize it. Just three days.
   It was autumn. We had to light the stove.
   Oh, how I hate the cold. Imagine, I saw
   My first snow as a sixteen-year-old girl.
   It never snows in Palermo. With you
   In Mantua—
ANINA   Ferrara. . .
FLAMINIA   I suppose it snows?
   Yes, you in the north are practically Germans.
   At the window
   A great day.
ANINA   Too lovely, almost. I wonder
   If we'll have a storm—?
FLAMINIA   If so, the faro
   Will start right after lunch. Good for Herr Bassi,
   If he plays with as much luck as last night.
ANINA   You took part?
FLAMINIA   No, Santis told me of it.
ANINA   He won also?

FLAMINIA   One can not compel fate.
  So he quit right after the game began.
  Then too, he doesn't like it very much
  When a player who borrows money sits
  At the table, and when the deadbeat's name
  Is unfortunately Casanova.
ANINA I thought he was rich?
FLAMINIA   Rich, him? In words, yes,
  In lies. Do you perhaps believe the tale
  He served up for us about his escape
  From the prison in which the Supreme Council
  Of Venice had for good cause locked him up?
  This digging, sawing, sliding, climbing, swimming,—
  And no one hears him, no one sees him, no one
  Recognizes him, and he sits on a roof
  In the moonlight, and takes another man
  With him—?! It's too silly.
ANINA   He did escape.
FLAMINIA Who knows? Maybe he was never in jail.
  And if, then he served his time like others.
  And if he fled, who says he succeeded?
  He plummeted from the roof, drowned—
ANINA   And lives. . . ?
FLAMINIA Perhaps not. It needn't be him, after all.
  A swindler.
ANINA   And the true Casanova?
FLAMINIA Either Casanova or true. But both—
  Never!
ANINA But you must be able to tell,
  Since you knew him years ago, after all.
FLAMINIA Knew him? I saw him. Spoke to him. Or not.
  He spoke, only he. I believe this man
  Has never heard another person's voice.
  Three times in my life I've met him, and each time,
  After we had barely exchanged greetings,
  He tells me the story of his escape,
  In the same words, in the same tone, almost.
  So it was last fall, and two years ago. . . .
  And seven years ago too, in Rome, when still

Almost a child, I saw him for the first time.
ANINA But wasn't that before he went to jail?
FLAMINIA Now you see, the whole thing was invented.
ANINA Still, it does seem you paid close attention.
FLAMINIA I was curious, dear, whether he would dare
    Put that old jest over on us again
    In my presence, and whether, considering
    His wicked lifestyle, his voice still retains
    The youthful ring which, so they say,
    Was very dangerous to women once.
ANINA Only once?
FLAMINIA   Yes, of course! His time is past.
    He arrived here alone. The last woman
    Gave him his walking papers in Brussels
    Three days ago. He told us so himself.
    Her name is Teresa. Former dancer.
    I saw her in Milan. A small round thing
    With a tiny nose. Any man could have her
    For ten ducats, —for two if she liked him.
    That calls itself a dancer. The singers
    Are just the same. Casanova's triumphs!
    Now she's danced away from him, or rather
    Rolled away—since she resembles a ball—
    And Casanova cries for her.
ANINA   I saw
    No sign of tears in his eyes yesterday.
    I found him gay, and his glance was radiant.
FLAMINIA You never saw him in his salad days.
    Today he's no more than a weeping willow.
ANINA *as if with pity* And still so young!
FLAMINIA   I assume Teresa
    Must know why she left him. And we've already
    Squandered too many words on a shadow.
    You are alone? Herr Bassi has gone out?
    I'll wager he's running through all the shops
    Searching after a pearl necklace worthy
    Of both his wealth and of your lovely neck.
ANINA He's not rich.
FLAMINIA   Today he is. And I hope

You'll be smart enough to seize the day's luck.
Indicating her own necklace
This we can always count on when the whim
Of the cards turns against their lord again.
You're smiling sadly? Don't tell me he's stingy?
ANINA Really, he's not. Yet he knows very well
That my heart does not pine for jewelry.
And if he's gone it's to stroll in the fields
And meadows alone, after his fashion.
FLAMINIA Oh, a philosopher, a poet even?
He looks it. Serious furrows in his brow,
The curly hair tangled but well cared for,
The dress distinguished yet a bit careless,
The eye veiled, although it can also glow. . .
A handsome man, his name too. . . *dreamily,*

Andrea. . . .

How long have you two been traveling around?
ANINA Three weeks,—*quickly* and we're going to be
married.
FLAMINIA So soon? Well, yes. We did it that way too.
Santis and I. Yes, I'm his wife. Don't repeat
This, my dear, because some men are scared off
By that sort of thing. The first man I loved,—
shrugging her shoulders
Well, that's what it's called!—I was just fourteen,
What does one know then,—he became my husband!
I have not regretted it. After all,
One can live and travel more securely
With so permanent an escort. We know
Each other, and that's worth something, surely.
You will see, my child,—if your destiny
Turns out akin to mine, as I foresee.
And why not?—The landlord—What do you think?—
He took us for sisters.
ANINA *almost alarmed* Really. . .
FLAMINIA   Really.
Naturally, you as my younger one. Well,
I was glad to let him because I'm so
Sincerely attached to you. Don't you feel

As if we have known each other for years?
I don't see it as a coincidence
That your carriage lost a wheel in the wood
Just outside Spa and you had to share ours,
But as providence.
ANINA   As providence even—?
FLAMINIA Santis also interpreted it so.
    Only today he told me: if two couples
    Like you and I, and Bassi and his girl
    Joined forces cleverly for work and play—
    It would turn out most advantageously
    For us all. Because—these are Santis' words—
    I must acknowledge Bassi as my master.
ANINA As master—? In what?
FLAMINIA   You're asking me, dear?
ANINA *alarmed* In gambling—?
FLAMINIA *by the by*   Perhaps in other things too.
ANINA He never touched a playing card before.
FLAMINIA *in disbelief* Oh, dear child—
ANINA *increasingly excited*   How ever should he
    have learned
    These sorts of—arts—in Ferrara, the son
    Of a highly respected merchant, or
    In Bologna at the University!
FLAMINIA   There or elsewhere!
ANINA   You're
    mistaken! His parents'
    Opposition—because I'm not wealthy—
    Drove us out—
FLAMINIA *interrupting her* Nonetheless, you are out now,
    That's how it starts. The flight becomes a trip,
    The trip, taken of necessity, becomes
    A cheerful journey, the mind grows easy,
    And things get learned abroad—mostly only
    Gradually—sometimes overnight—which
    The constrictions of home withhold from us.
    You're how old?
ANINA   Eighteen already.
FLAMINIA   Eighteen!

I'm twenty-four. And it has been ten years
Since Santis and I—! Oh, how young I was!
And when I think that Santis loved me then,
And does today, it might seem strange what he
Let me become. But one gets used to it.
And there is nothing more gay, believe me,
Than nestling heart to heart and whispering
Our latest adventures to each other.
How we laugh! Oh, because the world is dumb.
The more so, men—

SANTIS *enters. Over forty, tall and stout.*
ANINA, FLAMINIA

SANTIS   Greetings to you, ladies.
    To Anina, whose hand he kisses respectfully
    Did you sleep well, loveliest of women?
ANINA Excellently.
FLAMINIA   And what have you been up to?
SANTIS I've been offered a horse at a good price.
    I've tried it out on open ground, but I
    Believe it wants a less weighty rider—
    Say of Herr Bassi's well-proportioned frame.
    If he likes it I will let him have it.
ANINA You've already spoken with him?
SANTIS   Not yet.
    I thought of it just now, when I saw him.
ANINA *controlling her excitement* Where did you see him?
SANTIS   In
    the park, only
    From afar. I rode past. He was resting
    Upon a bench in the shade of dark trees—
    And I dare say he was dreaming! Not even
    The horse's hoofbeats could make him raise up
    His glance from the ground.
FLAMINIA   A philosopher!
SANTIS The mask becomes him very well.
ANINA *surprised*   The mask?
SANTIS Noble lady, who does not wear a mask?

It's hardly proper to show one's real face
In this carnival madness before midnight.
ANINA   And when does midnight arrive?
SANTIS   When we like.
ANINA   It seems you're the philosopher, Baron?
SANTIS   I really am! Yes, *in a new tone*   and thus always careful
That not a single hour be wasted.
It's a gorgeous day, let us savor it.
The table will be set up in the park—
I've given the order already, twelve
Settings—
FLAMINIA   Twelve?
SANTIS   I invited a few guests.
FLAMINIA   What sort of guests?
SANTIS   Gentlemen and ladies
Who seem worthy of so high an honor.
So, among others, a lord from England
Who, young and unwived, arrived this morning
In a splendid carriage, packed to the roof,
Engaged in his grand European tour.
Then a widow—comes here from Amsterdam—
Weighed down both by mourning and Dutch guilders
And very anxious to be rid of both.
FLAMINIA *to Anina*   You may quite trust his nose. He can smell gold
In trunk or pouch from a distance of miles.
ANINA   So, then we're going to dine with strangers?
SANTIS   To sit down with strangers—no doubt; however,
After a well-lubricated feast
With newly won friends to ride into nature,
Where we'll see how things develop. Gudar
Will join the excursion, Casanova
Too, if he's awake by then, for when I
Inquired after him at the "Lion" earlier
He was still sleeping off last night's bad luck.
FLAMINIA   You didn't speak with him?
SANTIS   His door was locked.
I'll fetch him later myself. He must come.

FLAMINIA Of course. It wouldn't be a real party
If he didn't tell his lead-roof legend.
SANTIS That wicked little mouth! Well, not the first
That he could quickly reconcile with kisses.
Good naturedly
And yet he seems not to desire yours.
To Anina
For the third time over the years he brushes
Past her—and now, as before, this man, else
So easily enflamed, remains unmoved.
FLAMINIA Look out, if ever I should want to move him.
But I wouldn't dream of it. The fool, the fop!
SANTIS *pointing out the window*
Here comes Herr Bassi.
ANINA *to herself*   At last.
SANTIS   Good morning!
FLAMINIA He barely returned our greeting.
SANTIS   Really,
He looks as if he had worked very hard
For last night's prize—and been cheated out of it.

ANDREA BASSI *enters.* FLAMINIA, ANINA, SANTIS.

ANDREA Oh, you have guests—
FLAMINIA   You didn't see us?
ANDREA   I did,
But I took this to be the Baron's room,
To Flaminia
Since I saw just you and not Anina—
off-hand
To whom I still owe a good morning kiss.
Kisses her fleetingly on the forehead
I bid the friendly visitors welcome.
He kisses Flaminia's hand, then extends his own to the Baron.
SANTIS What have you brought us from your morning stroll,
Andrea? A sonnet? Or some new tercets?—
What? Or a theory of the world's design?
ANDREA I wonder if I'd reveal the secret

If I did discover it! Tell me, Baron,
How did your morning ride agree with you?
SANTIS You saw me?
ANDREA   As one occasionally
Sees something with just the whites of his eyes.
But I wasn't pondering world enigmas,
Nor even a verse. The garden's fragrance,
The blue sky, the blowing of the spring breezes
Was ode enough for me; and I received
The immanent secret with reverence.
SANTIS Then our plans are in accord with your mood,
Since we've decided to conclude this day
With a delightful ride in the springtime
Breeze across open plains to a meadow
Superbly shaded by dark forest foliage;
There we'll have a small party, with dancing
And playing.
ANDREA   A party—?! This goes beyond
My inclination. Nonetheless, let us
Celebrate it with all the exuberance
Customary in so cheerful a place.
To Santis
Your winking tells me you have seen to that.
When night falls, unveiled forest nymphs will float
From bush to bush and squander their favors
On mere mortals—and woe to any man
Who recognizes them in the morning—
And—is my guess right?—instead of green cloth,
A luminous, white woman's body—fate
Will settle whose—will be our gaming table,
On which fortune will roll in golden waves—
And the loser—will be the big winner.
SANTIS *nodding in approval, to Flaminia* What did I tell
you? My master.
ANDREA   Baron,
You're flattering me. *In a new tone*
                      But on no account
Must the swords be forgotten! Well-honed ones!
Because one sometimes knows how a party

Like this begins, but never—how it will end.
FLAMINIA *to Santis* Why is he looking so wild, suddenly?
ANDREA *lightly* And that holds not just for parties, alas.
SANTIS *after a pause* If your disposition were not to change,
    You'd make for an irksome companion. Still,
    Before we meet again at the table
    Being set for us in the shade out there,
    One can see in the background waiters setting the table on
    the lawn under the trees.
    The sweet woman God granted you will smooth
    The somber furrows on your poet's brow.
    Come, Flaminia!
    Softly to her, as they leave
                There's a battle brewing!
    Santis and Flaminia exit left.

ANDREA, ANINA

ANDREA *calmly, with determination* You wrote him. What?
ANINA   Will you listen to me—?
ANDREA If I didn't want to listen to you
    I would not have asked. What did you write him?
ANINA Don't speak to me in such an angry voice.
    You know I neither want to lie, nor can.
ANDREA You wrote a letter to Casanova?
ANINA *surprised* You—didn't know it, Andrea—?!
ANDREA   I did, yes!
    I knew it. That boy. Tito is his name,
    And young as he is, pale from his vices,
    I saw him sneak in the gate of the inn
    Where Casanova lives. And right away
    I had a flash (no hunch has yet deceived
    This heart—!) A letter from you—! The pretext
    Too I know: lace! Whether that friend in Brussels,
    Of whom he spoke—(I heard with half an ear)
    Can really deliver it so cheaply.
    One pays three times as much in the shops here.
    I saw at once how you desired it;
    And Herr Casanova, as obliging

To lovely ladies as he always is,
Offered himself to serve as middleman—?
Stops, as if waiting for a reply.
ANINA   He did.
ANDREA   Yes, I heard him.
ANINA *with a sad smile*   With half an ear.
ANDREA   So you bother him about such trifles,
   As if you were in all that great a rush
   To be in touch with him, by a letter
   That will only send that spoiled man a sign
   That you're tempted to be in touch with him
   Before meeting him again in person.
   A letter to Casanova! Foolish child!
   And through Tito, yet! You lower yourself
   To a servant's joke by that—and me too.
ANINA *as above*   Which is even worse.
ANDREA *as if lying in wait*   What did he reply?
ANINA   Surely you know that Tito brought me none.
   In response to an impatient gesture on Andrea's part
   Nor will. Because you see, your hunch was wrong.
   I'd long since forgotten the Brussels lace,
   And there was no question in my letter.
ANDREA *slowly*   What then, Anina?
ANINA   A request only.
ANDREA   And of what kind?
ANINA   That he get out of town
   This very hour.
ANDREA   Casanova—?!
ANINA   He.
   Pause.
ANDREA   The danger was that great?—That unavoidable?
   That if you were to meet him one more time—
   wincing
   His glance—an indifferent conversation—
   Not a single word of it escaped me—
   And you have become his slave—? And I am
   Nothing more to you?
ANINA   Listen to me!
ANDREA   —Nothing!—

Why did you send him a messenger then?
Why not go yourself—fly into his arms?
Why still here, as if expecting my thanks,
As if you were not past recovery
Already, and forever lost to me,
Even if you never saw him again!
As if longing were not a thousand times
Worse than fulfillment, since rooting about
Unceasingly in the depths of the soul,
It muddies its pure course back to its source—!
But don't worry, he's not leaving, because
He read your letter after his fashion
As a dandy, and he will stay in Spa.
And he is right. You have the choice. Andrea
Or Casanova. No, you have no choice.
Because the one who is leaving is me.
Turns around to leave.

ANINA   He went before you.

ANDREA   And let you know?

ANINA   No.

ANDREA   Flaminia brought you the information?

ANINA   I've demanded that he get out of town
   At once—as thanks, which he can't refuse me.

ANDREA   As thanks—? For what—?

ANINA   For being his last night.

ANDREA *remains fixed, then goes up to her and stops in front
   of her; she remains motionless. Pause. He bursts out
   laughing.*   A bad jest, and it becomes you badly.
   You must have learned it from Flaminia.
   You complained to her—I know—that I torment
   You with my jealousy, so she advised
   A play of revenge done in the manner
   Of silly comedies, in which the maid's
   Faithfulness proves in the end to have been
   As shining as her man's mistrust was foolish.
   But such roles are foreign to your character
   As to my taste. Leave it to Flaminia
   And the likes of her to make sport of feelings
   Which can't be grasped by a heart for which love

Signifies a business, a commercial transaction,
Perhaps a joke, at best a fleeting pleasure.
By God, it galled me to find her and her
Ever-so-refined Santis, the Baron,
Acting the friendly neighbors in our room.
How could you dare!—And not enough that you
Allowed them to cross our threshold—Intimate
With such a pair, indeed, plotting with them!—
Because only they could have hatched this jest.
Really, I would never have imagined
That you, barely out of your parents' house,
Could get along so well with such people.

ANINA But not as well as you, Andrea, who
Already had a splendid conversation
With Flaminia in the coach—as at table,
Where you emptied one glass after another
With the Baron, and didn't find your way
Home from the card game until this morning.

ANDREA *sighing in relief* So that's it—?! One time and
never again!
But since by chance our journey turned out so,
I gladly used the opportunity
To look deeper into such goings-on
Than the usual day's routine allows.
And it turned out fairly well. Look, I won
he opens the secretary
This much. Enough gold for us to travel
About in style for another year and more.
But in the future, I beg you, let us,
Regardless if we break a spoke or shaft,
Beware of such questionable company.
I as well as you. And boldly turning
Away, escape from every temptation;—
Let the menacing tumult and danger
Of this place be shunned by us from this moment—
And let us ride away on the fast mail.
Get ready.

ANINA   I am. But I rather doubt
Whether our paths will run together.

ANDREA What's this, Anina? If I've forgiven
   Your all too nasty joke so readily,
   How can you continue angry with me
   That I forgot you for one night—the first
   And last—spent with drinking and gaming comrades.
   Not with Flaminia, who—you saw yourself—
   Withdrew from the company before you.
ANINA Do you enjoy misreading me, Andrea,
   And rather believe in grudges or revenge,
   Of which my heart knows nothing, than accept
   That with which your joyless, melancholy
   Mind darkened our youthful happiness,
   And—oh, grasp at last, what I myself can't grasp—
   What turned into reality last night.
ANDREA Say it.
ANINA   Yet again?
ANDREA   Casanova?
ANINA   Yes.
ANDREA *at first fixed, then he pulls out his sword and goes up to her.*
ANINA Lay on! Would I have said a single word
   If I'd not been prepared for such an end?
ANDREA He threatened your life! Gagged you! Mixed a potion
   In your wine at dinner! You didn't notice.
   He's well versed in that sort of trickery.—
   No sorcerer—but certainly a knave.
   Who doesn't know it? You advised him to flee—
   He can't be far.—Oh, do you think my sword,
   Which I crossed with nobler ones in Bologna—?!
   I will not defile it. *He puts the sword away*
                    In the galleys
   Let him be thrown, as the criminal he is.
ANINA Perhaps, but I have no right to accuse him.
   Long pause.
ANDREA *calmly* So, an accomplice, then—and you're still here?
ANINA Whether we must split is your decision.
   I want to hide nothing. But will you listen?

ANDREA *nods in silence, then lowers himself into a chair.*
ANINA   I was alone. The time dragged slowly by,
In vain I waited for you, sleeplessly.
My heart listened anxiously to the dark
Until touched by the silence all around,
It gradually grew mute and tired too.
I dozed off;—when from the garden's stillness
A suspicious rustling assails my ear;—
A coat brushes against bush and branches—
And gravel crunches under hasty steps.
At that I start. Who can it be but you—?
To the window. A light glows in the dark
softly
From my body.—And pale in the light stands
A man before my eyes, who is not you.
And I—as if extinguishing myself—
Rush back into the shadows of the walls,
But he—
ANDREA   Casanova?
ANINA   Casanova.
ANDREA   Whom you could recognize in your body's
Pale light.
ANINA   It was he. And before my lips
Can form a scream, he has brazenly swung
Himself over the sill, into the room,
Stands so near me that his breath wafts over
My eyelids, that his pulse trembles with mine;—
In his breath—which, cool and hot together,
Promises no kiss, much more a whisper
Without words, an entreaty, or a spell,
But finally, oh yes, craved by my mouth,
Becomes a kiss—all my being dissolves,
And upon the dream waves of this hour,
Conscious of neither past nor future ones,
It drifts away, as if freed from itself.
Pause.
As I awoke at dawn, I was alone
And lay with open eyes and knew full well
That what had taken place during the night

Would have appeared a few hours before,
Not just to others but also to me,
Andrea, as the heaviest offense—and not
As one committed only against you.
And yet—my soul was light and truly glad.
But this amazed me more than made me shudder.—
So wholly committed to you last night
That the mere idea of another man's
Touching my hand with impure intentions
Would fill me with disgust,—and next morning
To wake from a stranger's wildest embrace
As free of remorse as from a child's sleep?!
Yesterday still incomprehensible—
And today experienced?! And I'm the same
Person I was—as unchanged and unconfused,
And as worthy, Andrea, of your tenderness,
As if whatever cruel pain I cause you
And you return as anger multiplied
Must be scattered before these candid words
Which confess—freely—what one could conceal.

ANDREA *makes a gesture of scorn.*

ANINA It is so easy to tell a welcome lie.
Forgive my disdaining to offer it.

ANDREA Now I've listened. And only ask again,
Why are you still here?

ANINA   Because nothing happened.

ANDREA You mock me in the end?

ANINA   I'm yours alone.

ANDREA But you were his.

ANINA   That hour will not return.

ANDREA That is the way with hours. However,
From each one, as from each inn you've lodged at,
And were it to go up in flames behind you,
You will always wear the scent in your hair.
And that hour was.

ANINA *drawing close to him*
                But this one is now.

ANDREA And others will come. And in none of them—
Even if thousands were allotted me—

Would I ever forget that during one
Of them—even if it was half euphoria,
Half assault, and its magic caused your reason
To wither—during this one I lost you.
What avails your sending him off quickly?
Does he not take the hour's memories,
Your body's fragrance, the lingering taste
Of your kisses, the sound of blissful sighs
On his journey—even if it takes him
Across the ocean and to distant lands—?
Are you since last night not one more of all
The women he has taken for his pleasure—?
And when the lovely train of conquered beauties
Drifts naked past his mind's eye, will Andrea's
Bride not be among them? And when to amuse
His drunken friends he prattles shamelessly
About his adventures, will that circle's
Lascivious laughter not reward the rare,
Insolent jest, how Casanova sprang
Through a window from which, as otherwise
A bashful gleam from a lamp, this evening
A woman's white body showed him the way—
And how he delighted in the little bride,
While the groom sat at the gaming table?!
In breaking fury, at the desk, which he opens.
Here's the devilish gold, you will need it—
At least at first, until you've learned the rest
From Flaminia. I'm not worried for you.
Because you really do stand here unchanged,
As you boast. I only know you too late,
Who is so made, that she deceives her mother
First—
ANINA   For you.
ANDREA   Since I happened to be there.
   Then another came, and now I'm deceived.
   Here, take it, all this! Send a messenger
   After him, and let him know you've grown rich.
   He'll fly back. Or did you already plan
   To entice another languishing lover

Tonight with the pale gleam of your nakedness?
It's the same to me. The bond between us
Is torn forever, and I crush its shreds
Beneath my feet. Go! A short interval
Only, and this, the scene of my disgrace,
Will lie behind me like a gloomy fog,—
And behind me measureless delusion.
He rushes to the door.

ANINA Forsake me, as is your right, or rather,
After the conversation we've just had,
As has turned into your obligation,—
And mine, to order you out of my way.
Because, believe me, I feel more deeply
Still than you that out of this dark hour
No mutual path will lead us to the light.
But you may not, therefore, scorn those past ones,
The deathless hours of our happiness.
They are mine as well, I'll preserve my share
Even from you, as I would your picture.
But you, leave now, and take your gold with you.

ANDREA I'll not touch it, it's yours and no one else's,
As if he had paid it for your favors.
He turns to go. There is a knock on the door.

ANDREA Who is it?

TITO *opens the door, stands in the doorway.*

ANDREA   You, boy—*quickly shuts the desk.*

TITO   Herr Andrea Bassi?

ANDREA You know that's my name. A message for me?

TITO Herr Casanova desires to speak to the gentleman.

ANDREA   To
    me—Casanova?

TITO Yes, sir. He is waiting outside.

ANDREA   To me? You heard
    Right—to Herr Bassi—boy?

TITO To Herr Bassi, but—alone.

ANDREA   He may come in.

TITO *exits.*

ANDREA *locks the door behind him.* What is this?

ANINA   I don't

know. But whatever
It may be, consider well that the bond
Between us is torn. You will be sorry
If you act as if it still existed.
A knock at the door.
Flaminia will forgive my returning
Her visit while she is not in her room.
There may come a moment, perhaps, in which
You'll not be able to spare my presence.
Don't worry, I won't spy but I'll stay near.
And whatever his visit means, remember
Not my groom, nor my honor's attorney,
You are a stranger to me—as he is.
I'll make you regret it, should you forget.
Exits into the room to the left. Another knock at the door.
Andrea stands motionless for a while, then quickly opens it.

Curtain

II

ANDREA, CASANOVA

CASANOVA *enters, bows.*
ANDREA *thanks him coolly.*
CASANOVA First, Herr Bassi, thank you for seeing me.
ANDREA No reason for thanks. Your desire, Herr Casanova?
CASANOVA I would scarcely have dared—*interrupts himself*
                                        But you'll permit—
The window—
ANDREA *catching up the word*
                      Beg pardon?
CASANOVA   May I ask you—?
*He remains at the door and indicates by means of a gesture
that he would like Andrea to close the window.*
ANDREA
They think you gone?
CASANOVA   You'll understand at once.
But I beg of you, close the window first.
ANDREA *closes the window.*
CASANOVA *thanks him with a bow, steps forward*:
Now, for my request, which I don't deny
Would appear bold after an acquaintance
Of twenty-four hours—if I didn't feel
I stood face to face with you as a friend—
And as the proffered hand asks to be shaken,
So friendship asks for friendship as recompense.
He extends his hand to Andrea.
ANDREA *grasps it hesitatingly and releases it again right
away.*
CASANOVA Too, the fact that we are fellow-scholars—
ANDREA
You're a student?
CASANOVA   I was. I am. And think—
I always will be in a higher sense.
ANDREA
A student of law—?
CASANOVA   And philosophy.

True, not by the book, but still, with passion.

ANDREA You spent time at the school of Bologna?

CASANOVA Of Padua. But it was not granted me
To drink from wisdom's spring as I wanted,
For half out of whim and half for support,
I played in the orchestra there evenings.

ANDREA The violin?

CASANOVA Yes. And you're a flutist?

ANDREA *somewhat surprised*
What makes you say that?

CASANOVA   The slight deformity
In your lips betrays it immediately,
To the connoisseur. Do you love music?

ANDREA *reticently*
Who doesn't love it?

CASANOVA   True.
Begins to declaim
                    Oh, heaven's
Pure daughter, who floatest from star to star—

ANDREA
What are you talking about?

CASANOVA *smiling*   It's only
The beginning of an ode.

ANDREA   By—?

CASANOVA   By me.

ANDREA
You write poetry?

CASANOVA   Not worth the mention.
Here I am, chatting, while the ground is burning
Under my feet. To the point, then, Herr Bassi.
Quickly
I'm leaving. I must. For cogent reasons.
And quickly, at that. And it is very
Important to me before I leave town
To pay Herr von Gudar what I owe him.
He is not wealthy. You are, and had much
Luck last night. And thus I am asking you—
One nobleman to another—to lend
Me what I lost to him and he to you—

And what means much to him, nothing to you.
ANDREA *scornfully*
You're serious, Herr Casanova?
CASANOVA   My jests
Are funnier.
ANDREA *as above*
                    And you could think—
CASANOVA *matter-of-factly*   Around
A thousand ducats. That leaves a surplus,
Little as such trifles must concern you,
Of fifty ducats, which I paid you in cash.
I have already made out my note, due
Within thirty days. Here.
indicating the signature "Casanova,"
My autograph. I swear it's genuine.
ANDREA
But drawn on whom?
CASANOVA   On me, of course. Whom else
Do I trust? Although—Lausin in Brussels,
Also Raspetti, the Milan banker—
Not to mention others—would redeem it.
But I don't want that;—it would be an honor
For me, after the term elapsed, to pay
My debt in person, with compound interest.
ANDREA *looking at the promissory note*
In thirty days. . . .
CASANOVA   Yes, it says so right here.
But I wouldn't exclude a shorter term.
ANDREA
And how—forgive me, I'm not familiar
With financial deals—
CASANOVA   Among men of honor,
One's word usually suffices.
ANDREA   I'm sure. But—
CASANOVA You want security. I must commend you
For that. I shall provide it, and tenfold.
The note would be first. Second, I bear
The name Casanova. But you will ask,
Where will he get the ducats so quickly?

More quickly even than you imagine—
It could be I'll have the money by morning.
ANDREA You friend in Brussels—?
CASANOVA   Herr Lausin—perhaps.
  If I do not have a chance earlier—*smiling*
  I'm traveling with Gudar—
ANDREA   Whom you'll pay.
CASANOVA Of course. Above all. Then I'll invite him
  Into my coach to keep me company—
  A short game—on our trip, at the first stage;—
  And if fortune smiles on me as yesterday
  On him—and the odds are in my favor—,
  I'll have my money back before evening.
ANDREA My money.
CASANOVA *smiling* Rather, Herr Gudar's money.
ANDREA Who will then be left as poor as before.
CASANOVA Whoever plays must always be prepared
  For the malice of the cards.
ANDREA   Yet you felt
  Sorry for him.
CASANOVA How could I not?—Almost
  An old man, and was once as young as I,
  As you, even. He was an officer,
  And a hero—noble ladies loved him.
  You should have known him in his prime, as I did,
  When a secret mission took him to Venice—
  Where a still more secret one had brought me,
  And we—he still a man, I almost a boy—
  Emerged as friends from a bloody love-feud
  Of the sort that happens from time to time.
  One does not soon forget something like that.
  I don't know to whom I would rather owe
  A thousand ducats than my friend Gudar.
ANDREA I know; to me.
CASANOVA *cordially* Yes, to the younger friend,
  To the more fortunate one, above all.
  You're hesitating? Don't you trust my star?
ANDREA What does your star have to do with my gold?
CASANOVA That's how a tradesman speaks, not a poet.

However, I can respond to him too.
Pointing to the note, which he is still holding in his hand.
What does it say here? A thousand. Let's say
Two thousand, payable in two years.
ANDREA   And
   From where—?
CASANOVA   From where? The choice is difficult,
   Of course. First of all would be Herr Lausin—
ANDREA
   The one with the lace?
CASANOVA   Who for a whole year
   Has beseeched me to enter his business,
   Because out of kindness I recommend
   His merchandise to beautiful ladies
   Occasionally and have already won
   Several new clients for him this way.
ANDREA   But it strikes me, this sort of profession—
CASANOVA *quickly*   Is beneath your most obedient servant.
   I thought so too, and therefore turned him down.
   The more so since I—if one wished to risk it—
   With my little chemical invention—
   You've heard of it?
ANDREA *uncertain*   It seems—
CASANOVA *modestly*   People are talking
   About it too much. We're in the early
   Testing phase. But if future ones fulfill
   The promise of the first, a new epoch
   Will begin.
ANDREA   How so?
CASANOVA *as if inspired*
                   The colors sparkle
   Like luxuriant flowers in their southern
   Splendor and never fade. The richest silk—
   in a different tone
   Can not be damaged, even in the wash.
ANDREA *has to laugh involuntarily.*
CASANOVA   If your journey should take you to Paris
   In the near future, my confidential
   Agent, Doctor Retigneul, as carefully

As he safeguards the secret normally,
Will show your wife the loveliest samples.
ANDREA *makes an impatient gesture.*
CASANOVA *misunderstanding the gesture*
    Oh, none of them are offered for sale yet.
ANDREA *mocking*
    So that you can't expect substantial funds
    To come in so soon from this side either.
CASANOVA Soon, hardly. But then, sums without number,
    So that one could dispense with royalties
    From publishers and all such deplorable
    Income for the remainder of one's life.
    Meanwhile, of course—
ANDREA   You are earning money?
CASANOVA But sadly, as you may notice, not enough.
    Of course, if I could bring myself to tell
    The esteemed public something of myself,
    There would be plenty. Jan Groth in The Hague
    Has offered me three thousand guilders for
    A description of my imprisonment
    And amazing flight and deliverance.
ANDREA Three thousand guilders! And you declined? Why?
CASANOVA I hate to be the herald of my deeds.
ANDREA There was no evidence of that last night.
CASANOVA A critic yet? So, you advise me,
    How does one begin to resist the assaults
    Of lovely women. You heard them. They forced
    The account from me—as they always do.
    Truly, it would be much more convenient
    If, in place of every answer, one had
    A little book available for sale
    At a suitable price. Had the idea
    Struck me earlier, I would at least know—
    Even if I still owed Gudar money—
    How to settle the bill for my lodging
    And pay my driver.
ANDREA   What—? That too—? Is that
    How things stand with you?
CASANOVA   Momentarily.

It wouldn't be so bad if I did not
Have to leave.

ANDREA   Well, you shall have the ducats,
The thousand for Gudar, and the fifty—
The "surplus" which you wished so generously
To forego—for innkeeper and carriage.

CASANOVA   This is exactly what I expected.
From this day—take it in place of my thanks—
You have no truer friend in all the world
Than Casanova.

ANDREA   Not so quickly, sir.
You'll not have this gold a minute before
You've answered a question for me.

CASANOVA   So ask.

ANDREA   And answered without the least digression.
True to the last detail, upon your oath.

CASANOVA   What would I have to conceal from a friend?

ANDREA *slowly, but not too seriously*
What makes you leave Spa in such a hurry?

CASANOVA *after an almost unnoticeable hesitation*
The fact that my life is in danger here.

ANDREA   How is that?—Why? You swore, Casanova!

CASANOVA   And you doubt me in spite of it? What else
But imminent danger—

ANDREA   Are you the man
To flee from danger?

CASANOVA   From the overt, no,
But if it lurks in secret, maliciously,
As an assassin's knife on a dark street,
As a drop of poison in a wine-filled cup,
At a feast, as the drunken strangler's hand —
It might prove a bit awkward to tempt it.
Don't you agree?

ANDREA   Is there in this country—
Rather, is there any place where a man
Of your way of life, where Casanova
May imagine himself safe from deceived
Husbands, seduced maidens, and betrayed women?

CASANOVA   Oh, what words! None of them applies to me!

Did I ever seduce—? No, I was present,
Just when nature with its sweet sorcery
Began its work. Nor did I betray any,
For my heart remained grateful to each one.
And then that myth about deceived husbands!
Only spite could create such a senseless,
Vile word. Is he deceived who knows his fate?
Or he to be pitied, who never learned it?
ANDREA   Sophistry!
CASANOVA   Philosophy, my dear sir.
ANDREA   But only yours, not the deceived husband's—
in a different tone
As—if I am to understand your flight—
Is just being demonstrated anew.
CASANOVA
You suspect that?
ANDREA *very tense but controlled*
                  Perhaps. But I must know,
Before I exchange my gold for your note.
CASANOVA *after hesitating briefly*
Since your youth makes you so cautious, I will,
As if paying interest in advance,
Satisfy my debt with some good advice.
ANDREA
That might be?
CASANOVA   That you beware of Santis.
ANDREA
What does Santis concern me?
CASANOVA   Let's hope
It stays that way.
ANDREA   You're speaking in riddles.
CASANOVA   Flaminia cast her eye on you—I know.
But Santis insists on his spousal rights—
Which is why you must be careful, my friend—
According to whim and his chance for gain.
Now indulgent, as if he were deaf and blind,
Now lurking jealous like a Turk, enamored
Husband yesterday, a pander today—
In concert with his lovely one moment,

A Tartar on his own account the next—
And if yesterday he stood watch outside
Flaminia's door lest her lover be disturbed,
Another, whom he found disagreeable,
Might today expect the most cowardly
Of attacks from the Baron, insofar
with a tone of importance
As timely warning does not protect him.
The following very quickly

ANDREA But you've been—warned?
CASANOVA   I have.
ANDREA   You have—
  By whom?
CASANOVA By her.
ANDREA   Flaminia herself—?
CASANOVA   Who else?
ANDREA
  You—And Flaminia—
CASANOVA   Why should that surprise you?
ANDREA So it's an old hatred that threatens you?
CASANOVA
  It may well be.
ANDREA   After—these many years—?
CASANOVA I've crossed her path for the third time, but not
  Until last night did fortune favor me.
ANDREA Last night—and who betrayed you to the Baron?
CASANOVA *hesitating*
  I suspect that, well-concealed, he saw from
  The dark shadows of the lane—*breaks off*
ANDREA   Saw—what?
CASANOVA   How I leapt
  through the window into the garden.
ANDREA And why would he have been hiding out there?
CASANOVA Because a suspicion had been gnawing
  At his soul since our cheerful dinner
  Last night.
ANDREA   At which with even-handed grace,
  Both to your left and right, you made a gift
  Of your spirit's felicitous talents.

CASANOVA Yet that "grace" was not returned equally,
  As the apprehensive Santis perceived.
  And if Flaminia merely breathed those whispered
  Words to me—it appears that the Baron
  Knew very well how to interpret them.
ANDREA
  And these words—?
CASANOVA   Several men have heard their sound,
  And several more will after me.
ANDREA   The words—!?
CASANOVA
  "Come tonight at midnight, the door stands open."
ANDREA
  And stood open, in fact?
CASANOVA   I have no doubt.
  But I needed no door. She was waiting
  For me at the open window—and thus
  I chose the shorter path that so enticed me;—
  I took the same way back, and all too soon,
  As you know, I was playing cards again.
ANDREA And did the warning that forces your flight
  Resound together with the night's wild bliss?
CASANOVA Experienced women, my young friend, take care
  Not to end love's melody abruptly
  By means of some unwanted dissonance.
  Then too, I was well aware, as was she,
  That her room was divided by only
  A very thin wall from *with a slight bow*
                  —a chaster lady's,
  Who, as we didn't forget for an instant,
  Awaited her beloved in wakeful longing.
  Thus the time flew sweetly but mutely by.
ANDREA How then?—What?— Is it only your conscience,
  Is it a bad omen that urges flight?
CASANOVA Certainly not. A letter.
ANDREA   A letter?
CASANOVA Here, read it.
ANDREA *reads*   "If you are, Casanova,
  A man of honor, which I do not doubt,

You will surely not refuse a woman,
Whose wishes you divined, the only thanks
On which both her life and your own depend.
I can't see you again. Flee the city."
Lowers the letter
And nothing further—!
CASANOVA   I think it's enough.
ANDREA
I don't see the "warning."
CASANOVA   "Flee the city—
I can't see you again!" Tell me, what else
But fear for me elicits this cry from her?
ANDREA   Not a word—
CASANOVA   Because the sly creature thinks:
Should I frighten him with Santis' threat
Of vengeance, I'd be holding him spellbound
On this spot out of defiance, instead
Of promoting his escape. Therefore she
Demands it as thanks— who could refuse it?—
After a night of love.
ANDREA   All conjecture.
CASANOVA   Conjecture? If I tell you, sir, that Santis
In person was already looking for me
This morning at the inn—
ANDREA   So, he did that?
CASANOVA   But I didn't know it. The innkeepers
In Spa are experienced. They let me sleep,
He was sent away.
ANDREA   He let himself be sent?
CASANOVA
What else should he have done? My door was locked,
And since, as he must flatter himself, I will,
In the end, run into his net somewhere,
And since every single hour is precious
To a fellow such as this, he uses
This one too for another purpose;
To see whether he can catch new simpletons
For his games of chance or turn a profit
From horses, women, gemstones, or silk scarves;—

If he's not perhaps already hiring
For good money the dagger for the man
Who shamelessly remunerates a woman's
Kisses only with kisses of his own.
ANDREA *who has been listening with exaggerated gestures of*
assent, now goes to the desk and opens it
Here, take it—and quickly, here's five hundred,
Six, seven, eight—now I'm beginning to see.
Here, nine and ten—
CASANOVA   What do you mean?
ANDREA *acting clever*   His bearing
Was too odd. That of a madman almost—
I thought he was drunk.—
He is continuously occupied with the gold, tying up the bags
and handing them one after the other to Casanova
CASANOVA   You've seen him today?
ANDREA As closely as you. He stood on this spot.
Asked me to dine, they're preparing outside,
On an excursion—not so close, my friend—
He keeps Casanova from the window
To a party, and I don't know what else—
And grins—and his talk is strangely confused,
He rolls his eyes about, distorts his face,
And makes threatening gestures into thin air.
And now I recall that last night he stole
From the card table right after you did
And returned prior to your reappearance.
Now at last I understand. Here, the fifty
More, the surplus. And a hundred besides.
You want to go to Brussels? A bit close!
I would choose Holland—and be most careful
That every trail be wiped out behind me.
CASANOVA Ach!—His rage will be spent in a few days.
ANDREA That soon! Who knows! He doesn't look the type.
I'd take better care of myself in your place.
How about crossing over to England?
CASANOVA Or America maybe!
ANDREA   And why not?
CASANOVA The journey is long, and my means are short.

ANDREA   Does a man as free as you know distances?
   And where money is concerned, I will place
   Two, three hundred more at your disposal.
   I would be sorry for you. . . and my money.
CASANOVA   At higher interest then.
ANDREA   Not at all.
   Gives him more gold
   As long as you are safe, so is my gold.
   I'm only wondering how you'll escape
   From town undetected in broad daylight.
CASANOVA
   Have no fear on that score. There are small gates
   Here that only I know, and crooked lanes,
   And hidden paths, dark, dusky turns—And should
   I step into the light, who would know me?
   *He turns around for an instant, reverses his coat, alters his
   posture, turns back around and stands there wearing a small
   false beard; he speaks in a changed voice*
   You yourself doubt that it's me.
   He turns, resumes his former appearance; in his old voice
                                 It is me.
   Putting his gold bags in order
   So, this is for Gudar, this for the host,
   This for the trip. And now, thank you, my friend.
   You will not have to tremble for your gold.
   Even if I did not value my life,
   To preserve it for you is my duty.
   And a year from today, if not sooner,
   I will appear in Ferrara to pay
   My debt in person.
ANDREA *embarrassed* But I can't be sure
   Whether you will find me in Ferrara.
CASANOVA   I will. Because you're not a man who feels
   At ease in adventurous passages,
   Nights in strange beds, or lodging-house dinners
   With companions chosen by journey's chance.
   Your destination is peace, order, law,
   As homecoming is the ultimate sense
   Of your wandering. And in my mind's eye

I can already see you at your hearth,
Serenely welcoming your transient guest,
Who—along with the gold he owes, of course—
Brings respectful greetings to the noble pair,
Like the last reflection of days gladly
Forgotten.
ANDREA   The pair—? I'm not married yet.
CASANOVA Then you will be soon. And you'll thank the fate
That gave you, a youth, the gift of a wife
Lovely as Anina, bright and virtuous.
The bond formed early is strongest. Woe to him
Who seeks always; all good to him who finds.
ANDREA   Such a maxim from Casanova's mouth?
CASANOVA   I've not shared a wiser with any man,
Therefore preserve it in your heart with care.
ANDREA   You're too kind.
CASANOVA   Paltry thanks for your kindness.
Before departing I would have gladly
Offered my devotion to your lovely friend.
Greet her for me as befits a sister.
It's a brother, a friend, who takes his leave.
Exits.
ANDREA *alone, looks at the letter, then hides it on his person;*
he goes to the door left and opens it.
ANINA *enters.*

ANDREA, ANINA

ANDREA   We talked a long time, but not about you.
He borrowed gold from me for his escape,
For which he slyly made up a harmless cause,
And sends you—through me—his farewell greeting.
ANINA *smiling unnoticeably*
I'll take it along as the last one, then.
Now leave me alone a while so I can
Prepare for my journey undisturbed.
ANDREA   Where?
ANINA   Even if I knew where, you have no right

Any longer to ask. Leave me alone.

ANDREA Anina!

ANINA *goes to the right*

              All right, I'll leave as I am.

ANDREA And what Casanova told me otherwise
  Doesn't interest you in the least?

ANINA   I think,
  pointing to the open desk
  You spoke the truth—by all appearances.
  And say you did speak of me after all—
  Why should I care? My life is starting over.
  And no one has a part—not he, not you.
  Somewhat more vehemently, but still calmly
  Leave me alone, I have asked you twice now—
  Until I can gather up what is mine.
  *She goes to the armoire, opens it, and begins to take out
  linen and other articles of clothing.*

ANDREA *watches her as she begins to pack her things in the
  suitcase; after some hesitation, takes out the letter and throws
  it at her*
  If you're taking what's yours—then take this too.

ANINA *fixes him with a stare, then scornfully, bitterly*
  The gold for that—a deal?—Disgrace and folly!
  With sinking voice
  I only ask, whose disgrace, whose folly!

ANDREA Neither his, nor mine. He gave it freely.

ANINA Like you your gold. It still remains a deal.
  How dare you get that letter?

ANDREA *mockingly*   What do you care?
  You're starting life over.

ANINA   You broke your word.

ANDREA Did I promise that I wouldn't ask him
  Why he needs the gold, why he's running away?
  We did not speak of you.

ANINA   And my letter?

ANDREA Your letter? You and I know it, not he.
  He thinks it was Flaminia who wrote him.

ANINA *stands fixed.*

ANDREA You see, he thinks it was she, who waiting

For him—as had been arranged between them—
Stood in the window lighting up the dark;—
And thinks it was she who was his last night.
ANINA   And also thinks this letter is from her?
   Why would Flaminia write him such a letter?
ANDREA   To protect him from her husband's vengeance.
ANINA   And further—?
ANDREA   Nothing. You will understand
   That I refrained from enlightening him.
ANINA   You believe his delusion will last long?
ANDREA   It well might. It will—He's off to Holland. . .
   Perhaps to more distant lands.
ANINA *glances at the desk; with bitter irony*
                           You've done your share
   To help.
ANDREA   Not much. My winnings from gaming!
   Should I have refused him—? Not rather take
   The gold's being made so easy to give
   As providence—
ANINA   Providence?—
ANDREA   Don't you feel
   Too, that this wonderful turn of events,
   Sent us by fate, serves us as an omen,
   Which to misread—or to reject, even—
   Would amount to obstinacy, blindness—
   Blasphemy almost.
ANINA   You're gushing, Andrea.
   What has changed—? Has what took place suddenly
   Not taken place? And what was experienced,
   Now, abruptly, not experienced? Is my fault
   The slighter now? Or none at all? Your pain
   Mitigated—or dissolved to nothing?
   The hour I belonged to another
   Expunged from the rolls of its companions?
   And don't I carry its dark, unfading
   Vapor in my hair any more, like smoke
   From a rank hotel where I spent the night—?
ANDREA   And if the pain and guilt continued, still,
   Once more, I think fate is leaving us free

To consider if we should not forgive—
You, my foul words—I, your fouler deed—
ANINA Forgive—!
ANDREA   Understand, then, and willingly
   Forget.
ANINA Forget—? Is the abusive flood of words
   That rained down over me unspoken now?
   And have they been unthought now, those hateful
   Thoughts in which, as in a dense, gloomy fog,
   My very being was lost to your glance?
ANDREA But if I found it again— and you mine—?
ANINA How can I ever, and how could you? Does
   He not take with him the hour's memories,
   My body's fragrance, the lingering taste
   Of my kisses, the sound of blissful sighs —
   For all time—?
ANDREA   But not your image, Anina. . .
   So that whatever took place last night stays
   A secret between us; and if we swear
   Each other to silence and forgetfulness,
   Then it will never have happened at all.
ANINA Does a heart that seemed mortally wounded
   Recuperate so quickly just because
   One's vanity rids itself of its goad?
   Now I've really lost you—Get out!
   She wraps herself in her coat and is about to leave.
ANDREA   Anina!
   This is your answer? To my love for you?
ANINA I don't have another one. Let me go.
ANDREA Where are you going?
ANINA   Any place you're not.
ANDREA To him!
ANINA   That's not your business. Let me pass!
ANDREA Now I know you lied.
ANINA   Never.
ANDREA   You love him.
ANINA I do now. . . and now I'm really beginning to feel
   the happiness.
ANDREA If only it hadn't rushed off!

ANINA   I'll fetch it back.

ANDREA Unless I prove the faster, to appear
 To the escapee as herald of your love,
 But simultaneously as bearer, too,
 Of a somewhat more ominous message.

ANINA What would you gain by his receiving it?
 Even if you killed him, I'd tell the world
 That he and I were companions in love;
 And if he killed you, Andrea,—I would kiss
 The bloody hand that rescued me from you.

ANDREA Run to your mischief, then, your way is open!
 He opens the door to the right, at which instant Flaminia
 enters.

ANDREA, ANINA, FLAMINIA

FLAMINIA Hey, thanks! Some reception! Just like at court,
 Even if you didn't mean it that way.
 You're all set to go out—? That's fortunate.
 The others are keeping us waiting too long.
 So I thought I'd ask if you'd care, meantime,
 To sit with me at the table out there—?

ANINA
 Excuse me—!
 Attempts to go past her.

FLAMINIA *innocently*
     What—?

ANINA   You can see—

FLAMINIA   In your coat?
 Now I get it! You wanted—? Without him—?
 And without your luggage?—A lover's spat!
 We could see it coming. Did he perhaps—
 Gestures of striking
 Well, it happens.—Who runs right off right away
 On account of that? If every woman
 Acted that way after every quarrel—
 The half-packed suitcases would stand around
 In lodging-house bedrooms by the dozen.

ANINA *tries to go past her* Please—!

FLAMINIA   And you intend to hike out of town
   Like this, in such fine shoes? Because no more
   Coaches are to be had in Spa today.
ANINA   I don't care.
FLAMINIA   Besides, there's a storm approaching.
   Black clouds are gathering in the sky— thus
   Heaven itself warns against undue haste.
   Isn't that right, Herr Bassi? Do help me,
   Won't you, so that we can sit down at last.
   Why this obstinacy? You've had a fight—
   You'll make it up again. That's the custom.
ANDREA   Not everywhere. Do not block her exit
   Any longer. She's in a rush to steal
   From you a second time in broad daylight
   What she first stole from you last night.
FLAMINIA   How —?! What— ?!
   Oh no!—Now you had better just stay put.
   Another step—and I'll raise the alarm!—
   Stolen? And what? From my room—? My jewels
   I carry on me. So speak, Herr Bassi,
   Otherwise you're an accomplice! What? Were you?
   And both of you silent—! They'll make you talk!
   Help, someone, help!!
   Is about to shout through the door
ANDREA   Patience! Now then, Anina,
   You didn't want this to remain a secret,
   You must let her in on it, first of all.
   It is her business! So listen, Flaminia!
   He, for whom you waited in vain last night,
   Did unfortunately mistake the room
   And found such a friendly welcome next door,
   As you could scarce have intended for him.
FLAMINIA *unsure of herself*
   What is this joking—? Who waited for whom?
ANDREA   We all could see he was trying to win you.
FLAMINIA   I don't understand a word. Or should I—?
   Really—? He—? Who? And mistook the door— how?
ANDREA   Call it the window. But he found the way.
FLAMINIA   To whom? And who? So talk rationally.

Who found the way to her?
ANDREA   He whom you mean.
  But since she made him happy as Flaminia,
  She deems it her duty, resolutely
  To complete as Anina what began
  By chance as a frivolous masquerade;—
  And she is on her way to him just now.
FLAMINIA Is it possible? How? It's unheard of!
  I wait full of longing on my chaste couch,
  And this one snatches my sweetheart away—?!
  My arms reach thirstily into the dark—
  While hers are slinging themselves around him?!
  I drink in the night air, she his kisses—
  And while I, with eyes reddened from crying,
  Stare awake into the approaching dawn,
  Has this one here treacherously dozed off
  To sweet morning dreams that are rightly mine?
  Has such a measure of depravity
  Room enough in a woman's heart?
Turning to Andrea   And I,
  Good-natured fool, who in her own carriage
  Brought her to Spa, because her own broke down;—
  Accepted her with all my heart as a friend,
  As a sister;—and finally myself
  Introduced her to Casanova, whom she,
  Right after dinner, knows full well, as thanks,
  To entice into her lust-ridden bed—
To Anina
  A young miss, you? From a respectable home —?
  As if anyone would allow himself
  To be fooled by that pallid little mask
  Of innocence! As if one couldn't see
  The secret traces of villainous vice
  Deeply engraved on this soft, haughty face!—
  Where do you come from? From a servant's room?!
  From a house of pleasure! You, a young man's
  Honorable bride—? From a procuress
  He bought you, and he paid his honor over
  And above the agreed price. Ask Santis

Whether I didn't tell him right away!
A little tramp, I said, and the handsome
Lad—
to Andrea
      I mean you,—a fool, who'll regret it.
to Anina
And do you actually flatter yourself
That a man, a widely experienced man,
I mean Casanova, would allow himself
To be so clumsily deceived? That he
Did not perceive your trickery at once—
Though he knows nothing of me but my face,
My hand, and—my breath? And doesn't it dawn
On you that he betrayed nothing last night
Merely out of courtesy? You doubt it?
Well, here's proof: this morning, after the bliss
Had dissipated, leaving only shame
And chagrin, what did he do? To flee
The triumphant smile in your deceitful eyes
As well as my scorn and his own remorse,
He rode away on the express mail coach.

ANDREA
And how do you know—?

FLAMINIA   Because I just got
The information at "The Golden Lion."

ANDREA
You yourself were—

FLAMINIA   There; I don't deny it.
Because my waiting in vain for a man,
One whom I deemed worthy of the favors
He had long implored of me, is something
I experienced last night for the first time;
And I wanted the answer to the puzzle.
Now I have it. And angry as I am
That another woman's greed and cunning
Cheated me out of what was mine by rights,
That's how glad I am to learn I can offer
Forgiveness to my chosen blameless one,
And, generously to bring it to him

In person, I will forego dinner, drink
And party to fly after the dear man.
ANINA *has been listening to Flaminia, first motionlessly then
ever more relaxed and cheerful. The expression on her face
shows that she is beginning to grasp the humor of the situ-
ation, and to become increasingly willing to adapt to it.*
In such fine shoes—with a storm threatening?
FLAMINIA *disconcerted* She dares to mock me too, the
shameless one?
ANINA No carriage to be had—!
FLAMINIA   Six stand ready
For our excursion. I'll choose the fastest.
ANINA And which direction do you mean to take?
FLAMINIA No road which Casanova rides remains
A secret long.
ANINA   Perhaps he wants it to.
FLAMINIA Where has he gone—? Do you know?
ANINA   How should I?
And if I did, I would hardly tell you.
FLAMINIA *blocks her way again*
No coach will take you. I'll hire them all.
ANINA But none knows the way.
FLAMINIA   I don't lack the means
With which to make both host and driver talk.
ANINA If I am poor at present, my sweetheart
Will as soon as I reach him gladly pay
For whatever carriage brings me.
FLAMINIA   She's mad!
Take care! If you set foot outside this room,
I'll have you put in prison as a thief.
Don't smile! The judge in Spa is my friend.
ANINA   He too?
FLAMINIA And if he weren't my friend, he is just.
And theft remains theft. I'll scream if you dare—
ANINA But not so loud that Herr Santis will hear.
FLAMINIA What do I care about Santis? The whole
Town shall know it. Thief! Murderer! Villain!
Open the window, Andrea, so all may hear.
ANINA I'll gladly, myself—

as if she were about to go to the window
FLAMINIA   *holding her by the coat*
                              Depraved, shameless one!
in a different tone
Unhappy child! Andrea! Look at him—stands
There like a stone, and lets me, poor, weak woman—
As if it didn't concern him at all—
Andrea! You block of marble! Statue! Man!
Have you forgotten she's your bride? That you
Carried her off from her honest parents
Who are left at home, alone, despairing,
Innocent as she was, a child, basely
To sacrifice her to your lust? And now,
When she's merely doing what you taught her,
Incapable of grasping what she did,
Will you, cruel man, thrust her out in the street?
Yourself chase her into Casanova's snare?
That hypocrite, debauchee, blasphemer,
Who will corrupt her in body and soul.
Do not let her go, by your eternal
Salvation. If you take this on yourself,
No priest, no cardinal will absolve you
From such an outrage. Come to your senses,
Both of you. Leave him to one who better
Becomes him, and who made for it by God,
Will requite him all his sins a thousandfold.
ANINA   *apparently in earnest*
If those are your intentions, whoever
Loves Casanova must warn him against you.
FLAMINIA   You don't say! Why? Must you turn every word
Of mine into a snare? Don't you hear, rather,
From each one that I'm mad with love for him?
And now, as if a devil were toying
With me, the rare bird—surely I had him—
Flies, for the third time now, out of my hand,
Where he himself wanted to make his bed.
Oh nevermore! What evil possesses you,
That you want to take, to withhold from me
What's mine by rights?! You insatiable one!—

That you were his, whether through accident
Or lust, though certainly without dessert,
Is that not bliss enough? You want still more?
ANINA I was not his.
FLAMINIA   Who else?
ANINA   You, more likely.
FLAMINIA For him, but not for me.
ANINA   He doesn't know
That it was me, therefore it wasn't me.
FLAMINIA It wasn't me, since I know it wasn't me.
ANINA So it seems we both have title to him.
Hesitating
And whose is more valid, let him decide.
FLAMINIA Now she's completely mad! Let him decide!!
Ha! As if he didn't do so last night,—
And chose me.
ANINA   I wasn't a candidate then.
Much has changed during this one night—for him—
For you—for me. Now let him choose anew—
No, for the first time, truly!—Come, let's go.
FLAMINIA
With you—to him—?
ANINA   That we may learn our fate
From his lips, however it may turn out.
We'll go together, one of us will return.
FLAMINIA That would be unfair, you most just of women.
Not until I've granted him a night too,
Will our claims be equal. Then he may choose.
Not sooner. Isn't this noble enough?
I'll be nobler still. Listen, Anina:
You must leave him to me for just one night.
For one night, but without choice. And tomorrow,
I swear, I'll bring him back to you myself.
Then you may keep him for all eternity.
Do you ask for more?—here, my pearl necklace—
In response to a gesture on Anina's part
As a token of friendship, not as payment.
It's yours if you let me go alone.
Call it whim, if you like, an obsession,

Even yesterday I'd not have given
The least of these pearls for that Venetian
Any more than for any other man.
But today, and just because I want to—
ANINA   As if I'd sell him for a thousand pearls.
FLAMINIA   At your feet, then.—
She throws herself down before Anina.
ANINA   What are you thinking of?
FLAMINIA   One final time, let me entreat you, child.
You don't know me. Mild and good as I seem,
Whoever stubbornly denies my pleas—
ANINA   *tearing herself away from her*   I do.
FLAMINIA   *suddenly with great bitterness*
Then God help us both. Specially
You and your mild eyes. And since you're disposed
To find the dark night sweet, let it surround
You for eternity. With this needle—
*She has pulled a hairpin out of her hair and is about to
plunge it into Anina's eyes.*
ANDREA   *steps between them, takes Flaminia, then Anina by
the hand, which he does not let go for the time being. Thus
all three of them are standing in a row, their glance turned
to the left, at the instant when the door at the left opens and
Santis steps in.*

ANINA, FLAMINIA, ANDREA, SANTIS

SANTIS   *somewhat drunk, still in the doorway*
Flaminia!—I thought so!
Enters further   May I also—?
Get ready! The guests will be here at once!
And are we sufficiently beautiful—?
It may pay. A fine gentleman, my lord—
Just turned nineteen, resembles Adonis
And soaks it up as if he were Bacchus.
Already we are on familiar terms.
Drags his gold around in bars. Who'll snap up
This morsel—blonde or brown-haired?
To Andrea

Unless we go halves
In the transaction.—Well, philosopher?
Such a lord does not show up every day.
Holland is casting its nets already too.
FLAMINIA   The widow?
SANTIS   Yes, despite her thirty-nine.
Not men, I mean, but her thirty-nine years,
Maybe forty, though still fresh and well built,
She tippled too, spoke English with the lord.
And if I saw right, French under the table.
We'll take good care of them, Herr Bassi, what?
FLAMINIA   I should think there would be other guests too.
SANTIS   The young lady from Lyon, with her mother.
It strikes me the mother is the younger.
A manufacturer from Liege, bald but rich,
And—
Now he first notices how the others are standing there:
Andrea between Anina and Flaminia, holding them both by
the hand.
What—?! Practicing a minuet here?
But no, this is no dance. What's going on?
FLAMINIA *to Andrea*   Will you just let go of my hand?
SANTIS   I smell a fight! What's up? The girls—right? Why?
Over me—?
To Andrea
Over you—?
laughs   I should hope not.
ANDREA   No fight, Baron, the word is much too coarse.
A quarrel, hardly that. A slight difference
Of opinion—regarding an event.
No, not an event which actually occurred,
A philosophical spat, so to speak.—
Scarcely philosophical, though—
SANTIS   Figures.
ANDREA *as if suddenly struck by an idea*
And if anyone can settle it, it's you.
SANTIS   What?—Me?
ANDREA   Yes, precisely you. By your leave,
Ladies, I'll report in concise fashion

The beginning of the story again,
So the Baron might unravel the knot.

SANTIS *somewhat mistrustful and unsure of himself*
You passed the time of day here with stories?

ANDREA *quickly* In order to contribute my fair share
To the party, I intended to offer
The worthy company a merry tale.
I told it just now, to see what effect
It would have—and because its solution
Is so difficult, I had the idea
Of troubling the sweet ladies' acumen
Instead of my own mind. But, as it turns
Out, alas, my poor thread is not gently
Unraveled now, no, but wildly unrolled.
Therefore, Baron, before I tear apart
In angry impatience what I laid out
With so much artistry, you try your luck,
And untwist the capricious, tangled knot.

SANTIS The knot?—untwist—? Who can understand this?

ANDREA You will, soon. And whatever you decide,
We will comply with it.

FLAMINIA   That we will.

ANINA   Yes.

ANDREA And with the ending you find for the tale,
I will present it to your esteemed guests.

SANTIS With my ending?! I, an author? That would —!

ANDREA It does not require great art, just one word.
A yes, a no.

SANTIS   Just one word?

ANDREA   Nothing more.
Hastily
And I'll start fast, before the guests arrive.
Two sisters—wasn't it?

FLAMINIA   Two sisters?

ANINA *with certainty*   Yes.

ANDREA Both young, both beautiful and well-mannered.

SANTIS Well-mannered too? Why, I'm sure we shall see.

ANDREA Alike in figure, though not in their faces.

SANTIS But in figure! I smell something. Go on.

ANDREA The younger is engaged—the older free—
SANTIS Engaged to whom?
ANDREA *annoyed*   No matter. I'm abridging.
   So, the older—
SANTIS   The one not yet engaged—
ANDREA The free one, indeed.
SANTIS   How old?
ANDREA   Just nineteen.
SANTIS Just like my lord.
ANDREA   Who doesn't belong here.
SANTIS I asked him.
ANDREA   But not into my story.
SANTIS I'm listening.
ANDREA   But in silence, please.
SANTIS   Gladly.
ANDREA *quickly*
   Then one day a young man appears, with whom
   The older sister falls tenderly in love—
   As he with her; but since she's closely watched—
SANTIS Who watches her?
ANDREA   The mother, undoubtedly.
   The father's long dead.
SANTIS   May he rest in peace.
ANDREA So the two of them lack opportunity—
SANTIS Opportunity?—One makes it, if need be.
ANDREA She's closely guarded by day—
SANTIS   But at night—?
ANDREA She shares the bedroom with the younger one.
SANTIS The engaged—?
ANDREA   The younger, yes, I said so.
SANTIS Who is the intended?
ANDREA   A nobleman.
SANTIS When is the wedding to be?
ANDREA   Both sisters
   Wait for the solemn day with equal longing.
   Even more for that night; for when the one,
   The younger, newly wed, follows her husband,
   The other will—at last—without restraint
   And free, in the sisterly bedroom press

The well-beloved to her thirsting heart.
But—I haven't mentioned it yet—that youth
Was feared and hated for his bad morals—
Not by women, naturally—and thus
It came to pass that he was not invited
To the wedding; indeed, that to avoid
Every suspicion, he had been staying
Far away from town for days already.

SANTIS The town—?

ANDREA   Where what I'm reporting takes place.
Not until midnight, as they had arranged,
Does he approach and sneak across the park
On the familiar path to the window,
On the other side of which—he knows it—
The long yearned for, the promised bliss awaits.
And thus, with a bold swing over, he sets foot
In the dusky, fragrant bridal chamber.
But what he doesn't know and cannot know—
No message reached the all-too-well-hidden one—
Was this, that the wedding had been postponed,
Because a peculiar sort of event—
Of which more another time—prevented
The groom from appearing at the last minute.

SANTIS *greedily* And our young man finds instead of the one
Both of the sisters in the dusky room?

ANDREA No. Instead of the one he finds the other—
The bride, who exhausted by the torment
Of waiting, had sunk in heavy slumber.
Meanwhile, the one, cross and disappointed—
(She has no inkling, after all, that no word
Of the postponement had reached her sweetheart)—
Deprived of both sleep and consolation,
Leaves her resting place and in the garden's
Most remote lane devotes some useless sighs
To the distant youth who is oh, so near,
Until finally, tired with weeping,
She makes her way back to the joint bedroom.
But when, so as not to wake her sister,
She presses softly down on the door handle,

She thinks she hears the shuffling and gliding
Of steps inside, and opening the door
Full of misgivings, she just manages
To catch a glimpse of an individual
Hastily escaping through the window.
Although she only sees the figure's outline,
Still, there is never a doubt who it was.
And transfixed, in shame, pain, anger, she stands
In the silent room from whose dim shadows,
Faithlessly rumpled—a shining confession—
The white linen pillow greets her with scorn.
And nestled in it ("Would she were dead,"
Thinks the deceived one) sleeps her innocent-
Guilty sister who stole her love from her;—
The victim of chance, but thankful to it,
Maidenly-bridal before the sun set,
And before the new dawn—a stranger's whore.
Outide in the park, movement and noise.
FLAMINIA The guests already?
ANINA   It's the musicians!
ANDREA Time presses, so I'll say nothing about
    All that transpired in word and gesture
    Between the two sisters before morning.
    Only this will I report: both, by love
    Enflamed, lay equal claim on the young man-
    The one who was his, but without his being
    Aware of whom he held in his embrace-
    So that, not satisfied by pleasure obtained
    Surreptitiously, and thirsting anew,
    She aches for more pleasure, freely offered-
    The other, whom he fancied he embraced
    And who is left to sigh in unquenched yearning.
    And each one holds her claim alone to be
    Well-founded, and the other's null and void.
    But to let the young man choose between them,
    Which seems the obvious step, this they decline,
    For if he is no longer unsuspecting,
    As now, but rather consciously involved,
    Then it would become a new, totally

Different case, and the deciding word
Would be uttered on the basis of whim,
And not as they wish, or the tale's hidden
Sense demands, on the basis of justice.
So the question stands thus: to which sister,
According to pure right, does the youth belong?
And you, Herr Baron, who stand face to face
With the question as a man of experience
And, what's more important, with a clear mind,
Seem to us the best suited to solve it.
And lest time for mature consideration
Be lacking, we grant you time to ponder
Your answer until the end of the banquet.
ANINA No further delay. It's difficult to think
  Amid prattling guests and clinking glasses.
FLAMINIA His answer at once, as long as he's sober.
ANDREA As you wish, then. The Baron has the floor.
SANTIS But he gladly declines for now, and later.
  Because although I'll hardly be more drunk
  Afterwards than I am now, I do know
  That I'm not any smarter before eating
  Than after enjoying a good dinner.
  And as touches experience, I dare say
  You'll be able to learn the solution
  To such a tangled puzzle from several
  Persons who have traveled and looked around
  In the regions of love much more than I.
  And I know one who will, like a master,
  Without hesitation find a conclusion
  For this fine but unclearly conceived tale.
  Pause
  Shall I mention the name that hangs upon
  All our lips—?
ANDREA   You mean. . .
ANINA, FLAMINIA *simultaneously, in different tones*
                        Casanova?
SANTIS Who else?
ANDREA   Yes, if only we had him here.
  But unfortunately he left this morning.

SANTIS   That was his intent. But he stayed.
ANDREA   He stayed—?
SANTIS   And comes to dine.
ANDREA   He comes—?
SANTIS   An hour ago
  I managed, in person, to invite him,
  He'll be here soon.
ANDREA   A mistake, certainly;
  He did say he's taking a longer trip.
SANTIS   It was short—it ended a hundred steps
  Past the city gate.
ANDREA   And he's coming back?
SANTIS   In the same coach which was to carry him
  Off with Gudar—in pursuit of his sweetheart.
ANINA, FLAMINIA   Teresa?
SANTIS   Yes, the lovely faithless one.
  He'd found her trail and was following her.
  Why did I care? Well, it was my carriage.
  I had rented it for our excursion.
  So I had a perfect right to stop it.
  I did, before I knew who sat in it.
  And at the risk of my life. Look at me.
  He indicates his wrist.
FLAMINIA   You're wounded?
ANINA   Blood?
SANTIS   By Casanova's sword.
ANDREA   An adventure! How ever did it happen?
SANTIS   After my morning snack with the young lord—
  None but I drank him under the table—
  Wanting to take a walk in the fresh air,
  I took the road towards the open country,—
  When a speeding coach roars ever closer
  Behind me in the swirling dust of wild hooves.
  I wait, look, recognize carriage, driver—
  "Hey, where to with my deposit, rascal?"
  And rooted in the middle of the street
  I signal him to stop. But he swings his whip,
  Striking the horses so that they snort past,
  Till I, falling into rein and bridle,

Force them to a stop. But in that instant
There leaps down from the carriage a fellow
Of suspicious appearance: his hair down
Over his forehead, a small goatee, wrapped
In his coat, sword in hand, menacingly
Rolling dark piercing eyes, and he bawls at me:
"If you don't march off this instant, you're dead."
Fortunately, the horses remain still,
Leaving both my hands free and I'm ready
To defend myself with my sharp weapon.
The blades are whizzing already, touching,
Scratching—he too was hurt—when the carriage
Spits out another. Him I knew. It was Gudar.
He calls: "Come to your senses, Casanova!
What's the idea?!" And with wide-open eyes,
Falling back in amazement, not in fear,
I really recognize Casanova,
Our friend, in my wildly disguised foe.
And lowering my weapon: "Are you mad—?
It is I, Santis, not a highwayman,
And I stopped your coach because I rented
It this morning at an outrageous price
For an outing in cheerful company.
Hey, driver, right?" And at the same time hit
The scamp one across the back with my blade.
"I asked you too, that is, you were still sleeping
When I came to your guest-house this morning.
You appear to be in a big hurry,
Where to? And masked yet! You too, Gudar, why?"
They both remain silent. Casanova has
Gotten rid of the ridiculous mask
And stares like one scared awake by a nightmare.
"Well, as you please," I say, "I have no right
To hold you up if the distance beckons.
But I fear it means continuing on foot.
Bon voyage!"—And swing myself up into
The coach, smack the driver: "To Spa, rascal!"
But as he starts to turn, Casanova
Leaps up as well and, I don't know if it

Was his intent or the jolting of the coach—
Hurls himself at my neck: "Santis, dear friend!
You've been sent by fate. I was all ready
To rush off after a faithless woman,
I, an incorrigible fool for love,
On a foul road to disgrace, perhaps death.
The sign came in time. You are my savior!
Now let's dine, drink, play, laugh and be merry,
In spite of all the intrigues of women.
Gudar will join us!"—he'd gotten in too—
And so the coach brings the three of us,
Crowded together, quickly back to town—
And here we are again.

ANDREA   You we can see;—
   Not Herr Gudar, nor Casanova, either,
   That incorrigible fool for love, who,
   Safe from further signs from fate, may now be
   Rushing off in your coach a second time
   After the faithless one he loves so much.

SANTIS He swore a sacred oath to forget her!

FLAMINIA Where is he, then?

ANINA   Why does he keep us waiting?

ANDREA The guests are gathering.

SANTIS   He will be here.

ANDREA They're sitting down.

SANTIS   Let us do so as well.

ANDREA I hate impoliteness above all else.
   I'll eat at my own expense, and alone.
   *Turns towards the door on the right. Movement outside in the
   garden.*

SANTIS What's the matter?

FLAMINIA *goes to the window* It's him.

SANTIS   Casanova?

ANINA   He!

   Anina and Flaminia open the window.

Curtain

III

In the background, under trees, the set table is visible, around which the guests are informally grouped. Not all of them have taken their seats yet; prominent among them are those mentioned earlier, especially the LORD *and the* WIDOW *from Holland. Further in the background, striding forward through the lane,* CASANOVA *becomes visible, dressed in light-colored finery, richly adorned with rings, chains, snuff boxes, etc.*

SANTIS *through the open window*
    Welcome, esteemed guests!
VOICES *of the guests*   Thank you, Herr Baron.
SANTIS Welcome, Casanova!
VOICES   Casanova!
LORD Oh, Mister Casanova, enchanted!
    He shakes his hand.
MOTHER *from Lyon, to Casanova* Over here!
DAUGHTER No, sit next to me!
WIDOW   No, to me!
SANTIS But first, Casanova, a word with you.
CASANOVA *has come closer*
    What can I do for you? *Noticing Anina and Flaminia*
                Greetings, ladies.
    Anina and Flaminia, standing on either side of the window, acknowledge Casanova's bow in a barely noticeable manner.
ANDREA *is still standing, unseen by Casanova, at the door to the right, facing away from the interior of the room.*
SANTIS I shall tell you instantly.
CASANOVA   If you please—
    My thirst and hunger are more than trifling.
SANTIS But you must first earn your meal.
    To Anina and Flaminia   Am I right?
    It will take a minute. Just one question.
CASANOVA Go ahead and ask.
SANTIS   You must step closer.
FLAMINIA Do come in.
ANINA *pointing around the corner*
        The entrance is over there.

CASANOVA   Why lose more time? Please, with your per-
mission.
He leaps over the sill into the room.
SANTIS *laughs* He's used to it.
CASANOVA *bowing* Here I am.
   Notices Andrea   Oh, Herr Bassi,
We meet again sooner than we expected.
SANTIS *admiring Casanova's suit*
My, how splendid!
CASANOVA   Isn't there a party?
One simply dresses up as best he can.
SANTIS The chain! New?
CASANOVA *incidentally* I guess.
SANTIS   And the box? Emeralds—
CASANOVA Only one. Flawed.
SANTIS   Hardly noticeable.
CASANOVA *handing him the snuff box*
Here, Baron, please take it.
SANTIS   On no account.
CASANOVA My savior, take it!
SANTIS   I want to buy it.
CASANOVA I wouldn't sell it for fifty pieces
Of gold.
SANTIS   Well, you are forcing it on me.
Puts it in his pocket; commotion outside.
ANDREA It seems your guests are getting impatient.
SANTIS So they are.
   Calls   Start serving dinner! Pour the wine!
Forgive us, we'll be out in a moment.
CASANOVA *hiding his impatience, courteously*
Now, for that question. I'm waiting. Please speak.
SANTIS The question, hmm. How can I state it clearly?
FLAMINIA Herr Bassi, you ask him.
ANINA   Ask him, Andrea!
ANDREA It wasn't I who had the bright idea
Of asking Casanova for the answer.
SANTIS Well, then I'll try it. Pay close attention.
*Begins simply, but quickly talks himself into a state of self-
indulgent enthusiasm.*

Two sisters, beautiful and young, the one,
However, younger than the other, and
The other, a bit older, but both young—
ANDREA We'll be here all night.
SANTIS *unperturbed*   And both beautiful.
Lovely of figure, of softest white skin,
One blonde, one brown-haired, and fairly well-mannered,
Yes, just fairly, as will appear at once.—
ANDREA You're jumping ahead.
SANTIS   But revealing nothing.
Mannered—up to the start of the story.
CASANOVA The story? So? What is the author's name?
FLAMINIA Andrea Bassi.
ANINA   But it lacks a conclusion.
SANTIS Exactly, that's what you must find for us.
CASANOVA Well, I really don't know—but still, go on!
SANTIS No interruptions! All right, two sisters,
From a good home with a garden, which night
Overspreads.
ANDREA   That doesn't come till later.
SANTIS Well, it's been said, and Casanova knows it
For later, when he'll need it. The father died.
Of what? We do not know. Perhaps poisoned.
ANDREA This is going nowhere.
SANTIS   But the mother
Is alive, the sisters rejoice.
ANDREA   Why?
SANTIS   Why?
With pride
Because they're not sufficiently depraved.
But suddenly, one day, who'd have guessed it,
The younger gets engaged to a nobleman.
Oh happy groom, Oh blissfulness!
ANDREA *in despair*   Baron!
SANTIS The Baron be damned, I'm a poet now.
Exactly like you, and I'm very pleased.
Where did I break off?
CASANOVA *courteously* The one is engaged.
SANTIS Quite right. Engaged the one, while the other

Full of longing, wallows in her chaste bed.
ANDREA Where will this lead?
CASANOVA   Go on. The Baron narrates
   Most poetically and suspensefully.
SANTIS One day a young man shows up, and she burns
   With love, notwithstanding that her mother
   Guards her with authority and that she
   Sleeps in the same bedroom as her sister.
CASANOVA The mother?
SANTIS   No, the sister.
CASANOVA   I thought so.
SANTIS She's looking forward with delight, this sweet
   Flower of innocence, to sacrificing
   Herself on love's altar, as many girls
   Have done before and many will do after.
CASANOVA God grant it.
SANTIS   But it came to pass otherwise.
   The wedding day had already been fixed.
CASANOVA The same day for both sisters, I suppose?
SANTIS No, just for the one. The crowd of wedding
   Guests is assembled, the bride is decked out—
   And yet, oh misery without measure,
   One is missing: the groom, a noble man,
   Is detained by urgent business matters.
   The bride sobs, the mother's tears overflow,
   The guests are whispering, "What a bridegroom!"
   And shaking their heads in untold number.
ANDREA Enough.
SANTIS   How so? I'm just now beginning.
ANDREA And are so deeply tangled in nonsense
   Already that the end is nowhere in sight.
SANTIS One does what one can. One learns gradually.
   Had I known how fine it is to compose,
   I'd have gotten started when I was young.
ANDREA *hastily* Leave the story's plot for another time,
   If Casanova wishes to hear it.
   In few words, as with a mathematics problem,
   I'll state the question that awaits his answer.
   One night, by chance, a young man embraces,

Not the lady who promised him her favors,
But another, who does not expect him.
SANTIS The sister.
ANDREA   That's all the same, it's a problem.
Dumb with fright and lust, she firmly believes
He knows with whom he is attaining bliss.
The following morning, the young man leaves.
But the two ladies, in conversation,
Unintentionally confide—reveal—
To each other the past night's adventures.
And as they realize what has happened,
Each looks on herself as the cheated one;—
The one who had sighed for him in vain, while
He, enchanted, fancied he lay in her arms;—
The other, whom he had embraced in fact;
But now that she discovers that his ardor
Was not meant for her, the soothing afterglow
Of ecstasy turns to painful longing.
So each one, by jealousy confounded,
Determined to give chase to her young man,
Each, convinced that her claim is the better,
The only valid one, affirming right
With might, seeks first with words amicably
To move the other to renunciation;
But soon, words do not suffice, no curses
Or threats have an effect; eyes blaze hatred,
The voice breaks, one lunges at the other
With a sharp pin; finally, a dagger flashes—
SANTIS Oho! Let's rein in that fancy! If such
A thing should strike the heart, it's all over
For the lady, and for the problem too.
CASANOVA Still, I assume that the daggers were blunt,
And since the word, no matter how well aimed,
Lacks the power to kill, I assume that—*with irony*
Luckily for both problem and young man—
The beautiful ladies are both alive.
But for me—do I guess right?—it remains
To decide which of them is cheated most—
Since no doubt both are, and at the same time

Casanova in Spa 67

Both cheaters—guiltless, indeed—but they are.
The one, who withheld the promised favors—
However it happened—from the young man,—
The other, who yielded the utmost gift
To him, but—it happens—not as herself.
And so it seems in this coincidence
That neither one sister nor the other,
But the good young man is the most deceived.
ANDREA The young man?!—What—deceived!? Who properly
Speaking was twice blessed?
CASANOVA   No, twice disappointed.
And should he chance to boast of his triumph,
Both women would have to call him liar.
Since rightly considered, he had neither one.
*Noise from outside. Voices, increasingly loud, become
audible.*
GUESTS *in the park*
Where is our dinner?—Bring some wine!—Hey, waiter!—
Is that a storm approaching?—That's nothing!
Baron! What's keeping you?—Hey! Wine!— Have we
Been invited in jest?—Let's call the host!—
The Baron is our host! He's standing there!—
SANTIS *goes to the window*
What's the matter? You still haven't been served?
Pardon me, noble ladies, worthy sirs—
Hey, the platters on the table, the bottles!
Where's the waiting staff hiding? None here yet?
Damned mess! Hey! You sleeping? Here, you miscreants!

TITO *enters from the right.*

TITO Herr Baron—
SANTIS *at the window, turning towards him*
Here's one. Toddle off into the kitchen.
Serve the meal! The bottles from the cellar!
Quickly, why do you stand and stare at me?
TITO I've been ordered by my boss to tell you that no platter
will be served and no bottle uncorked until the bill has been
paid.

SANTIS How dare you, boy? Has your boss gone crazy?

TITO Pardon me, Herr Baron, the boss says it was expressly
arranged this way. Here, Herr Baron. *He produces the bill*
All in all, it comes to fifty-nine ducats. Naturally, everything from before is included in that.

SANTIS Get a doctor, the host is ill! I'll pay
When I get up from dinner, not before.
Only in dives is it done otherwise.
Out with you! Take the message to your boss.

TITO *remains standing* And my orders are: not a morsel on
the plates, not a drop in the cups, prior to the bill's being
paid in full. *He turns to go.*

SANTIS Hey, wait a second. *Looks the bill over*
                              Fifty-nine. Too much
By half. Deceit, extortion, trickery!
Here you are, nine. The balance this evening.

TITO Fifty-nine, Herr Baron! I am not permitted to accept
less.

SANTIS Oh, unheard of gall! As if I were not
Good for fifty, a hundred, a thousand.
If you want a pledge, then take this snuff box,
Set with flawless precious stones.

TITO My boss has expressly instructed me to accept only
cash, since, unfortunately, he has frequently had bad
experiences with precious objects.

SANTIS   Flaminia,
Your pearls, take them off! Just for a few hours.
Even if the innkeeper's a rascal,
I won't let my guests wait any longer.
Give them here. What's keeping you?
He tries to open the clasp of Flaminia's necklace himself.

FLAMINIA   It's useless.
I've had it soldered shut. My only means
Of making sure it stays my property.
*Casanova's facial expressions proclaim his conclusive under-
standing. Automatically, he reaches for his own neck. He
looks at Anina, who returns his glance without smiling, then
at the window, then at Flaminia; he nods to himself and
smiles, more or less as if to say, "Now it's all clear to me."*

SANTIS Wicked woman! By God, I'd love to give
  You and your chain as a pledge to the host.
TITO That may perhaps be open to discussion, if the Frau
  Baroness—
  Gestures as if inviting her to leave the room with him.
CASANOVA *suddenly in front of Tito*
  Hold your mouth, boy, here, take this and get out!
  He gives him a bag full of money
  Count it outside and keep whatever's left
  Yourself, and tell your boss to remember this:
  Where Casanova has been invited,
  No innkeeper need tremble for his bill.
SANTIS *as if this were not acceptable*
  I will never—
CASANOVA   Hush, my savior. It's nothing.
  He orders Tito to withdraw by means of a gesture.
TITO *exits with repeated bowing.*
CASANOVA *to Andrea*
  And I still have enough left to make good
  My debt to you at the same time, Herr Bassi,
  Since during our ride I won back again
  From Gudar the sum I had repaid him.
  Here is your gold—and once more, I thank you.
ANDREA You had good luck.
CASANOVA *giving the bags of gold to Andrea, who takes them
  with some hesitation*
                  You have it too, my friend.
  Is the amount right?
ANDREA   It's right.
CASANOVA   That's that, then.
  *In a new tone, looking out the window where the guests are
  visible sitting at the table.*
  And now, the wine is twinkling, the platters
  Are steaming, I believe it's time to dine.
SANTIS Not yet. First your verdict.
CASANOVA *as if he were bored* Didn't I give it?
  Cheated all three: the young man doubly so,
  The women but once, each in her own way.
  So it was all settled, and I declare

The whole adventure to have been invalid.

ANDREA   That's easy to say. Unfortunately,
However, you're forgetting that the ladies
Are still standing there with naked daggers.

CASANOVA   Only in the fiction. Because, my friend,
At the core of the philosophical
Problem, there's no dagger, passion, or murder.
The bill has been settled—Let's have dinner.

ANDREA *blocking his way in childish obstinacy*
The problem is settled, I will allow.
But how, I ask you, does the story end?
Where what has once taken place does not let
Itself be dismissed as if it had not;
In which, since it is an imitation
Of nature, memory is not extinguished;
Where true and false are wonderfully entwined
And passions go on affecting people
Both in the short term as well as the long;
Where—in the story just as in real life—
There is no lack of daggers that flash, kill,
And arms of other kinds,—of blood and tears. . . .

CASANOVA *looking out the window*
Rhine salmon with green sauce—there'll be none left!

ANDREA   And where—to return to the present case,
One claim stubbornly opposes another,
And the enamored ladies aren't inclined
To relinquish, much less to share the man.

CASANOVA *speaking out the window*
Ruby red glistens the Burgundy wine—
The young lord is on his second bottle.

SANTIS   The widow from Amsterdam on her third.

CASANOVA   To dinner!

ANDREA   Not yet; you are making it
Too easy for yourself. You must first earn
The meal.

CASANOVA   Even now that I'm the host?

SANTIS   Our roles are reversed, but in exchange
I have found the solution to the problem,
And found, simultaneously, the story's

Conclusion.
ANDREA   Is that so?
SANTIS   Pay attention.
   The young man—twice happy, as Andrea thinks,
   Or as Casanova finds, twice deceived—
   Who of a night held one in his hot arms
   But in his soul embraced another's picture,—
   In order that all three have justice, he must
   During a night as dark as the one past,
   While blissfully pressed against the second
   One's breast, visualize the face of the first—
   And once again, flee before break of day.
CASANOVA *at hearing these words, has glanced in accordance
   with their tenor, now at Flaminia, now at Anina.*
SANTIS *proudly*   I've solved the problem as a philosopher,
   And as a poet conclude the story.
ANDREA   And applaud yourself like a simpleton.
SANTIS   Huh? What? *Wants to attack him.*
CASANOVA   No further delay, if you please.
SANTIS   I'll answer your simpleton for dessert, sir!
CASANOVA   And now to dinner; ladies, if you please—.
ANDREA *placing himself before the door*
   There's a first course. Let's see which one of us
   to Casanova
   Will still enjoy the dinner afterwards.
CASANOVA   So great a hurry?
ANDREA *drawing his sword*   Draw!
CASANOVA   What a fragrance
   From that roast! Truffled pies, Hungarian wine!
   To Andrea
   Two bites and a swallow, after that, death!
ANDREA   First our course, and only one of us,
   I swear, will continue to dine on earth.
   Either you or I, the other in hell.
CASANOVA   In heaven, if you insist, but right now.
SANTIS *gradually understanding*
   What? Why? Was it perhaps not a problem?
CASANOVA *has drawn too, takes up his position opposite
   Andrea.*

FLAMINIA *between them* Hold it! I forbid it! My Casanova!
SANTIS *thinking he comprehends*
    Flaminia—? With you last night—can it be?!
    With you, instead of Anina?—now I see.
    Your Casanova! Ha, not bad, truly—
    Am I not your husband, your lord anymore,
    That you should choose your own sleeping partners?
    You'll be sorry for that. But not before
    Your Casanova!
    Goes towards him, drawing his sword
                From you I demand
    Satisfaction for seducing my wife.
    And that at once.
CASANOVA *courteously*
              You'll have to wait your turn.
    Kindly step aside, if I may ask you,
    And now, Andrea, my friend, I am ready.
ANINA I won't have it. Put your sword away, Andrea,
    Have you forgotten? You no longer have
    The right to kill for me; and even less
    Of one to die for me.
ANDREA   You fool, for you—?!
    You think it really involves only you
    When Casanova and Andrea fight?
    A greater struggle will be decided here.
CASANOVA You overestimate us both, I fear.
    And yet your words are nice, and one of us—
    You, I hope—shall keep them for the next world.
    They begin to duel.
    Outside, the guests have gotten up from the table and
    approach the window; some of them look inside.
THE GUESTS How?—Look here!—What's this?—Oh!—A
    duel?!—For fun!
    Capital!—No, they're serious!—They fight well!—
    Of course—Casanova!—And the other?
    Who is it?—A handsome lad!—so young!—Go on!
    Stop that music!—Yes!—Why?
LORD   Go on! Go on!
    A hundred ducats on Casanova!

The door at the right opens suddenly, Gudar enters, looks the situation over.

GUDAR What's this?—Just in time!—
Steps between them, knocks their swords asunder.
                                        Come in, Teresa!
Here's the man you're seeking!

TERESA *stops at the door for only a second, then up to Casanova*   Casanova!
Now I've got you again, my lover, you!
She rushes into his arms.

THE GUESTS *at the window*
  A jest!—Did I tell you?!—Damn!—All over!
  Who's that little thing?—One can imagine!
  Will nothing come of it, then? Pity! Let's eat!
  They gradually withdraw from the window.

TERESA *from Casanova's arms*
  I hope the company will forgive me.
  Acquaintances too?—Flaminia! Dear friend!
  She embraces her. To Santis.
  Baron!

SANTIS Teresa!

TERESA   Well, so we meet again.
  With a slight bow to Andrea and Anina
  My name is Teresa, dancer from Naples.

GUDAR *introducing* This is Herr Andrea Bassi from Ferrara
  And Frau Anina, his attractive wife.

TERESA Yes, most attractive!
  To Andrea   Will you permit me, sir?
  She embraces Anina
  Now, what's going on? What did I interrupt?
  I dare say swords were being crossed?—But why?
  And who's fighting whom? I see three swords bare.
  To Gudar
  Truly in the nick of time, Herr von Gudar.
  What was it? No one answers? Casanova!

CASANOVA I think if one has questions to ask here,
  It's me, not you.

TERESA   Lover, unfaithful one!
  Embracing him again

I have him again—and so ask nothing.
Let your swords be sheathed—whatever happened!
Be glad with me, there's more joy in the world!
CASANOVA *partly amused, partly annoyed*
You can say "unfaithful one"? You to me?
TERESA   What then? Weren't you unfaithful? Didn't you—
I don't know how—steal away from my heart;—
And my poor heart, suddenly empty, stood
There, open—
CASANOVA   And let somebody else in.
TERESA   I don't remember. And why the questions?
Aren't I back?
CASANOVA   And where's the other one?
TERESA   Dead! Like Rhampsinit—like Alexander—
Like my great-great-grandfather and others
Who are lying in their graves. What concern
Of yours are the dead?
CASANOVA   Is he in his grave?
TERESA   Much deeper! In oblivion! No more, now,
If you love me. Am I asking questions?
And I could—right?—
To the others, but especially to Anina and Flaminia
                  And could also—*quickly*
                              But I won't.
I have you again, so everything's fine.
In a different, more determined tone
And now, my darling, a speedy farewell
From your friends, dear as they are to us both.
We're leaving!
CASANOVA *laughing*   What are you saying?
TERESA   My coach
Waits outside the gate, right, Gudar?—you saw it.
GUDAR   And what a coach, and how richly harnessed!
TERESA *to Casanova*
You have just enough time to pack quickly,
We have to leave at once. I'm on my way
To Vienna, to the Imperial Court Theater.
Six thousand gulden salary. My first role,
The slave in "King Rhampsinit."

GUDAR   The second—
I'll wager, Roxanne in "Alexander."
TERESA Or maybe Ariadne; it all depends.
GUDAR How divinely you danced both roles in Rome!
CASANOVA And you believe I'm just going to go
To Vienna with you?
TERESA   You've yearned to go there
A long time. There's never been a better
Opportunity.
GUDAR   Nor sweeter company.
TERESA And there are women there—
CASANOVA *laughing*   And men—
TERESA *also laughing*   Thank God!
CASANOVA So, all the best. As far as I'm concerned—
I'm expected elsewhere. In Petersburg,
In Brussels, Madrid—
TERESA   So you'll choose Vienna. . .
CASANOVA I couldn't possibly, even if I
Wanted to leave. Some pressing matters hold
Me here.
To Santis
Right, Baron?
SANTIS   What's that? You mean me?
If that's all it is, go, God be with you.
I know nothing more of it. Here's my hand.
CASANOVA And here, sir, is mine.
TERESA *believing she understands*
                         What, Flaminia, you?
I thought so right away. The wild red mouth—
The divine figure—how well I understand.
She sighs, impetuously embracing Flaminia at the same time.
GUDAR *applauds.*
TERESA Now, Casanova, let's be on our way.
CASANOVA I see one other who might stop my leaving—
ANDREA *bitter* Who can stop anyone from anything?
Sheathes his sword.
SANTIS Spoken like a philosopher.
ANDREA   Cheap scorn.
SANTIS You called me simpleton, now we're even.

CASANOVA Andrea, your hand.

ANDREA *gives it to him* Good luck on your journey!

TERESA *to Anina* You too, my sweet child? Well, naturally,
Who can resist him? What was your name again?

GUDAR *answers for Anina* Anina.

TERESA Sweet and innocent. How else
Could it be? Anina—let me hug you!
Embraces her impetuously.

TITO *enters in haste* Beg pardon—

CASANOVA Looking for someone?

SANTIS What does the boy want?

TITO My message is for the famous dancer Teresa from
Naples.

TERESA For me?

CASANOVA What do you want from Teresa?

TITO *bows deeply to Teresa* Oh, I thought so right away.

TERESA What do you want?

CASANOVA Speak!

TITO It's for the lady only.

CASANOVA We keep no secrets here.

TERESA Go on, speak.

CASANOVA Well, shall we hear it today?

TITO But I do beg of you, not to make me suffer for it if it
should be somehow disagreeable to the ladies and gentlemen.

CASANOVA Quick, without preface, who wants Teresa?
A man?
To Teresa
That's why the rush? A pursuer?
To Tito
Now speak! A gentleman? A young gentleman?

TITO No, two.

CASANOVA What are you saying? Two of them?

TITO But they don't belong together.

TERESA Well, then—

TITO They arrived at practically the same minute, each in a
different carriage, and both asked me whether the famous
dancer Teresa had put up at this inn. Each in secret. Neither
is aware of the other. I don't suppose they even know each

other.

GUDAR   How should they, if the one is Rhampsinit,
And the other the great Alexander!
Where should those two have become acquainted?

TITO   They didn't say their names. Perhaps they're called
that, but I can't say anything for certain.

TERESA   I don't know them, let them go to the devil.

CASANOVA   You don't know them?

TERESA   And whoever they are—
I don't know them now.

CASANOVA *to Tito*   Where are the gentlemen?

TITO   Well looked after for the time being. Since both of
them struck me as very excitable, and one can never tell
what such excited people have up their sleeves, I have for
the time being led each one into a different room and
locked the door behind him.

CASANOVA   Locked up?

SANTIS *to Tito*   This could turn out badly for you.

TITO   I can manage to keep them under lock and key for half
an hour. The windows open up onto a courtyard, no one
will hear them if they happen to make noise. In the meantime, the ladies and gentlemen will have time to take care
of whatever is necessary here.

TERESA   I like this boy. Listen Casanova,
We'll take him to Vienna as our servant.

CASANOVA   We? No. But I—whether just to Vienna,
Remains to be seen. Possibly—to Lisbon.

TERESA *to Tito*   You're coming to Vienna with me.

CASANOVA   To Lisbon.

TERESA   Get ready immediately, we're leaving.

TITO   Can this really be true? The famous dancer Teresa
wants to take me into her service? What luck!

CASANOVA   For the time being you're serving us both.
And later you'll choose where you wish to stay.

TERESA   He shall never choose—
To Casanova   I'm yours eternally.
Throws herself in his arms.

GUDAR   Life may be long—eternity is short!

CASANOVA   So, get ready, boy, our journey begins

An hour from now.
TERESA   Not until then? Why?
All sorts of things can happen in an hour.
CASANOVA If hell itself should punish my delay,
I'll not set off until I've eaten lunch.
SANTIS By the God of champagne, truffles, and pies—
He has surely earned it. And we no less.
Though the best morsels are already gone,
Still, if the divine Teresa shares it
With us, we'll call it a regal repast.
TERESA   Who can withstand words like these? I'll dine
too. . .
With a glance at Anina and Flaminia
If these two lovelies remain at my side.
Flaminia and Anina give her their hands which she keeps in hers.
And just for an hour; then—
to Casanova   my darling,
Off to Vienna in my winged carriage.
Exits through the door to the right, leading Flaminia and Anina by the hand; Santis and Gudar follow.

CASANOVA, ANDREA

CASANOVA *was about to follow as well; but when he notices Andrea standing motionless at the door, he stops there too.*
And you?
ANDREA *courteously*
                Please don't linger. It's time to dine.
CASANOVA Not without you, else I'll think you're angry
With me and that would spoil my appetite.
ANDREA Very funny.
CASANOVA *goes closer to him*
                I am your friend, Andrea.
ANDREA But I'm not yours, Casanova.
CASANOVA   Winning
You over would be an honor for me.
VOICES *from the park* Casanova! Casanova!
ANDREA Go, they're calling you. No one's calling me.

And it's right this way. This is not my world.
It is yours. They're calling you, do get out!
CASANOVA   Even if you persist in scolding me
So rudely, I would never leave you here
With so wounded a heart.
ANDREA   What business of yours
Is Andrea's heart?
CASANOVA   Fine; let it be closed to me.
But I call it childish obstinacy
If it scorns to receive the consolation
It longs for, even from hands lovelier
Than those of an unwelcome friend;—to take
It thankfully from the beloved's hands.
ANDREA   Shall I really believe, Casanova,
That this morning's shamelessly glaring light
Lit up the depths of my soul so little
For your deep-seeing eye?
Passionately, not violently
                              Do you believe
Andrea could ever be reconciled with,
And approach as her lover, a woman
He'd loved and who'd been unfaithful to him?!—
The way other men can, the way in which
To my amazement, Casanova can,
Who is granted the choice among thousands
And who chooses the most unfaithful one.
CASANOVA *unembarrassed*
Whom do you mean?
ANDREA   You ask?
CASANOVA   Ah, Teresa!
Right?
ANDREA *somewhat confused*
            She herself, so it seemed to me, confessed.—
CASANOVA   Confessed. Well, yes, but for all there is for her
To confess and to keep hidden from me—
I ask you, is there greater faithfulness,
Is there, to be more precise, any other
On earth between men and women, Andrea,
Than what Teresa just demonstrated?

She returned to me. That is faithfulness,
The only kind deserving of the name;
Because everything else we consider
To be the guarantees of faith will not
Stand up to rational examination.
Is it proof, perhaps, when virtue itself,
After a hard struggle, sinks into your arms
Amid hot tears of passion? Who can tell
Of whom she is dreaming while in your arms!
A sacred vow? Friend, women know as well
As we: God uses his lightning sparingly.
Does she court danger? That spices pleasure.
Does she kill herself, by this ultimate
Sacrifice to conquer her lover's doubts—?
At heart she merely hopes—as a blest spirit
To gloat over his tears of repentance—
ANDREA And nowhere faith—?
CASANOVA   Oh, yes! I just told you:
The coming back, from wherever it be.
ANDREA Yes, if it were homecoming, then maybe.
CASANOVA Homecoming?—A phantom! As if one could
Flatter himself that he's "home" to another.
Is wandering not the soul's eternal call?
What yesterday was alien and chill, does
It not hug us today, warm and familiar?
And what we called home, was it ever more
Than a stop on the way, as short or long
As it lasted? Home and abroad—dead words
For him who does not, in bourgeois fashion—
Oppressed by prejudice, intimidated
By the law, and cowardly entangled
In the bedlam of conscience,—invent order
For himself in the chaos of his heart.
The man of open mind and free spirit—
places a hand on Andrea's shoulder
One like us, lives extemporaneously.
ANDREA You're no philosopher, but a sophist.
CASANOVA Could be. Hence I'm fated to make mistakes.
Only from case to case; it's not my fate

In an obnoxious philosophic way,
Fixed glasses on my nose, to see the world
Always the same, yes, but always wrongly.
TITO *enters with a small suitcase in his hand*
Here I am, all set to go, as you ordered.
CASANOVA   Ay, already? I'm not yet.
ANDREA   Don't blame me.
CALLS *from the Park*   Casanova!
CASANOVA   I know. It's getting to be high time now.
   Andrea—
As if he were about to invite him to come along.
TITO *amazed*
The gentleman still wants to have lunch?
CASANOVA   You have no
   objection, I hope?
TITO   I wish only, most humbly, to call your attention to the
   fact that the two gentlemen have become a bit restless in
   their rooms.
CASANOVA   The two departed ones? Right, I forgot.
   *Noise from above the room which was already audible
   earlier.*
TITO   They have practically expired. I'm afraid the innkeeper
   will hear them in the end, after all, unlock the doors, and
   what will happen then. . . . Perhaps it would be good for us
   all, dear sir, if we, before—
He makes gestures of disappearing.
CASANOVA   Careful and saucy at the same time, boy?
   Louder noise from above.
You unlock the doors, and immediately.
And bring both—
interrupting himself Do they look respectable?
TITO   Not only respectable, but fashionable and very hand-
   some.
CASANOVA   Did I ask that? I'll invite them to dine.
TITO   To dine, the two excitable gentlemen?
CASANOVA   I will ask them to grant me the honor
   Of joining me at a modest meal prior
   To my leaving for Vienna with the famous
   Teresa. What are you waiting for? Shall I

Find legs for you?

TITO *exits*

ANDREA   Truly, Casanova,
I've never yet met a human being
So well disposed, so hospitably inclined.

CASANOVA You will really get to like me at table!
*He takes him by the arm, as if he wanted to link arms with
him, suddenly points to the park*
Look, my friend—

ANDREA *without following his glance, as if still sulking*
What's there to see?

CASANOVA Teresa, Flaminia and Anina. . .

ANDREA *looks outside, starts*
Arm in arm.

CASANOVA Yes, arm in arm.

ANDREA   And chatting. . .

CASANOVA Smiling—

ANDREA   Laughing—

CASANOVA All three strolling on the lawn—the bright sky
Above them—in sisterly unity.
What a picture—

ANDREA *bitter*   Yes, what a picture, indeed!

CASANOVA A lovely one.—If men could ever be
Brothers the way all women are sisters—
In response to a movement by Andrea
Are sisters in their deepest souls—In truth,
Life would be a far less difficult thing.

ANDREA What, it's still not easy enough for you?
I'm afraid you're being unreasonable.

GUDAR *enters* What's new? I have been sent to see whether
You stabbed each other to death after all.
Laughter outside.

ANDREA The anxiety doesn't seem to be
Very great, exactly.

GUDAR   But the longing
For your company, great beyond measure.

CASANOVA *pointing outside* There they are now; they don't
look at all bad.

GUDAR What? New guests?

CASANOVA   And Teresa, marvelous—
  As if she'd never seen the two of them.
  He calls outside
  Music! It's stopped too long.
TERESA *calls from outside*   Casanova!
CASANOVA *calling out* Welcome, gentlemen!
GUDAR   I see.
  Rhampsinit
  And Alexander. Handsome young men both.
  Flaminia's already flitting around them.
  Music.
CASANOVA Andrea, friend, I will not wait much longer.
GUDAR The Baron scents something too. I'm afraid
  They will depart poorer than they arrived.
CASANOVA *to Gudar*
  Perhaps we'll find a little time after lunch
  For a short game. What do you think, Gudar?
GUDAR You go to Vienna and leave them to me.
VOICES *from outside* Casanova! Casanova!
ANINA'S VOICE *from outside* Andrea!
CASANOVA   You're being called too. That was Anina's
  voice.
  And if you still hesitate now, you will
  Deserve nothing more than to be deceived.
  In response to a gesture of Andrea's
  For the first time.
VOICES *from outside*
                        Casanova! Andrea!
ANINA *from outside*
  Andrea, will you come out here, finally?
ANDREA *prepares to go.*
CASANOVA *delighted*   With me, Andrea,
  my dear chosen brother!
  *Exits with him, arm in arm. The rejoicing with which they are
  received outside is audible.—The music resounds more loudly.*

GUDAR   *stands at the window, looks out into the park*   Oh, to
be young again—!
The music grows particularly clear, then suddenly dies away.
But, I was once!

*Laughter and music. Gudar steps away from the window in
order to join the others in the park.*

The curtain falls.

SEDUCTION COMEDY

CHARACTERS

AURELIE
JUDITH
SERAPHINE
MAX VON REISENBERG
ULRICH BARON VON FALKENIR
ARDUIN PRINCE OF PEROSA
AMBROS DOEHL
GYSAR
WESTERHAUS, *a bank president*
JULIA, *his wife, Judith's sister*
ELIGIUS FENZ, *an opera singer, Seraphine's father*
ELISABETH, *his younger daughter*
LEINDORF, *a lieutenant, Elisabeth's fiancé*
FRANZISKA PRINCESS OF DEGENBACH
BRAUNIGL, *a district attorney*
SKODNY, *cavalry captain*
RUDOLF VON HEYSKAL, *councilor*
ALBINE and IDA, *friends of Elisabeth*
MEYERHOFER, *retired chamber singer*
MADAME DEVONA, *retired chamber singer*
HANSEN, *hotel manager*
GILDA, *his daughter, fifteen years old*

Strollers, masked persons in fancy dress and in dominos, hotel waiters, including a small black man, footmen, servants. The first act takes place in the Prince of Perosa's park, during a public celebration on the night of May 1, 1914.

The first scene of the second act takes place at the small mansion of the Countess Aurelie von Merkenstein on the Salesianergasse; the second at Judith's, in the Westerhaus apartment; the third at Seraphine's, in her father's house. All three scenes take place on one day, in mid-June 1914.

The third act takes place in Gilleleije, on the Danish coast, on August 1, 1914.

ACT ONE

An evening spring festival in the park of the Prince of Perosa. The park rises moderately towards the rear. Far in the background, the Prince's illuminated, not very large palace, in Baroque style. In the center of the stage, but not filling it, a stone-rimmed pool, in the middle of which stands a statue. A usable path runs all around the pool. Stone benches are right, left, and front. Walks towards the right and left. At right front, inside a tent-like structure, a fully laid buffet, in front of it several small tables with chairs. As the curtain rises, one can hear the music of a small orchestra from a distance which soon dies away, becoming audible again from time to time. Ladies and gentlemen in summer outfits, several in dominos. The movements of the public take place almost exclusively in the background. As the curtain rises, two gentlemen and a lady in front of the tent, on the point of withdrawing.

Inside the tent, Princess FRANZISKA VON DEGENBACH *and* JUDITH ASRAEL. *Captain* SKODNY *and* RUDOLF VON HEYSKAL *are just approaching from the left. The Princess, a dainty blonde, is past forty but makes a younger impression.* JUDITH ASRAEL *is around twenty, of medium stature, with dark eyes and hair. Both are wearing light summer dresses.*

PRINCESS *mechanically* Would you like champagne, gentlemen? —Oh, here are some dear acquaintances! Good evening, Captain.

RUDOLF VON HEYSKAL *introducing himself* Sektionsrat von Heyskal. *He notices that the Princess does not recognize him right away.* Your humble servant, Princess. *Kisses her hand* Good evening, Fräulein Judith. May I have a glass of champagne?

SKODNY And me. . . .

PRINCESS *pours a glass for Skodny.*

One of the Princess's footmen has come forward from the rear of the tent and whispered a few words to her.

JUDITH *Pours a glass for Heyskal, but there is not enough cham-*

pagne to fill it up quite.

PRINCESS But just ask for it in the palace. There is surely still enough champagne in the cellar.

JUDITH Oh, that was our last bottle!

PRINCESS Another load is coming right away. I've already sent for it.

The footman has exited.

SKODNY This really is a marvelous party. I trust Your Highness is satisfied?

PRINCESS Oh, yes, we've taken in an immense amount of money for our charity.

SKODNY I dare say this is the first time in living memory that the Perosa Park has been open to the public?

PRINCESS If you think it was easy to get permission from Prince Arduin. . . .

RUDOLF VON HEYSKAL *to Judith* I just now had the good fortune to see your beautiful sister, Frau Westerhaus.

JUDITH You recognized her?

RUDOLF VON HEYSKAL Naturally, she took her mask off while she danced.

JUDITH So, she danced?

RUDOLF VON HEYSKAL With Herr von Reisenberg.

JUDITH Oh, Max von Reisenberg is here too?

A second footman has brought a few bottles of champagne. One is opened immediately.

PRINCESS Well, thank God.

A gentleman and a lady approach the tent.

PRINCESS A moment's patience, please, my friends.

JUDITH *pours a glass for Rudolf von Heyskal.*

PRINCESS *pours for the others.*

RUDOLF VON HEYSKAL Aren't you in the mood to dance as well, Fräulein Judith?

JUDITH I'm on duty now, as you can see, Herr von Heyskal. Perhaps later.

Bank President WESTERHAUS *enters; approximately forty-five years old, large, broad, energetic, with a somewhat ruthless face; he is wearing a white summer suit and white gloves. With him, the district attorney,* EMMERICH BRAUNIGL, *over forty, with a youthful, sharp-featured face; he is wearing an open domino over a summer suit.*

WESTERHAUS *to Braunigl* My little sister-in-law will surely still have some champagne for us. *At the buffet, in greeting* Your Highness—

PRINCESS Good evening, my dear Herr President. I must still thank you on behalf of the committee for your generous contribution.

WESTERHAUS *introducing his companion* Permit me, Your Highness—District Attorney Emmerich Braunigl.

PRINCESS Your name is well known to me, Herr District Attorney.

BRAUNIGL Your Highness has an interest in the courtroom as well?

PRINCESS I always read about the court proceedings immediately after the theater and art news. After that come the local news and the classified advertisements. It's only with politics that I want nothing to do.

RUDOLF VON HEYSKAL And it is just politics, Your Highness, which may not be so uninteresting nowadays.

JUDITH *hands Westerhaus a glass of champagne.*

WESTERHAUS Thank you, Judith. *Drinks* The night lighting becomes you. I had no idea that you are so good-looking.

JUDITH *lightly* Pity.

PRINCESS Where is your beautiful wife, Herr President?

WESTERHAUS That is something you must not ask the husband, Princess. Disappeared, lost, perhaps kidnapped.

RUDOLF VON HEYSKAL I saw the Frau President dancing just now. *To Judith* Does it still not tempt you, Fräulein Judith? It is a rare sensation. . . in the open. . . under the stars.

WESTERHAUS *throws a number of gold pieces onto the buffet.*

PRINCESS But Herr President! This is almost too much.

WESTERHAUS Don't people like us have a difficult time of it, Your Highness? We are considered either stingy or ostentatious.

BRAUNIGL *with a glance at the gold pieces* Such a degree of generosity is almost immoral.

SKODNY Oh, what is money? Money is actually just a fiction.
BRAUNIGL Nevertheless, one can buy oneself any number of things with it.
WESTERHAUS Everything.

The painter GYSAR enters. He is over forty, with smooth black hair and a dark Van Dyke beard. He is wearing a summer suit and a half open domino.

PRINCESS *waving to him* Master Gysar! Over here, Master Gysar. There's champagne.

Gysar walks over, kisses the Princess's hand somewhat too familiarly, then observes Judith, who hands him a glass of champagne.

JUDITH I am Judith Asrael. You painted my sister Julia, three years ago.
GYSAR Ah, but they hid you away from me. *He drinks to her* When may I begin your portrait?
WESTERHAUS Wait until Judith has become a famous singer, Gysar.
GYSAR You are going on stage, Fraulein?
WESTERHAUS A student of the opera singer Fenz's, and soon of Jean de Reszke's.
GYSAR You must make a marvelous Carmen.
PRINCESS How do you like our party, Master Gysar?
GYSAR The people are having a great time.
WESTERHAUS It's not likely to be a party to Gysar's taste, Your Highness. They have parties of a different kind in his garden.
RUDOLF VON HEYSKAL More magnificent than this?
GYSAR More honest, perhaps.
WESTERHAUS That is the question. Or do you mean to say that nakedness does not lie, Gysar? *Out of control.* And if you could tear open their breasts. . . their hearts would still be lying.
JUDITH *stares at him.*
  In the background, movement of people drawing closer.
VOICES CALLING OUT Long live the Prince of Perosa!

PRINCESS Ah, there comes His Highness.

RUDOLF VON HEYSKAL Ambros Doehl at his side.

BRAUNIGL The author—right?

SKODNY His Highness enjoys condescending.

GYSAR Perhaps, Herr Captain, it is Ambros Doehl who is condescending in this case?
The attention of the company is drawn to the right.

ARDUIN *and* AMBROS DOEHL, *coming around the pool, approach.*

RUDOLF VON HEYSKAL *to Skodny* Have you taken a close look at the Princess?

SKODNY Yes—and?

RUDOLF VON HEYSKAL Well, then go to the Modern Gallery sometime soon and look for yourself at the slumbering Venus with the red rose at her breast.

SKODNY . . . Titian's?

RUDOLF VON HEYSKAL No, Gysar's—in the Modern Gallery.

SKODNY You see a resemblance?

RUDOLF VON HEYSKAL Resemblance? Don't you know, then, that he paints two pictures of every woman who sits for him? The official one, dressed, and then another one. . . .
Arduin and Ambros have reached the tent. The Princess has stepped outside the tent.

PRINCESS Well, my Prince, how does popularity suit you?

ARDUIN *in the uniform of an Austrian Hussar General, but nevertheless wearing a black satin domino over it, so that the uniform is only barely visible. His head is bare.* Dearest Princess, I leave it gladly to those enviable individuals who are accustomed to that sort of homage.

AMBROS *wearing a light colored summer suit covered by a domino, extends his hand to Judith.*

ARDUIN May I introduce you to Herr Ambros Doehl, Princess?

PRINCESS That won't be necessary, Highness, the name of Ambros Doehl is becoming world famous, after all.

AMBROS *bows.*

JUDITH *hands him a glass of champagne.*

ARDUIN *moves forward a little with the Princess* One question, Princess, if I may. Hasn't your pretty niece, the Countess Aurelie, arrived from Merkenstein?

PRINCESS I don't know anything about it, Highness. In fact, I haven't even seen her since Shrove Tuesday at my house—which of course does not exclude the possibility of her still showing up here.

JUDITH *goes up to Ambros, gives him a rose* Take this, Ambros, as a thank you.

AMBROS For what?

JUDITH For your terza rimas.

AMBROS You read poetry, Judith?

JUDITH Yours, Ambros Doehl.—You are friends with the Prince?

AMBROS Friends? I'm only a kind of secret revolutionary for him.

RUDOLF VON HEYSKAL *to Judith, pleading* Fräulein Judith!

JUDITH Yes, right, dancing.—Here I am!
Nods to Ambros in passing, leaves with Heyskal.

PRINCESS *to Arduin* May an old, devoted friend be permitted to give Your Highness a humble bit of advice?

ARDUIN Please.

PRINCESS *somewhat surprisingly, in a new tone of voice* Just simply ride out to Merkenstein, Highness, and fetch Aurelie for yourself.

ARDUIN You have funny ideas, Princess, as always.

PRINCESS Once again, forgive me. But for my part, Highness, I don't believe in any of your love affairs.

ARDUIN *smiling* Oh!

PRINCESS Everything only out of spite. But I wouldn't put it off much longer in your place, Highness. Aurelie was always so unpredictable. That time at my house, on Shrove Tuesday, she surfaced completely unexpected, indeed, uninvited, after two years of total seclusion.

ARDUIN She was in mourning after the death of her parents.

PRINCESS That was long past, already.—I think anything is possible with her. *Arduin looks at her, surprised* Even that she might disappear into a convent one fine day.

ARDUIN *smiles, as if pacified, turns to Westerhaus, who has been standing apart with Skodny, Gysar, and Braunigl* Well, my dear President, what do you think? Will we have war?

WESTERHAUS Your Highness is asking me? This is too great an honor.

ARDUIN Who else? If you are so inclined—together with your professional colleagues in France, England, America, Japan, then we will simply have war.

WESTERHAUS Your Highness is overestimating us bankers a little. *After a short hesitation* Still, if Your Highness wishes to undertake an undisturbed cruise in your new yacht, I would not wait until midsummer.

ARDUIN Hmm, pity that my ship will probably not be finished before July.

WESTERHAUS One hears wonderful things about it, Highness. It is said to be truly a fairy-tale yacht.

PRINCESS May one ask, Highness, where you will take it on its maiden voyage?

ARDUIN If I knew that, then it wouldn't really be a fairy-tale yacht. For the time being I know only that it will be launched in Denmark. Hennings in Copenhagen is building her. Several things are still missing, especially where the artistic embellishments are concerned. *Turning to Gysar* Would you like to paint a picture for my sleeping cabin?

GYSAR Your Highness is too gracious, but unfortunately I lack the talent to work on commission. . . . Nevertheless, it will be a great honor for me, at a suitable time, to offer Your Highness a picture which I painted without a commission.

ARDUIN I love your pictures, Gysar. I may well take you at your word.

A singing voice has been audible for a short time, the sounds of a violin are soaring above it.

ARDUIN Just listen to that, Ambros. Who is that singing so beautifully?

WESTERHAUS That is Judith's voice.

AMBROS And a violin is soaring beautifully above it.

ELIGIUS FENZ, *already visible earlier, steps closer; a smooth-shaven actor's face, thick, almost completely white hair, and a lively glance.*

ELIGIUS FENZ   The violin is being played by Fräulein Seraphine Fenz, my daughter; the singer is Fräulein Judith Asrael, one of my most gifted students. Engaged in Dresden for the coming season.

PRINCESS   Good evening, Herr Fenz.

ELIGIUS FENZ *notices now upon what a distinguished company he has happened, and first of all kisses the Princess's hand* May I ask the favor, Your Highness, to be introduced to this noble company.

PRINCESS   But who does not know Eligius Fenz, our famous opera singer, member of the Imperial and Royal Court Opera.

ELIGIUS FENZ *as if to ward her off* Past member. An honorary member for a long time now.

WESTERHAUS   Well, your students will spread your fame if I may judge by Judith.

PRINCESS *hands Eligius Fenz a filled glass* Please, Herr Fenz.

ELIGIUS FENZ *bows, then drinks to all the others* To the good health of the illustrious company!
He empties his glass.

PRINCESS *pours a second glass for him. Westerhaus and Skodny stand closest to him. Arduin and Ambros have moved together in the meantime. The activity in the background grows livelier for a while; louder music blares up again.*

PRINCESS *to Gysar* But now I too want to plunge into the bustle. Your arm, Gysar.
The Princess and Gysar exit to the rear. Fenz has taken a seat at one of the small tables and drinks alone. Westerhaus and Skodny, still with Fenz at the outset, soon withdraw. Ambros and Arduin have come left forward together.

ARDUIN   Well?

AMBROS   Your Highness?

ARDUIN   She is not here.

AMBROS   But there is still an hour to go before midnight.

ARDUIN   I'd have to know if she were here. No one saw her come. My park has no secret entrances, at least not tonight. She's not in Vienna at all. I know it. The doors in her little mansion on the Salesianergasse are locked and the windows covered. Aurelie has stayed out in Merkenstein and is laughing at us all. It was a carnival jest, nothing more.

AMBROS Do you really believe that, Highness?

ARDUIN We were fools to have taken it seriously. You and I, I mean, I am not including Falkenir, of course.

AMBROS Why not?

ARDUIN He is no more here than Aurelie.

AMBROS Your Highness is mistaken. The Baron is here at the party. We've already greeted each other from a distance.

ARDUIN So, he is here? Well, he could just as well have stayed in Rome. Don't you agree, Ambros? I wonder how many years older than Aurelie he is. Ten or fifteen, certainly.

AMBROS How little would youth be if it were everything. And by the way, he's barely past forty.

ARDUIN Not more? He was after all a friend of Aurelie's father and, after both parents died, Aurelie's guardian or something like that. His first wife committed suicide, by the way. His first, I'm saying, as if he were sure to get a second one. Not a soul knows why. She was a Princess Rodenberg.

AMBROS I did not move in those circles very frequently back then.

ARDUIN He retired from his diplomatic post at the time, and from the world generally, and now he lives in Rome as a recluse.

AMBROS As a scholar, Highness. Last year he published an article about the latest excavations on the Palatine.

ARDUIN That too. The Falkenirs were always odd. His father devoted himself to Buddhist studies. I would just like to know what suddenly induced this Falkenir, after he had been as good as dead, to appear at the Princess's ball. He didn't even have a reason to suppose that Aurelie would be there. No one knew it. Do you know, the Princess hadn't even invited her? All of a sudden, unexpectedly, there she stood, like an apparition from another world. . . among us mortals, I nearly said.

AMBROS I imagine we are something of the sort, Highness.

ARDUIN And Aurelie is not?

AMBROS There are gradations, evidently.

ARDUIN *more seriously* You may be right, Ambros Doehl. . . . It was the night of a ball like a hundred others —and in that instant when Aurelie came in—it seemed like the beginning of a fairy tale.

AMBROS   It was Aurelie, how should it not be a fairy tale?

ARDUIN   Indeed. *Smiling* The Countess and the three suitors
. . . . Only, is it certain there are no others whom she bewitched that evening?

AMBROS   It's difficult to say. In any case, it is only you,
Prince Arduin, the Baron von Falkenir, and I who have been
ordered here at midnight tonight, in order to learn Aurelie's
decision from her own lips.

ARDUIN   She will not come. How ever could we take such a
crazy affair seriously? Even during these past three months,
I did not think of this appointment as of something real,
something that could lead to any real continuation. Even my
own courtship of her seemed like something unreal to me—or
at the very least like something incomprehensible. Hasn't it
been something like that for you, Ambros?

AMBROS   If it had been like that for me it would be easier to
explain. The courtship by a thoroughly middle-class young
author for the hand of a Countess of Merkenstein after a
deferential friendship of barely half a year—it has been no
longer than that, Prince Arduin, since you had the kindness to
introduce me to the Countess—was, to say the least, a
somewhat bolder undertaking than the courtship of the Prince
of Perosa and Rodegna.

ARDUIN   Do you think so? If it didn't concern Aurelie, then
perhaps you would be right. But even I, who have known
Aurelie since her earliest youth—as children we played here,
around this pool, Ambros—had until the night of that ball
never so much as dreamt that I could ever desire her for my
wife. And during these past three months, while we were
forbidden to see Aurelie—she absolutely slipped away from
me. She and the memory of that night slipped from me into
the unreal, the improbable, into something that had never
been. And only now, since we have been speaking of her
again—

JULIA   *wearing a domino and a mask, enters from the left*
Arduin, I have to talk to you.

ARDUIN   Is that so, pretty mask? Only, I'm afraid I won't have
time for that.

JULIA Don't you know me, Arduin?

ARDUIN You were presumably my lover once—how should I know you?

JULIA *takes the mask from her face* It's me.

ARDUIN We're not alone. Why are you taking your mask off?

JULIA Does one keep secrets from Ambros Doehl?

AMBROS True, unfortunately. I used to wish sometimes that people would keep secrets from me, but neither they nor I succeeded at it.

JULIA I have to talk to you, Arduin.

ARDUIN What for? It's over.

AMBROS *slowly walks over to Eligius Fenz's table.*

JULIA I know that. Am I not worth a farewell? Are you afraid of me? I swear to you, I will not strangle myself in your bed.

ARDUIN Come!

Arduin and Julia exit right.

ELIGIUS FENZ *to Ambros, who has sat down at his table* My daughters ask for you, Herr Doehl. Why don't we see you at our house anymore? Because the noble circles attract you. Take care of yourself, Ambros Doehl. Princely favor is dangerous for an artist.

AMBROS I hear you could tell quite a story on that score, Herr Fenz.

ELIGIUS FENZ How do you mean that?—Oh, you're thinking of that old story. . . about the Archduchess? Incidentally, she was not an archduchess, but simply a countess.

AMBROS *in order to please him* You had to spend an entire cold winter's night on the balcony—isn't that so?

ELIGIUS FENZ There are two different versions of that. According to the one I did in fact spend the night on the balcony. Then again, another version maintains that I jumped down from the first floor, into the garden.

AMBROS And remained lying there, dead.

ELIGIUS FENZ That would be the third version.

SERAPHINE *joins them. Blonde, of medium height, voluptuously slim, with a simple hair-do, wearing a white summer dress; of unpretentious appearance* Is it possible? Our friend Ambros? It's a wonder that we should see you again.

ELIGIUS FENZ You played splendidly, my child.

SERAPHINE *a modest gesture.*

AMBROS You've made great strides, Seraphine.

SERAPHINE *pointing to the roses in order to interrupt him* What marvelous roses.

AMBROS May I offer you one?

SERAPHINE Thank you. *She takes the rose* They glow in the darkness.

AMBROS Yes, they are bloody like the tears of betrayed love. What was that piece you were playing before? It was such a passionate melody.

SERAPHINE Improvisations. Such as my heart suggested to me.

AMBROS In that case I'm surprised they were so sincere, Seraphine.

SERAPHINE Do you think so? The violin did not reveal everything. And it couldn't, really. It was not mine. I borrowed it from one of the musicians.

ELIGIUS FENZ And now it is consecrated for all time.

SERAPHINE You are carrying on today, father.

ELIGIUS FENZ Believe me, she is going to become a great artist. She is lacking perhaps one more thing: the great adventure—the great happiness, the great suffering.

SERAPHINE Enough, father, enough. *To Ambros* One never knows where he will end up once he gets started.
Gently strokes her father's cheek.

ELIGIUS FENZ *kisses her hand.*

AMBROS One must make all manner of sacrifice for art's sake. Virtue is the least of it.—Oh—your sister.

SERAPHINE Yes, it's her.

ELIGIUS FENZ And always with the Lieutenant! You should not allow it, Seraphine.

SERAPHINE Yes, with Lieutenant Leindorf. Prepare yourself for a surprise, father.

ELIGIUS FENZ I have a suspicion.

AMBROS This really seems to be turning into a family reunion. Good-bye! Give my regards to Elisabeth.

SERAPHINE She would be glad. . . after all, she is still in love with you a little.

AMBROS I imagine we will see each other again.

Exits right.

ELISABETH, *Seraphine's sister, resembling her, but a little sharper in her manner, also wearing a plain, white summer dress, and Lieutenant* LEINDORF, *a handsome young man, enter from the left.*

ELISABETH *to Seraphine* Wasn't that Ambros Doehl? *Without waiting for an answer* Where is your overcoat, father? Karl will get it for you from the wardrobe.

ELIGIUS FENZ It's a summer night, my child. I left the coat home.

ELISABETH *shaking her head* And so close to the pool. *Running her hand over the edge of a bench* The benches are all damp. Oh, you two, one should never let you out of one's sight.

SERAPHINE And yet, one must occasionally.
Takes Elisabeth's head between her hands.

ELISABETH *quietly frees herself* Oh, well. *To Leindorf* Well, Karl, it's your turn, say something already.

LEINDORF My highly esteemed Herr Fenz. I have the honor of asking you for your daughter Elisabeth's hand.

ELIGIUS FENZ You get right to the point, Herr Lieutenant.

ELISABETH Do the same, father, and say yes.

ELIGIUS FENZ Are you in such a hurry to make me a grandfather, my child?

ELISABETH It would be quite good for you, father. You might finally realize, then, that you're not a youngster anymore.

ELIGIUS FENZ *sits down on a bench* Have a seat, first of all, Herr Lieutenant.—What do you think, Seraphine?

SERAPHINE I suppose we'll have to say yes, father.

ELIGIUS FENZ Have you thought everything over thoroughly, Elisabeth? He is a soldier. War could break out tomorrow or the day after. You might remain behind with three unprovided-for children.

LEINDORF The rumors of war are without foundation, Herr Fenz.

ELISABETH Stock-market maneuvers, everyone knows that. We want to get married on June 15th at the latest. We will honeymoon in Carinthia, first because Karl's new garrison is in Klagenfurt, and second because his parents have an estate nearby.

ELIGIUS FENZ Ah!

LEINDORF A small estate at best.

ELIGIUS FENZ Well, there is something to be said for it, in any event, if one of you were settled.

ELISABETH Things will be settled wherever I am. But I wonder how things will be with you if I leave?

Two female dominos walk by.

FIRST FEMALE DOMINO Good evening, Eligius Fenz.

SECOND FEMALE DOMINO Greetings to you, handsome singer.

They both laugh and disappear again.

ELIGIUS FENZ Strange people. They are making fun of me.

SERAPHINE What an idea, father! Aren't you young, aren't you handsome?

ELIGIUS FENZ *nods, then adds* But the people don't know it. That is the pity.

LEINDORF My promotion to first lieutenant is imminent. I will be a captain in three years, at the most.

ELIGIUS FENZ And then a major and lieutenant colonel and colonel and general. And as general or field marshal you will retire. Yes, you soldiers have it good. We civilians, we have to come back down off the mountain. Ever further and further down. One becomes a captain again, a sergeant, a private; in the end, no one salutes any more.

SERAPHINE *somewhat moved* But father!

The female dominos reappear.

FIRST DOMINO Don't you want to hear what we have to say, Count Almaviva?

SECOND DOMINO Aren't you at all curious, Don Juan?

They withdraw more slowly than before.

ELIGIUS FENZ What do you think, Seraphine? It would not be out of the question for these two masked women to have something important to communicate to me. There are supposed to be all sorts of things going on at the opera. A change of director and the like. *Standing up resolutely* Goodbye, children!

ELISABETH *who, with Leindorf, has barely paid attention to the dominos as yet* You're leaving, father?

ELIGIUS FENZ Forgive me, my dear ones. I do have to try to get to the bottom of this. Just a moment or two.

ELISABETH And you'll get home at noon tomorrow!

ELIGIUS FENZ What are you talking about, Elisabeth. I have to give a lesson at ten in the morning. Well, my dear prospective son-in-law, you will give us the pleasure of your company at table tomorrow. We will discuss the matter further then. Good-bye, children!

He follows the dominos; all three can be seen disappearing.

ELISABETH How will things turn out in the house when I'm gone, I wonder? You will have to hire a girl in any case.

SERAPHINE We won't be at home much. The concert tours are beginning now, you know. And father is coming with me.

ELISABETH You will not have an easy time with him, Seraphine. Nor father with you, either. Will you at least look out for each other?

SERAPHINE Really, don't worry, Elisabeth! Nothing will happen to us. And the only sad part is that it's all over now—forever—with our bedtime chats.

LEINDORF You must play in our officers' casino in Klagenfurt some time, Seraphine.

SERAPHINE All right, if it can be arranged.

MAX VON REISENBERG, *perhaps 24, in a gray summer suit covered by an open domino with silver gray silk lining, comes past the pool on the left.*

SERAPHINE *has already noticed him earlier; when he wants to continue on his way, almost half the stage away from her, Seraphine quite suddenly, as if surprising herself, throws a rose at his feet. He does not notice it, is about to continue on his way.*

SERAPHINE *throws another rose at his feet.*

MAX Was that for me?

SERAPHINE It may very well have been.

MAX *picks up the rose.*

SERAPHINE And there is another one.

MAX *now picks up the first rose too.*

SERAPHINE *throws a third rose before him* And here is a third one while I'm at it. So you will at least know that they are good things.

MAX *not too near, holding the roses against his chest* Oh, Miss, if only I could thank you as you deserve—with like talent and with like fragrance. Still, hidden somewhere, a white lilac blooms.—Linger here but a little while—I'll bring it thee.

SERAPHINE *in a drawl* "Thee?"

MAX To thee, sweet child, to whom else?

SERAPHINE I am not wearing a mask, Sir.

MAX I believe you are. Only you do not know it. Your eyes, your mouth, your smile—all a mask. And what good is it, my child, soon I will know your face. I'll fetch the lilac now. Then we'll dance.

SERAPHINE Don't bother, Sir. By the time you return I will long since have forgotten you.

MAX Oh grievous words! Shivering, I can already feel myself sinking in floods of forgetfulness. Still, if fortune wishes me well, I'll rise again to the surface. *He bows and withdraws in the same direction from which he came.*

Short pause.

ELISABETH Has anyone ever seen such an affected person? Didn't he speak in verse, even?

LEINDORF It sounded as if it came from a play. *Romeo and Juliet*, perhaps.

ELISABETH *to Seraphine* What ever were you thinking of? And he addressed you so familiarly too. Do you even know who he is?

SERAPHINE He walked by as I was playing the violin. I think that's the reason it sounded so beautiful.

LEINDORF He should have introduced himself at the very least, in my opinion.

AMBROS *who has been standing at the rear, by the pool, approaches from the left; speaks to Seraphine* I saw everything. Is that how you treat my roses, Seraphine?

SERAPHINE Do you know him? What's his name?

AMBROS Good evening, Elisabeth.

ELISABETH Good evening, Ambros. Permit me to introduce my fiance. Herr Lieutenant Leindorf. Herr Ambros Doehl.

AMBROS Congratulations.

Shakes hands with Leindorf and then with Elisabeth.

ELISABETH *sighing softly* I would rather tell you right away, Karl, I was in love with this man once, before he became famous or moved in the highest circles. He even wrote some poems to me.

LEINDORF This is very flattering to my bride.

ELISABETH I recently read in a newspaper that you had introduced a new tone to literature. . . or something like that.

AMBROS The newspapers are not always quite reliably informed about such things.

SERAPHINE *to Ambros* Well, Ambros, what's his name?

AMBROS Whom are you talking about? Oh, yes, the young man who now has my roses is named Max von Reisenberg.

SERAPHINE Oh, he has a last name too. Actually, Max would suffice.

ELISABETH A horribly affected individual.

AMBROS That would not be the worst thing! But dangerous!

SERAPHINE Is that possible?

AMBROS Beware of him, Seraphine. All the women fling themselves at him. They all fall in love with him.

ELISABETH Reisenberg. Isn't that the jeweler on the Neuer Markt?

AMBROS The jeweler was his father.

LEINDORF The jeweler Reisenberg, surely that is the same one who fell in a duel a few years ago.

AMBROS Yes. The Count of Merkenstein shot him.

SERAPHINE The one who has the beautiful daughter?

LEINDORF The duel took place in our barracks. It caused quite a sensation at the time.

AMBROS One could almost have predicted that end for the jeweler Reisenberg. He had altogether too much success with women.

SERAPHINE And his last with the Countess of Merkenstein?

AMBROS Yes. It had been a very good marriage. Then this man came along and destroyed it.

SERAPHINE I imagine they split up after the duel?

AMBROS No, they made up. That is to say, they stayed together and tortured each other to death—since shortly thereafter they both died, in the same week, I believe.

ELISABETH So this affected young man is a jeweler?

AMBROS No. He sold the business shortly after his father's death. Only the name of the firm remained.

SERAPHINE So what is he up to now?

AMBROS All sorts of things. He draws a little, plays the piano not at all badly—

ELISABETH And writes poems too.

AMBROS Occasionally. But bad ones. It is altogether incredible how many things he can not do. But that is of no consequence either. The fact is he came into this world only to make as many women as possible unhappy.

SERAPHINE Or happy.

AMBROS Yes, it may well start out that way, generally.

SERAPHINE Then one has something beautiful to remember in one's unhappiness.

ELISABETH *to Seraphine* And I am leaving you alone.

AMBROS Elisabeth, *pointing to Seraphine* nothing will happen to her! And if in time she should have ten lovers, she will stay eternally pure.

ELISABETH What are you talking about, Ambros. My sister must not take a lover, she must become a good housewife in spite of her violin-playing, a wife, a mother, that's what she is born to.

SERAPHINE A mother! Oh, yes, that must be really beautiful. How do women manage to find the right father for their child, I wonder?

LEINDORF Fräulein Seraphine!

ELISABETH She isn't serious, Karl.

Livelier music has been audible for a while.

ELISABETH Shall we dance, Karl? *Stands up* Well, Seraphine, you really intend to wait here for your affected Herr Max?

SERAPHINE That's all I need! We want to dance too, right, Ambros? And Herr Max can come looking for me if it is of any consequence to him. Come, Ambros.

Leindorf and Elisabeth have already exited.

JULIA *comes quickly up to Ambros, just as he is about to exit with Seraphine.*

JULIA Just one word, Ambros.

AMBROS *hesitates.*

SERAPHINE Oh, I don't want to fight anyone over you. Good-
  bye.

  Leaves quickly.

AMBROS Julia?

JULIA *removing her mask, hastily* Westerhaus is looking for
  me. If he asks you, you will tell him that I've been chatting
  with you here by the pool the whole time. There he comes
  already, with Judith, naturally.

BRAUNIGL *comes from the same side as Julia, as if he had been
  looking for her as well* Finally, I have found you again.

JULIA May I introduce you?

BRAUNIGL *is about to say his name.*

AMBROS I've already had the pleasure.

  Westerhaus and Judith come in.

WESTERHAUS Good evening, Julia. It is a nice party, isn't
  it?

JULIA A beautiful party.

AMBROS We've let it sweep past us here.

WESTERHAUS So, you have—?

MAX *enters with three lilac branches.*

  Braunigl, Julia, Westerhaus, and Ambros stand together.

JUDITH *steps quickly up to Max* Give me the lilac.

MAX Whatever you desire, lovely mask, even myself, if you
  please.

JUDITH I'll do without that. The lilac.

MAX It's been. . . promised. *After hesitating an instant* Still,
  as there are three branches, one shall be yours.

  Hands her one branch.

JUDITH *takes it, breaks it in two, throws it at Max's feet.*

MAX So, Judith!

JUDITH *takes off her mask.*

MAX You could just as well have left your mask on. I would
  have recognized you just from this.

WESTERHAUS *greets Max cursorily* Good evening, Herr von
  Reisenberg. Let's go home, Judith.

MAX So early, Herr President?

AMBROS It's barely midnight.

  *Westerhaus, Ambros, Max, and Judith are standing together
  now.*

JULIA *stands apart from them.*

BRAUNIGL *taking advantage of the opportunity* Julia!

JULIA Be careful!

BRAUNIGL You disappeared. Where were you?

JULIA Where might I have been? Most likely with a lover.

BRAUNIGL When will you be mine?

JULIA You are mad.

BRAUNIGL Ask of me what you will. My life, my honor. . .

JULIA We shall see.

WESTERHAUS Well, Judith wants to stay. I will send the car for you. Julia! We're going!—Why so silent? *Uncontrolled* Are your lips sore from so much kissing?

BRAUNIGL *starts.*

WESTERHAUS Why are you staring like that, Julia? As enraptured as if you were still dreaming in his arms?

JULIA *beside herself* Let me go!

WESTERHAUS Not today. Perhaps tomorrow. I haven't had enough of you yet. Come on!

BRAUNIGL You have lost your senses, Herr President!

WESTERHAUS What business is it of yours, Herr District Attorney?

AMBROS Herr President!

WESTERHAUS What is it you gentlemen want? She is my wife, a female, a thing, bought like any other. Purely a transaction, gentlemen. Please God there may be no worse! *He has grabbed Julia by the arm and quickly exits with her. Braunigl and Ambros stand together.*

BRAUNIGL Have you ever heard such a thing? What a state of affairs! A swamp!

Ambros and Braunigl exit.

MAX, JUDITH

MAX It is unthinkable for you to stay in that house any longer, Judith.

JUDITH Nor do I intend to. I'm going to London soon, to continue my studies with Jean de Reszke, and I've already signed my contract with Dresden.

MAX You're going to Dresden?

JUDITH In the fall.

MAX Wouldn't you allow me to accompany you there?

JUDITH In what capacity? As impresario? As voice coach?

MAX Why not as your husband?

JUDITH Oh, yes, this is a masquerade party! I forgot.

MAX You don't want to take me seriously, Judith.

JUDITH And you don't take me lightly enough. I, someone's wife. . . grant someone rights over my person? No, I was not born for that. I want to do things more honestly than—the others. I want to enjoy my youth, without owing an accounting to anybody.

MAX To hear you talk like that, Judith, one could get worried about you.

JUDITH Worried? Because I know what I want? Because I am being honest with you?

MAX If one knew at least that much with certainty.

JUDITH I'm not with everyone, you know. And will be with very few. But with you I am, with you, Max, I can feel it, I can be, must be honest. We two, I have always sensed it, we two are of the same blood.

MAX Say it right away: brother and sister.

JUDITH Comrades.

MAX I like that better. That does not—exclude anything.

JUDITH And you shall see right away how much I am your comrade and friend. I have something important to tell you.

MAX Wasn't all this important enough?

JUDITH *in a matter-of-fact manner* You have a large deposit in my brother-in-law's bank.

MAX *hesitating somewhat* Yes. . . from my father's time. My entire fortune is in Westerhaus's bank. I never had any reason to change that.

JUDITH You will have it immediately. Give them notice that you intend to withdraw your funds, tomorrow morning, if possible.

MAX But why? They are—how shall I say—very obliging to me. The interest I draw—

JUDITH Is higher than elsewhere. I know. It may conceivably go even higher.

MAX Your brother-in-law is considered a financial genius.

JUDITH And he is. But in spite of that—or because of it, he has more than once already been very close to. . . it was only a year and a half ago that I tore a pistol out of his hand one morning.

MAX You?

JUDITH Who then? Julia maybe? He trusts only me. He was standing at the brink of ruin back then. Well, fortunately it turned out all right. A few days later, the Bank was saved and Westerhaus a few million richer.

MAX And Julia got her celebrated string of pearls.

JUDITH And I a bracelet. I still have it. Do you see? Beautiful, isn't it? I wear it all the time.

MAX I knew it, Judith, you are in love with Westerhaus.

JUDITH I do not deny it, my dear comrade. Too bad he didn't notice anything while there was still time.

MAX And what has been missed, when all is said and done?

JUDITH By him—everything, I'm afraid. By me—only one thing, to be sure. But one so important that its loss has changed my life fundamentally.

MAX Judith—

JUDITH *warding him off* No more about that. Will you do as I advised?

MAX I'll think it over.

JUDITH There may no longer be any time for that, Max.

MAX Judith, please, enough of business for tonight. Let us dance, rather.

JUDITH *eagerly links arms with him* I'm at your disposal, comrade.

MAX *passionately* Judith!

JUDITH Not a single word, Max. I know what you want to say to me. But it would be too cheap. Now let us dance. *Both exit.*

AMBROS *and* FALKENIR *run into each other. Falkenir, wearing a summer suit, around forty, clean shaven, with dark hair graying at the temples; he extends his hand to Ambros.*

FALKENIR Isn't it a remarkable coincidence, how now, for an instant, the paths of two lives intersect which under different circumstances would have run past one another for all eternity?

AMBROS   I rather believe we would have had to meet some time in any event, Baron Falkenir—and possibly for longer than an instant.

FALKENIR   Well, *hesitating somewhat* whatever the next few minutes might determine with regard to our future lives, let us hope that our meeting today will not remain our last.

AMBROS   I am convinced of that. Rarely—if I may say so, Baron Falkenir—have I felt myself so drawn to a person with whom I had exchanged barely a hundred words as to you. Please forgive the frankness of this admission, but in such a fateful hour one would rather appear to be somewhat importunate than too cautious.

FALKENIR   I can assure you, Herr Doehl, that I find your sympathy not only flattering but pleasing as well. This should not surprise you. I am, after all, somewhat better acquainted with you, probably, than you with me. I know your poems. I read them just recently, in Rome, with considerable interest, and I was—now I will be somewhat importunate too—most deeply moved by them.

AMBROS   Moved? Really? Just that I seldom hear. I thank you.

PRINCE ARDUIN *enters,* AMBROS, FALKENIR

ARDUIN *extends his hand to Falkenir* Good evening, my dear Baron. Well, it seems we are all here—with the sole exception of the leading character.—You have come directly from Rome, Baron Falkenir?

FALKENIR   Yesterday morning I rode past the castle of Perosa.

ARDUIN   Why only past it? You should have stopped off. My mother would have been pleased to see you again—even if she had not remembered you at all. She is very lonely. I intend to visit her this summer. Did you speak with the Crown Prince in Rome?

FALKENIR   I live in Rome as a private citizen, Highness.

ARDUIN   I've heard.—And do you now intend to devote yourself entirely to your research?

FALKENIR   For the time being. I'm careful not to devise any long-range agendas.

ARDUIN That is very wise. May I come see you if I should come to Rome? You must be my cicerone through the ruined imperial palaces, palaces that are in even greater ruin than the ducal castle of Perosa. And you, Ambros Doehl, you will come to Italy with me. That way, this carnival joke that has been played at our expense will at least have served some purpose. *Midnight bells sound from a tower* Midnight, gentlemen, the time is up. There may yet be some very merry goings-on in this park tonight. What would you think, gentlemen, if we mingled among the public? I wouldn't mind playing Harun-al-Rashid. We could choose one from among the local lasses. We should all do that, gentlemen, and tomorrow ride out to Merkenstein together and introduce our brides to the Countess. They need not be brides, exactly. That would make for a cheerful revenge. Don't you agree? A jest for a jest.

AMBROS It is not a carnival jest, Your Highness, but a fairy tale, and the fairy tale has its laws, just like reality. They are called punctuality, patience, and faith.

ARDUIN It's midnight.

AURELIE *standing behind them in a dark dress* And here is Aurelie. Greetings, my friends.

ARDUIN *and* AMBROS Aurelie!

AURELIE The three months are up. I promised to give you my decision at midnight tonight, here by the pool, in the park of Perosa. Each of you give me your hand. Arduin, Ambros, let us remain friends. Yours I hold fast, Falkenir. It is you I have chosen.

Pause.

ARDUIN Farewell, Aurelie. *He exits right.*

AMBROS Aurelie, farewell. *Exits in the opposite direction.*

AURELIE Farewell to you both!

AURELIE, FALKENIR

AURELIE How long have these three months been! How long haven't I heard your voice, Falkenir. Do you want to keep me waiting even longer?

FALKENIR *remains silent.*

AURELIE Is it happiness that leaves you speechless? Then I will be doubly happy about your silence. But if your silence signifies something other than happiness, then tell me. And I will do what I can to insure that nothing but happiness will remain.

FALKENIR Me?—Me, Aurelie, from among these three, me? Is it possible?

AURELIE What is the matter with you, Falkenir? Didn't you ask me to marry you like the others? Were you here tonight like they were? And now you don't dare believe that you are the one I've chosen?

FALKENIR Are you really sure, Aurelie, that you're not making a mistake?

AURELIE Falkenir!

FALKENIR That you're taking for love what—is perhaps something fundamentally different—trust—friendship—

AURELIE *about to interrupt him.*

FALKENIR Hear me out, Aurelie. When your father and mother died, I was your adviser and friend. As young as you were, I let you get some sense of—let you know, what I had experienced and suffered. The other two are less known to you by far. I almost feel as if I had an unfair advantage over them, and to exploit it would strike me as downright treacherous—against them and also against you.

AURELIE *has been listening to him with changing expression: smiling, irritated, impatient, calm* You don't say, Falkenir! I did not know the other two? I did not know Arduin, my childhood playmate, my sports and hunting companion of former times? We were the best of friends, when he didn't happen to forget me in favor of his adventures and silly pranks—or when he became all too impudent, which also happened from time to time. Do I know Arduin!—And Ambros Doehl—

FALKENIR *quickly* With whom you have certainly not spoken a half dozen times before today!

AURELIE But how long and how well do I already know his poems; for a long time before I met him in person. And I know some of them by heart. And the few conversations we've had in our small park of Merkenstein—they led us so far, so deep, that his very being concealed scarcely any secret from me, nor, I believe, mine from him. And then his letters! Yes, Falkenir, he too wrote me;—rare letters, all too rare, it seems to me today—Oh, and how I know him!—I know them both, the poet Ambros Doehl and the Prince Arduin von Perosa. I could never ever learn anything new about them.

FALKENIR   What a mistake, Aurelie. No one knows them. They don't know themselves yet. They are young, barely twenty-five. What do you know, what do we know about them? About the deeds, the works, that lie still dormant within them? And just you, Aurelie—yes, maybe just you were created to rouse into fruition the great deed, the timeless work in one or the other.

AURELIE *in a purposely light tone* Imagine, Falkenir, even this task does not excite me in the very least, neither for one nor the other. And if the one were to lay a crown at my feet or the other raise me up to immortality with himself—what significance would I, I personally have had in the end?—to Prince Arduin, among any number of things that he might fight for and conquer, one bit of booty or one triumph more—to the poet Ambros Doehl, among a thousand representations and transformations of existence—one more image. To you, Falkenir, I know full well, I will be neither triumph nor image; to you I am Aurelie.

FALKENIR   Yes, you are Aurelie, in your name resound all the wonders of your being. But what am I to you, Aurelie? What may I, what can I be to you? I, a man without future or enthusiasm, whose temples are beginning to gray, who has nothing to give but himself and is nevertheless condemned to make demands, so inexorably and without measure, as if he had a world to give in exchange.

AURELIE   So demand! Since I chose you, I gave you the right. In your voice I hear the echo, in your eyes I see the reflection of the world. I want nothing else, nothing more from it than what is echoed and reflected by your soul.

FALKENIR   This modesty, Aurelie, does not become you— especially you. If anyone does, surely you have a right to the real world, the living, immeasurable world, which can never be encompassed for you by one person, however dear to you he may be.

AURELIE It does not entice me, this world, this "living" world. What I have heard, seen, understood of it gives me no desire to become more closely acquainted with it. I have seen how my mother, returning from that world you're talking about, sank down at the threshold of our house, tired and shattered. I saw other women as well, women who emerged from heavy destinies as well as from light ones. None of their faces reflected peace of mind, and my heart ached for them all. For those who thought themselves fortunate almost more than for the wretched ones. Seekers and pursued, insatiable or intoxicated is how they all appeared to me, the fortunate as well as the wretched. The world from which they came moved me rather to a shudder than to any longing.

FALKENIR What you call shudder, Aurelie, will likely turn out, actually, to be nothing more than longing in the end.

AURELIE Falkenir. . . !

FALKENIR Longing that is ashamed of itself.

AURELIE Why do you distrust me, Falkenir?

FALKENIR It is not distrust, Aurelie—it's knowledge. A more painful, deeper knowledge—even about you, than is granted, or can be granted to you yourself.

AURELIE *after shaking her head seriously* Shadows of the past are benighting you, Falkenir.—Oh, I know, you do not dare be happy—as if you had to atone for something *in a livelier tone* of which you are not guilty.

FALKENIR Isn't foresight guilt? Doesn't it have the mysterious power to conjure up what it wants to avert? And if it were to succeed in averting it, would it still have been foresight then?

AURELIE You're torturing yourself, Falkenir. The woman you are thinking of at this moment, did she not depart this world of her own free will? Did she not in her madness seek out death?

FALKENIR And if it was madness, was it not I who drove her to it?

AURELIE Surely you loved her, Falkenir?

FALKENIR That's just it. Because I loved her, I knew the

thoughts she herself would never have dared to think, I knew the deeds she would never have dared to do. All the possibilities of her being were obvious to me—and each bore within itself the seed of reality. Madness her death? It was meant to bear witness that she was mine alone and that she was mine alone for all eternity. Vain sacrifice! I recognized her death, too, as what it was: her flight from herself—and from me.

AURELIE So you had definite grounds to suspect her?

FALKENIR No, Aurelie, but it is given me to hear the rushing of the eternal streams—the dark, eternal streams that flow ceaselessly from man to woman and from woman to man, from one sex to the other. And that is what condemns me to loneliness, even with the truest—even with the best loved heart. And that, Aurelie, is why—

MAX *comes from the left rear past the pool. After hesitating briefly, he steps up to Aurelie* I beg your pardon, but I found this piece of jewelry over there by the pool a few minutes ago. *He produces a necklace with a pendant* I have reason to assume that it belongs to the Countess of Merkenstein, and I dare say I have the honor to be standing before her.

AURELIE *surprised, accepts the necklace* It belongs to me. I am the Countess Aurelie von Merkenstein. I thank you, Sir.

MAX *bows and wants to leave.*

AURELIE But how could you know—I was wearing this necklace for the first time today.

MAX *hesitating* My father made it. Excuse me that I didn't . . . at once—*bowing slightly to Falkenir* My name is Max von Reisenberg.

FALKENIR Falkenir.

AURELIE I thank you, Herr von Reisenberg. Strange that the clasp opened.

She is still holding the piece of jewelry in her hand.

FALKENIR And strange that just you found it, Herr von Reisenberg, and recognized it right away. Do you know every piece of jewelry that came from your father's studio?

MAX Not every one. But this was the last one that my father made personally, and it was I who furnished the design for it.

AURELIE   And your father brought it to Merkenstein personally?

MAX *nods.*

AURELIE   So, this piece of jewelry had to be the last one. This, therefore—. My mother never wore it.

FALKENIR *in a purposely light tone*   If you were superstitious, Aurelie, you could never again put the necklace on, or you would have to throw it into the pool here at once.

AURELIE *finally putting the necklace on now*   I don't believe that either curses or blessings attach to things or to people. Fate is not accustomed to dealing with us mortals so simply. I thank you, Herr von Reisenberg.

MAX *about to leave.*

AURELIE   Oh, you must not steal away like this, as if you had done something wrong. So you are the son of the man whom my father—

MAX   The way I preserve my father's picture in my memory —he surely wished for no more beautiful conclusion to his life than—

AURELIE *completes his thought*   Than to die for a woman he loved.

MAX *remains silent.*

FALKENIR *in a purposely light tone, which sounds forced*   So you are safe from blood revenge also, Aurelie.

AURELIE   My father and my mother are dead. I would have worn this necklace today in any event, even if I had suspected. . . . How distant this all is, how long ago. I feel no revulsion to this necklace. And I will be glad to meet you at any time, Herr von Reisenberg.

She extends her hand to him.

MAX   I thank you, Countess. And may I be so bold as to request another, more meaningful sign that I represent just as harmless a specimen of humanity to you as the next person?

AURELIE   Shouldn't my assurance be enough for you?

MAX   It would be confirmed most magnanimously if the Countess were so kind as to grant me a dance.

AURELIE *coolly*   Thank you, Herr von Reisenberg, I do not wish to dance.

FALKENIR *quickly*   Why not? Why don't you want to dance,

Aurelie. This is a party. And if Herr von Reisenberg were to
see you dance with someone else later, he might really take
it that you are not entirely free of superstitious prejudices.

AURELIE *looking at him in surprise* If I were to dance tonight,
the first dance would surely belong to my fiance. Don't you
think so?

FALKENIR I hardly ever dance. Herr von Reisenberg has asked
you first. His prerogative is beyond question.

MAX Oh!

AURELIE If you wish it, Falkenir. *She still hesitates a very
short while, then* Please, Herr von Reisenberg. But only a
short turn. Are you staying here, Falkenir?

FALKENIR You'll be able to find me.

Max and Aurelie exit right.

FALKENIR *remains standing motionless, looks after them.*

ELIGIUS FENZ *comes past the pool and up to the tent accompanied by the two female dominos* Here we are at the right
place. Please, ladies. Oh, the Princess is not here anymore?
But it must be the devil's own work if I couldn't still find
a couple of bottles of champagne here.

*He enters the tent, bends down, as if looking, but finds only
empty bottles. In the meantime, two young persons have drawn
nearer; they, together with the dominos, quickly disappear to
the right rear.*

ELIGIUS FENZ *raises his head again* Nothing. Unfortunately
nothing, my dear ladies. *Notices that they are gone. Presently
comes out of the tent, takes a few steps, then goes up to
Falkenir who has continued standing there motionless* I beg
you pardon, sir. Could you perhaps tell me—I had two ladies
on my arm just now.

FALKENIR Yes, I thought so too.

ELIGIUS FENZ And they've disappeared without a trace. Has
the earth swallowed them up? That doesn't happen with real
things.

FALKENIR There are all kinds of magic, Herr Fenz.

ELIGIUS FENZ Oh!

FALKENIR Ulrich Falkenir. There is no reason for you to remember me. A gentleman from the audience, nothing more.

ELIGIUS FENZ Oh, I know you, Herr Baron. *Recollecting*

One moment. Second floor, left, loge five or six. The Herr Baron attended all my performances in former years.

FALKENIR   Others too, occasionally, when circumstances permitted.

ELIGIUS FENZ   With your dear mother. I can still see her before me. She always wore black, a pearl hairpin in her hair.

FALKENIR   You have a good memory, Herr Fenz. My mother has been dead for sixteen years.

ELIGIUS FENZ   Is it possible? I feel as if I still. . . three years ago, still yesterday—To be sure, it's been a long time since I set foot on the stage. The customary term for it is "honorary member," Herr Baron.

FALKENIR   I saw you for the last time, if I am not mistaken, as Don Juan. It was a wonderful performance.

ELIGIUS FENZ   Oh, do not speak of that, Herr Baron. I trolled the role of Don Juan but did not sing it, I played him but I did not become him. Now, Herr Baron, now I'd be ready. But the people don't know it. "Honorary member." We can't win against that damned myth, Herr Baron, the myth about old age. Do you know what old age is, Herr Baron? Nothing but a plot contrived against us by youth. Well, yes, it's easy for youth. . . . Outward appearances speak against us. The myth must be destroyed. Well, and as far as Don Juan is concerned, · I want to let you in on a secret, Herr Baron. At his peak, he was older than people usually assume. Only a sixty-year-old can sing Don Juan. Life begins at sixty in a certain sense. Round about fifty we have some bitter days, of course. That is the basis of the myth, and one runs the risk himself, at times, of surrendering to it. Many, many are defeated by it. But those who escape it—oh, Herr Baron, I assure you—my voice, for example, convince yourself.

He sits on the buffet, an empty champagne glass in his hand, and begins to sing the champagne aria from "Don Juan."

SERAPHINE *entering*   How beautifully you sing, father. But don't you think—the night air—

ELIGIUS FENZ *sings a few more measures, then breaks off abruptly, making introductions*   This is my daughter Seraphine. Baron von Falkenir. You have heard the name, my child, an old, very old family. The Baron is a connoisseur. An old admirer, if I may be allowed to say so.

FALKENIR   Your father is allowed to say so, Fräulein.

ELIGIUS FENZ *still sitting on the buffet, has put his arm around Seraphine's neck*   Also an artist, Herr von Falkenir. Violin.

FALKENIR   A professional artist, Fräulein?

ELIGIUS FENZ *answers for Seraphine*   Certainly, Herr Baron. We've just done a very successful concert.

FALKENIR   I was away from Vienna, unfortunately.

ELIGIUS FENZ *excuses him with an indulgent motion of his hand*   There are prospects for a tour, on terms that are not at all bad. The contract will be signed one of these days.

SERAPHINE   This may not especially interest the Baron, father.

FALKENIR   It does, Fräulein. Where will the tour take you?

ELIGIUS FENZ   We will play in the larger spas and watering resorts in Bohemia and Germany, Karlsbad, Marienbad, Wiesbaden, and so forth. Then we'll head north. Denmark: Klampenborg, Skodsborg, Marienlyst, Gilleleije. Have you ever heard this name, Baron? Gilleleije! What melody in that word.

The PRINCESS *and* GYSAR, *in conversation, enter from the left.*

PRINCESS   But I find it simply mad. *She notices the others, first of all Seraphine and Fenz*   Oh, here is Fräulein Fenz. Good evening, Fräulein. *To Eligius Fenz*   I congratulate you on your daughter. The concert really came off splendidly. Just keep it up. What, am I seeing straight, Baron Falkenir? Back again from Rome?

FALKENIR   Since this morning, Princess. *Kisses her hand.*

PRINCESS   I'm very glad to see you again. But what do you say to this? Have you heard? The Prince is making a gift of the park, and of the palace with it.

FALKENIR   A gift? To whom?

PRINCESS   To the people. To humanity, as the Emperor Joseph did with the Augarten. Beginning tomorrow it shall be a public park, like the Stadtpark or the Volksgarten.

ELIGIUS FENZ   What truly princely generosity.

PRINCESS   He must have been terribly angry about something. It's the only explanation I can find for this gesture.

GYSAR Why didn't he give the park to me, rather? What are the rabble to do with a gift like that? They will make noise, eat bread and butter, and smell bad.

Aurelie and Max enter from the left.

MAX *kisses her hand and disappears.*

AURELIE Well, this feels like a homecoming.

PRINCESS Aurelie! You are here, Aurelie?

AURELIE *kisses her hand* Good evening, dear aunt. Yes, I'm here. What is so wonderful about that? Good evening, Gysar. *Seraphine and Eligius Fenz stand off to the side but have not withdrawn entirely, although Seraphine is obviously trying to drag Fenz off.*

GYSAR *kisses Aurelie's hand* You've been taking part in the dancing, as I see, Countess. May I ask, perhaps—

AURELIE No, Master Gysar, I've had enough for today. Don't you agree, Falkenir? *To the Princess* May I present to you my fiance?

PRINCESS What? The Baron Falkenir? One surprise after another. My best wishes. Congratulations, dear Baron. But when did you get engaged?

AURELIE Soon it will have been an hour.

GYSAR I take it one must ask the fiance for permission now, if one wants to have a dance?

FALKENIR *to Aurelie* You danced more beautifully than ever. It is a joy to watch you.

GYSAR Well—Countess?

AURELIE I'm a little tired already. And if I dance still another round tonight, then only with you, Falkenir.

FALKENIR But if I tell you, Aurelie, that it would give me real pleasure—

AURELIE All right, then, but only because you insist. Here I am, Gysar.

Exits with Gysar, left.

PRINCESS *to Falkenir* So that is why you returned from Rome?

FALKENIR Not at all, Princess. An hour ago, neither one of us knew anything about it yet.

PRINCESS How odd. She really does dance splendidly. And when is the wedding actually to take place? *They have both exited right during this conversation. Eligius Fenz has already disappeared earlier. Seraphine and Max come towards each other from different directions.*

MAX But where to in such a hurry, Fräulein?

SERAPHINE Excuse me, my father has suddenly given me the slip again.

MAX Do let him go. You'll find him again all right. Here is the lilac. Go on, take it, it's yours.

SERAPHINE But this is really much too much.

MAX Oh, there was even more. There were three branches. One has already been snatched away from me.

SERAPHINE So hold on to the third one at least. You'll surely find use for it yet.

MAX Why do you make that assumption, my Fräulein?

SERAPHINE I do not assume it, I know it.

MAX But you barely know me.

SERAPHINE Oh, I already know you a little. I don't think it's especially difficult to know you.

MAX Really? So, do tell me something about myself. I've wanted to know for a long time what sort of person I actually am.

SERAPHINE I believe I could tell you that in a few words. An unspeakably conceited human being is what you are!

MAX Conceited? Well, yes, I think highly of myself, but not very much about myself. And further?

SERAPHINE And further, you're unfaithful.

MAX You surely understand something completely different by that than I do. Perhaps even the exact opposite. Because to me it seems the worst kind of unfaithfulness to persevere in one place while one has long since wanted to be in another.

SERAPHINE A somewhat convenient interpretation, but still, one could let it pass. And you are quite certainly frivolous.

MAX Granted. It is certainly not my style to run into anxiety's arms. For what? It always meets us halfway anyway.

SERAPHINE *smiling* It seems to me that you actually manage to pass all your faults off as virtues.

MAX And if I didn't come to your assistance, Fräulein—what is your name, actually?

SERAPHINE My name is Seraphine Fenz.

MAX —Then you would find nothing at all good about me, Fräulein Seraphine?

SERAPHINE Oh yes, one thing.

MAX And what might that be?

SERAPHINE That one cannot be angry with you.

MAX That would make it more a good quality of yours, then.

SERAPHINE Oh no. With others I could be. . . for example, if I loved a person, or if he were very dear to me—I could probably also be angry with such a person under some circumstances. Not with you. But now we've chatted enough for the first time. Good night, Herr von Reisenberg.

MAX My name is Max.

SERAPHINE Sleep well, Herr Max von Reisenberg.

MAX What kind of abrupt farewell is that? What entices you away all of a sudden? One could almost conjecture—

SERAPHINE Oh, go right ahead and say it.

MAX That somewhere hereabouts, in a secret walk—an adventure awaits you.

SERAPHINE God preserve me from it! Adventure! How distasteful I find the very word.

MAX Well, then, if there is no one else, why do you leave me alone?

SERAPHINE Now I want to tell you a secret, Herr Max von Reisenberg.

MAX —?

SERAPHINE Namely, that one can also go home. There are people who simply go home after midnight.

MAX I would like so very much to see you again soon, Fräulein Seraphine.

SERAPHINE What for? It could surely never again be as beautiful as it was tonight.

MAX Much more beautiful still, I believe.

SERAPHINE Consider—

MAX What?

SERAPHINE That you still have a lilac branch left.

MAX *offers her the branch.*

SERAPHINE Oh, just keep it. I only have enough gratitude in store for one. Its fragrance is glorious. I'm sure it will retain it a while longer yet.

MAX   When may I see you again, Seraphine?

SERAPHINE   What for? Don't you go imagining that I could fall in love with you. I've been warned.

MAX   Warned? Ah—my friend Ambros Doehl.

SERAPHINE   You're supposed to be a very dangerous person. You know nothing about that, Herr Max von Reisenberg? And I have no time for dangerous things.

MAX   Then you'll just have to take the time. You are an artist. Well, that is simply part of being an artist.

SERAPHINE   How do you know I'm an artist? I am just enough of one to know that I can never become what I myself understand by the word, and I am just little enough of one that I'm not excessively vexed about it. And it would not have taken much—you will not repeat this to any one, right?—for me to have become a telephone operator.

MAX   But I've heard you play. Wonderful.

SERAPHINE   You probably don't understand very much about it.

MAX   But I do a little. I'm fairly musical. I play the piano myself.

SERAPHINE   Oh, yes. Of course. I can even picture fairly precisely how you play the piano. You have a soft touch, at times a little too sweet, not very much rhythm; you also fantasize on occasion and smoke a cigarette while you do.

MAX   My, but how you know all this.—

SERAPHINE   You are not all that mysterious.

MAX   Nor do I want to be—for you, Seraphine.

SERAPHINE   And where there is no mystery there is no danger.

MAX   All the better. Then you won't take it ill if I ask you whether I may practice with you occasionally.

SERAPHINE   *somewhat sternly* I practice with my sister. I am sure she plays better than you, Herr von Reisenberg. I have no time to play the dilettante now. I'm rehearsing for my tour.

MAX   You're going on tour? In summer?

SERAPHINE   In mid-June it begins.

MAX   But that's not the season.

SERAPHINE   It's a kind of trial tour of watering resorts and spas. To Bohemia, Germany, and the North. And I even have a tentative contract for America already.

MAX It seems like you've made plans for your entire life.

SERAPHINE Only a tentative plan.

MAX Wouldn't you like to conclude such a tentative contract with me too?

SERAPHINE I do not at all like frivolous remarks, Herr von Reisenberg.

MAX You've misunderstood me, Fräulein. Might I not listen in some time, perhaps, when you're practicing with your sister?

SERAPHINE That could not be very interesting for you. Besides, we live far out in the suburbs.

MAX Oh, how splendid. I love the suburbs. Of course you have a small garden too.

SERAPHINE That's true, we have one.

MAX Then one could stroll up and down and chat in the open of an evening, after you've practiced diligently.

SERAPHINE What would we have to chat about? I think we have pretty much told each other everything there is to tell.

MAX Oh, then you don't know me very well. I always know something more. And there is so much that occurs to a person when he's permitted to look into two such dear, clever, kind eyes.

SERAPHINE Do not depend on my kindness too much.

MAX Yes, you are kind. You are so—sisterly. How lovely it must be to be able to tell you everything that moves one's heart, how beautiful to unbosom oneself to you, cry one's eyes out in your lap when one has been cheated or deserted by someone.

SERAPHINE Cry your eyes out? You, Herr Max von Reisenberg, crying? I can no more picture that than I can picture you burst out laughing brightly over something. You are much too elegant for that.

MAX I believe you're making fun of me, Seraphine.

SERAPHINE That may well be possible, Herr Max von Reisenberg.

ELISABETH *enters with Lieutenant Leindorf* Here she is. Let's go home, Seraphine. Haven't you seen father?

SERAPHINE *with an appropriate movement of her hand* He must be over there somewhere. This is my sister Elisabeth.

ELISABETH And you are Herr von Reisenberg. We've already heard who you are.

MAX With commentary, as I hear.

LEINDORF *introducing himself* Lieutenant Leindorf.

ELISABETH My fiancé.

MAX Delighted. The ladies want to leave the party already?

ELISABETH Tomorrow is another day. We live pretty far out. And this young warrior is on duty tomorrow, as usual.

LEINDORF Oh, that doesn't matter. If it pleases the ladies to stay a while longer—

SERAPHINE No, it really is time to go home. Don't worry, Father will find his way home by himself.

ELISABETH But when?

MAX May I put my my car at your disposal, perhaps?

ELISABETH You have a car?

MAX I take one when the occasion warrants it.

SERAPHINE The occasion is not at hand.

ELISABETH We don't want to trouble you in any way or to take you away from here.

MAX I have nothing further to look for here.

SERAPHINE But to find, perhaps. Good-bye, Herr von Reisenberg.

MAX And when will I have the good fortune of seeing you again, Fräulein?

SERAPHINE *hesitatingly* If the trip is not too long for you, then visit us some time.

ELISABETH *looks at her, surprised.*

SERAPHINE Herr von Reisenberg has kindly offered to accompany me on the piano from time to time. *More sure of herself* It's a lucky coincidence, perhaps,—because now you will— *with a glance at Leindorf* not have so much time, after all, to practice with me—

MAX So—I may really come?

ELISABETH But of course, Herr von Reisenberg. One is not so particular in an artist's family. This sort of thing is quite beautiful. It's called love at first sight, isn't it?

SERAPHINE Oh, no, it is not called that. Isn't that so, Herr von Reisenberg? He only wants to cry his eyes out on my bosom after a woman has made a fool of him, isn't that so?

MAX   More or less. Actually, I said I would like to cry my eyes out in your lap.

ELISABETH   Well, I'm not sure that's really any more respectable. Good-bye.

MAX   So, I may not take you home?

ELISABETH   We're walking.

LEINDORF   It is a beautiful night.

MAX   That long way on foot?

ELISABETH   You already know that too, that we have a long way?

SERAPHINE   You may escort us up to the park gate, no further.

They all exit.

AMBROS *and* ARDUIN *enter and meet.*

ARDUIN   Did you see, Ambros?

AMBROS   —?

ARDUIN   Aurelie is dancing.

AMBROS *as if this were to be expected*   It is a carnival party, Prince Arduin.

ARDUIN   If a quarter of an hour after becoming engaged, the Baron Falkenir lets his betrothed dance with other men, then there is something behind it, either foolish or malicious.

AMBROS *gestures as if he were about to respond.*

ARDUIN *putting him off*   I'm afraid for Aurelie. Individuals who kill someone I can understand in the end. I even feel related to them in some way. But a person for whose sake another being kills himself—I find such a person sinister. I'm sure you see that as well as I do, Ambros. We should let Aurelie know—before it's too late, perhaps, Ambros—that she may count on us in any event, on our—friendship, Ambros.

AMBROS   If Aurelie should ever need a friend, she will know how to find one unerringly.

ARDUIN   I am by no means convinced of that. As in her choice of a husband, she might also go wrong in her choice of a friend.

AMBROS Let her be a hundred times mistaken—each mistake will only reflect the truth of her soul.

ARDUIN You're creating a poetic Aurelie to your own taste, Ambros.

AMBROS That may well be the right one.

ARDUIN With all due respect for your attitude, don't you think people notice your disappointment.

AMBROS To be disappointed where we had nothing to hope for is a bit of courtesy we owe to fate.

ARDUIN And resignation, with however much wit it disguises itself, still remains a cheap gesture.

AMBROS Certainly it is a greater one, my dear Prince, to give away a castle and a park—even if one has several more still remaining, not to mention a magical yacht.

ARDUIN It isn't one any more, now, Ambros Doehl, nor will it ever become one.

AMBROS Who knows.

ARDUIN Now it's a matter of risking the voyage into the unknown without Aurelie.

AMBROS Into the unknown?

ARDUIN *lightly* As any voyage may in fact turn out in the end, more or less. . . . By the way, may I invite you to the launching?

AMBROS Your Highness is very kind.

ARDUIN *hastily* It'll take place at the end of July. It'll be a particular pleasure to see you among my guests. Where can I send you word around that time?

AMBROS I will be quite near Your Highness, in a small spot on the Danish coast, where I've been spending my vacation for years.

ARDUIN You told me about it once. A fishing village.

AMBROS It was at one time, Highness. But there is an ambitious hotel director there who has gotten the idea in his head to turn the fishing village into a world famous bathing resort. To be sure, it has not gone that far yet, but the solitude is long since a thing of the past. A few years ago it was really still a fairy-tale beach—a truly Mediterranean landscape under a pale northern sky—

ARDUIN   Oh, I remember—in one of your most beautiful poems—what was it called—

AMBROS   It was a short cycle.

The music has become livelier during the past few minutes. Movement at the rear, masked persons going past amid laughter and cheers.

AMBROS   The mood really is becoming overly merry.

ARDUIN   Yes, the people are feeling at home now. It's strange to be suddenly walking about here as a guest. And for the last time.

AMBROS   How's that?

ARDUIN *quickly*   Come Ambros, let's put on masks and be part of the public like the others! I smell adventure in the air.

AMBROS   Forgive me, Highness, if I prefer to leave, although I was only a member of the public before too. But for me this party has had just about enough highlights.

ARDUIN   Well, farewell, then, Ambros. We'll probably not see each other again for a long time. Tonight, I am sleeping in the—former—Perosa Palace for the last time, most likely.

AMBROS   And tomorrow?

ARDUIN   I don't know. Somewhere else, at any rate. Goodbye, Ambros Doehl. What was the name of that little fishing village?

AMBROS   Gilleleije, my Prince.

ARDUIN   That has a beautiful sound—of fairy tales, adventures, and poems. I will remember it.

He puts on his mask, exits left, Ambros exits right.

The movement at the rear continues.

AURELIE, GYSAR

AURELIE *releasing herself from Gysar's arms as they are dancing*   That's enough, Gysar, I can't any more.

GYSAR   What a dance that was, Countess! I will never forget it.

AURELIE   Now I want to be alone, Gysar.

GYSAR *after bowing*   May I remind you, Countess, that you still owe me the answer to a question?

AURELIE   What all did you not ask! I don't know any more.

GYSAR It was always the same question. Shall I repeat it?

AURELIE It's hardly necessary, since I am obviously not in the mood to answer.

GYSAR So, I will not ask any more. I will simply say it. I want to paint your portrait. Countess. It is no longer a question or a request. I only want you to know, Aurelie, I will paint a picture of you.

AURELIE You are audacious, Gysar.

GYSAR I dare say one has to be—if the very meaning of one's life is at stake.

AURELIE One could say that the meaning of your life has changed a number of times already.

GYSAR The pictures I have painted until now signify nothing, less than nothing. Today I know it. I am ashamed of my fame. Everything I have accomplished ought to be effaced, the world would be no poorer for that—and I perhaps happier.

AURELIE If you always carried on so impetuously for the sake of a new portrait, then the effort could only rarely have been worthwhile.

GYSAR Did I ever have to beg? I had the choice among hundreds, among thousands. Why did I decide on this or that one? It could always have been another one too. The women were of secondary importance and the portraits no more. Only with yours, Aurelie, could I become the person I am.

AURELIE *remains silent.*

GYSAR When may I begin your portrait?

AURELIE Now is not the time to talk about it.

GYSAR Precisely now. It is perhaps the last time. You are engaged. In the next hour he could already forbid you to pose.

AURELIE What a fool you are.

GYSAR It's not my fault, Aurelie, that the request of the artist sounds no different to you than the courtship of a man.

AURELIE Go away, Gysar.

Falkenir can be seen approaching.

GYSAR I swear to you, Aurelie, that I will not begin another picture until I've completed yours. *He leaves.*

AURELIE, FALKENIR

AURELIE *going towards him* Now, finally, Falkenir, our dance.

FALKENIR The music has stopped.

AURELIE Really, it still kept sounding in my ear. Well, all the better that it stopped, so we can talk, Falkenir. Let's talk about the future. Where shall we live? You are drawn to Rome, I suppose? With pleasure, Falkenir, with pleasure. Let's go there in the fall. But during the summer we'll travel. Isn't that so? And when will the wedding be?

FALKENIR *mildly* Enough, Aurelie, I no longer want to hear you say words that have become senseless.

AURELIE What—are you saying, Falkenir?

FALKENIR Nothing other than what you yourself feel, Aurelie. We will not get married.

AURELIE Am I dreaming?! Or are you joking? I should be angry with you. Because I danced with another man? And it was you, Falkenir, who well-nigh ordered me to. Wasn't it all the same to me, whether this one or that one swung me around in a circle? Did I dance differently than you had seen me dance at other times? Uglier, more impudently than other women?

FALKENIR You danced as beautifully as ever. More beautifully than ever. It was in your dancing that I first understood you fully. Tonight, while you were dancing, I felt as if I were seeing you yourself for the first time.

AURELIE So it was something like a test? Is this worthy of you—or of me, Falkenir?

FALKENIR No test, Aurelie. Perhaps—a sign.

AURELIE If you still had need of a sign, how could you think of courting me?

FALKENIR Forgive me. In that hour I barely knew as yet how much . . . what you mean to me. Not until we were apart did I become, day by day, more deeply aware of my love, of my boldness, of my injustice. I comforted myself with the painful-consoling conviction that you could not possibly choose me. But as it happened nonetheless, the promise of an incomprehensible happiness—I did not keep it a secret from you—sank under my anxious misgivings. I was determined to propose a new period of reflection to you. Now it is no longer necessary. It is beyond all doubt: if there are two people on earth who must not tie their destinies together, then they are you and I, Aurelie.

AURELIE *with increasingly vehement movements* And you courted me and stood here today—and I chose you!

FALKENIR That you believed you had to choose—today or some other time—that it appeared to you as your preordained fate, as your mission in life, to choose one man among three, among a hundred, who should be your husband, your lord, this was your mistake; this was the compulsion which you thought yourself subject to. Your true being was hidden beneath the all-enveloping prejudices of your birth, of your education—even from yourself. You did not know yourself yet, Aurelie, you did not yet trust yourself. Now you must no longer be deceived about yourself. Believe me, Aurelie: if you had, free of all outer and inner compulsion, followed your deepest impulses, you would not have returned, even from these first dances which bore you away from me—

AURELIE Falkenir!

FALKENIR Not here, not to me! You would have whirled away, flown away—God knows where.

AURELIE What can you be thinking of, Falkenir, that you insult me this way?

FALKENIR It is no insult, Aurelie. It is homage—to the woman you are without having suspected it. To the multi-faceted, inexhaustible, splendid woman who was created to squander herself, and yet, in all her extravagance, always to hold back her innermost self. That's how I have long sensed you to be, that's how I saw you tonight, Aurelie, that's how you are. How you soared away, to unknown distant places, a winged impulse towards them in your gliding steps, a mysterious reflection from them in your twilight glances, a yearning presentiment of them in your unlocked soul. Understand, Aurelie, and be glad: all those distant places are yours, and the gates leading out into the world stand wide open for you.

AURELIE And this is how you're pushing me out—?

FALKENIR No, Aurelie, I am taking my hand from yours—and I am pointing your path out to you.

AURELIE —Leaving me alone?

FALKENIR I am giving you back your freedom—to become what you are, Aurelie.

AURELIE *after a pause* Well, then, let us part. Farewell, Falkenir.

She turns as if to go.

FALKENIR Not this way, Aurelie.

AURELIE How else, Falkenir?

FALKENIR You've misunderstood me terribly if you intend to leave me with bitterness.

AURELIE How we left each other, that we will know some time in the future, perhaps.

Turns again as if to go.

FALKENIR There may yet be a number of things—there are many things yet, Aurelie, for us to discuss. Naturally, this is neither the time nor the place for that. But I trust you will grant me the opportunity to discuss them with you, before we—bid each other farewell.

AURELIE What for? Such a conversation, in feigned inoffensiveness, as if we were—taking up as good friends again— would that not signify a profanation of our farewell, Falkenir?

FALKENIR *after a brief silence* We will see each other again.

AURELIE That's certainly possible. But we should not wish it—either one of us.

FALKENIR Aurelie!

AURELIE Live happily, Falkenir.

She extends her hand to him.

FALKENIR *grasps her hand, kisses it, and exits.*

AURELIE *stands motionless a while, then decides abruptly to go.*

MAX *comes towards her, alongside the pool, is about to greet her.*

AURELIE *noticing him, automatically reaches for her neck, unclasps her necklace and throws it into the pool.*

MAX Well, superstitious after all, Countess?

AURELIE *makes no reply.*

MAX What's troubling you?—You're alone?—What has happened, Countess? *Looks all around* Am I—to be blamed somehow in the end?

AURELIE *shakes her head* You have no reason either to re-

proach yourself or to imagine anything.
She turns to go.

MAX *determined* Forgive me, Countess, but I won't let you leave this way. Where is Herr von Falkenir? Has there been a misunderstanding here? Obviously. I'm at your disposal.

AURELIE There is nothing, nothing at all.

MAX You're distracted, Countess Aurelie. I mustn't leave you alone.

AURELIE *laughing absent-mindedly* You're worried about me, Herr von Reisenberg?

MAX The party is over, permit me to escort you to your car, Countess.

AURELIE *gradually changing her tone* Why? I'm not much in the mood to go home.

MAX The park is emptying, the lights are going out, the music is over.

AURELIE Pity. It was such a beautiful party.

MAX Yes, that it was. A strange, a fairy-tale-like party.

AURELIE Do you think so, Herr von Reisenberg? I wonder how those fairy tales which do not end with a wedding come out.

MAX They all end with a wedding. It only takes a while sometimes to get to that point. And there are adventures to be gone through along the way.

AURELIE Dangerous adventures.

MAX Harmless ones too. And merry ones. But in the end, without fail, comes the wedding.

AURELIE Or death.

MAX A fairy-tale death, not such a bad thing, I imagine.

AURELIE Look, the party is continuing. Or is a new one beginning so soon? There, between the trees, it looks like torchlight.

MAX Those aren't torches, Countess, that's the dawn.

AURELIE Is morning so near—?

MAX A spring morning. *Quietly hesitating* Aurelie—

AURELIE Yes, it smells of lilacs.

MAX What smells of lilacs, I imagine, is this branch. *Hesitates* It's yours, Aurelie. I've saved it for you. I knew I would meet you again tonight.

AURELIE Did you really? *Takes the branch* I thank you. And now good-bye. Yes, now I want to be off. Not home, somewhere out in the open. *Presses her face to the lilac branch* Shall we take a ride out into the open, Herr von Reisenberg?

MAX *greatly moved, bows to her.*

AURELIE . . . Out into the Spring morning. . . . Or are you afraid?

MAX *with an uncertain smile* Aurelie!

AURELIE *serious again* Perhaps you're right. One never knows.

MAX And were it death itself. A ride with you, Aurelie, on a spring morning—that would surely be worth nothing less.

AURELIE *the lilac branch against her lips, glances at Max with a distant smile* Come!

She exits.

MAX *after a barely noticeable hesitation, follows her.*
The stage is empty. The last light from the palace goes out.

Curtain

ACT TWO

Scene One

At Aurelie's mansion.

A small parlor in the Merkenstein mansion in the Salesianer-gasse. The door to the balcony stands open, giving a view of tree tops. To the right, a door to the anteroom; to the left a smaller door. Gysar is standing in front of an easel, painting. The picture is not visible. Aurelie is sitting on an armchair.

GYSAR   What are you thinking of, Aurelie?

AURELIE   I hope to find that out shortly from the portrait you're painting.

GYSAR   Your soul is flying off all too far into the distance, Aurelie.

AURELIE   One should be able to paint that too, when all is said and done.

Pause.

GYSAR   Your head a little to the side—glance directed a little higher—over past the tree tops, if you would be so kind, Countess.

AURELIE   Why so subservient, Gysar? It goes against your nature. Go ahead and command, where you may. Shouldn't I rather prop my arm up on the chair? Or how would it be if I stepped out onto the balcony and leaned against the railing—the way we tried it at first—I wonder when that was?

GYSAR *to himself* I don't know.

AURELIE   Just about the end of May we began, so, two weeks ago.

GYSAR   I thought—yesterday.

AURELIE   Shall we take a break for a while? You're not in the right frame of mind, Gysar.

GYSAR   To put it mildly. I'm beginning to despair.

AURELIE *always steadily cool* Perhaps the lighting is to blame. The sky seems a bit dreary for a summer day.

GYSAR   Dreary light—overcast sky—excuses, vain excuses. I

am losing myself—with every passing day, I am losing my-self more. I began for the third time yesterday—and it keeps drawing further away from me—the picture—and you, Aurelie.

AURELIE Perhaps you're further along than you think. If you would only let me see the portrait once—

GYSAR *defensive movement.*

AURELIE Or if we showed it to an expert—

GYSAR *without emphasis* To Herr von Reisenberg for example?

AURELIE *ever cool* To him or to another whose judgment you trust.

GYSAR I would recognize only one authority: the Baron von Falkenir.

AURELIE It would be difficult to summon him here. He is in Rome, as I hear—

GYSAR He's there. One of my friends, the painter Beraton, spoke to him recently. He wrote me about it—incidentally —among other things. *Since she remains silent, he continues* He has taken up his researches with Dr. Grimani on the Palatine again. Imagine, *painting* in the last section of the imperial palace to be excavated, in the sitting room of the wife of Tiberius, they found an excellently preserved mural, a portrait of the Empress. The colors are said to shine like on the day they were painted. Most likely they owe their brightness to the fact that the painting was buried for two thousand years.

AURELIE To be buried for two thousand years—isn't that too high a price for brightness?

GYSAR It really makes no difference when posterity begins. *He continues painting, looks at her, shakes his head.*

AURELIE This is right, isn't it? My glance is directed out over the tree tops, just as you wished.

GYSAR *looks at her, then at the portrait. Suddenly he draws several heavy brushstrokes over it.*

AURELIE *stands up, fairly unmoved* Well then, farewell, Gysar.

GYSAR You are dismissing me?

AURELIE Really, you're doing that yourself.

GYSAR You have misunderstood me, Aurelie. Give up on your portrait?—I would be giving up on myself at the same time.

AURELIE *mildly* Do let us interrupt it for the time being—for a few months—or years. You will rediscover your genius in some other work in the meantime. And both the world of art and I will have the enjoyment of it.

GYSAR There is no longer any other work for me in this world than your portrait; you know it, Aurelie.

AURELIE The Prince of Perosa has asked you to do a painting for his yacht. You could let your imagination run free there.

GYSAR I've given the Prince to understand that I am not in a position to accept commissions.

AURELIE How much more there would be for you to do!

GYSAR Nothing.

AURELIE A hundred women wait with longing.

GYSAR Let them wait. Before you, after you, no others.

AURELIE And the models—the famous models, who wait for a sign from you?

GYSAR I have long since sent them all to the devil.

AURELIE To hell—directly from heaven? How inhuman, Gysar.

GYSAR *with increasing urgency* I am alone; my house and my garden wait. Only for you alone. Don't refuse me any longer what I have begged of you again and again. I want to paint you under the open sky.

AURELIE *cooly* We could try it once. I'll have your easel put up in the park.

GYSAR I want to paint you in the sunshine. Heaven's light over your hair, over your forehead, your throat, your neck, your hips, Aurelie. My house stands alone. High walls around the garden. We'll be like on an island in the ocean. Come, Aurelie.

Pause.

AURELIE And if this picture should also turn out to be a failure in the end? How will you compensate me for the loss of time—and for whatever else may be lost?

GYSAR With my life, if you like.

AURELIE You know very well that I wouldn't ask for that. And what good would it do me?

GYSAR It would become a portrait, Aurelie, such that a person who saw it in a hundred or a thousand years could go mad at the thought that he was born too late to see the original.

AURELIE And what if you're only imagining all this? If it should turn out that you are really no artist?—What then, Gysar? If in the end it amounted to nothing more than to a kind of deceitful enticement?

GYSAR Well, then you would have simply given yourself away, Aurelie.

AURELIE To you—?!

GYSAR You would have made a person who adores you happy. Is that so little? Why so stingy? Aren't you free? Must you render an account to any one?

Arduin is suddenly standing in the doorway to the right.

ARDUIN Why do you ask that, Gysar. I beg your pardon for coming in unannounced. Good morning, Aurelie.

AURELIE You are in my house, Arduin. You forgot to greet Master Gysar.

ARDUIN Later. First I desire your answer, Herr Gysar. By what right do you ask Aurelie if she owes anyone an accounting?

AURELIE By what right do you ask him?

GYSAR Your Highness would perhaps do better to dispense with my answer for as long as we find ourselves in this house.

ARDUIN So come. Let us continue our conversation, wherever you please.

AURELIE *quickly* You may both do what you like. Nonetheless, should this conversation be destined to continue in any form, then I swear, that neither one of you will ever lay eyes on me again.—I think you're not a boy anymore, Arduin. And you, Gysar, are a man, even. And I—to answer both of you—owe an accounting to no one except myself. *Smiling* The matter is herewith chivalrously settled. Give your hand to one another, gentlemen, as is customary in such cases. I ask it of you.—I desire it.—I command it!

ARDUIN *extends his hand to Gysar.*

GYSAR *grasps it fleetingly.*

AURELIE *nods, smiling* By the way, I'm astounded to see you here, Arduin. I thought you were God knows where.

ARDUIN I arrived this morning.

AURELIE If I had had any idea—If we had known a half hour

ago—*To Gysar* You would surely have accepted the Prince as an expert?

ARDUIN *understanding, in a conventional tone* I see. You are being painted.

AURELIE Was being painted. The Master was not satisfied. That is why he has obliterated the picture.

ARDUIN *as above* Pity.

AURELIE For the third time.

ARDUIN Really? Then I suppose for the last time too?

GYSAR *agitated movement.*

AURELIE *quickly* Oh, no. *To Gysar* You were right, Gysar. This is not the place to finish a portrait. One is too exposed to interruptions. And regardless of how welcome they might be, they remain interruptions all the same. So, we're agreed, Gysar, if the sky doesn't cloud over again by tomorrow counter to expectations, I will be at your house around noontime.

ARDUIN *starts.*

GYSAR *kisses Aurelie's hand, partly to control his emotions, bows slightly to Arduin, who barely returns the greeting, and exits.*

AURELIE Don't you want to sit down, Arduin?—Where are you coming from actually?

ARDUIN We can talk about that later.—It is not seriously your intention to set foot in Gysar's house?

AURELIE The house and the garden;—if the sky remains clear. —You were in Greece and Italy?

ARDUIN *quickly* And in France and England.—Do you really know where you'll be going if you go to Gysar's?

AURELIE To the studio of a great artist.—Were you on a secret mission, as people say?

ARDUIN A studio? The police will come before long and raid that nest. There are women running around there the way God created them.

AURELIE A strange idea, to entrust you with diplomatic missions.

ARDUIN What has happened to you, Aurelie? I spoke to the Princess.—I want to hear it from you. What people are saying doesn't concern me. Are you Falkenir's fiancée or not?

AURELIE I am not anybody's fiancée.

ARDUIN Then I will court you a second time. If you accept my suit, I will ask nothing further. And if it matters to you—if only it were so—then Falkenir will have a bullet in his forehead even before the two of us stand before the altar.

AURELIE You don't say! And I suppose during the funeral you'll leap over the coffin on your horse.—I think you could leave this foolishness alone. The time for it is past.

ARDUIN I love you, Aurelie! Weren't we destined for each other from the beginning?—Created for each other from childhood on? Everything I've done, was only for your sake—the good and the bad, all for you. And if they make me a ruler or a king somewhere, some time, it will again have been only for you, Aurelie. I knew it, I knew it could not last with Falkenir.—I was a fool to go away—not to come to you right away the next morning.

AURELIE Do you think so, Arduin?—What makes you so sure you wouldn't already have been too late, the next morning?

ARDUIN Aurelie! What have they done to you? Tell me, Aurelie. What have they done to you? This is not you talking like this!

AURELIE It is me. I'm that too, Arduin. And who knows what else. . . .

ARDUIN You're playing. Yes, Aurelie, you are jesting and playing comedy. Now I recognize you again. Yes, those are your childhood eyes. You looked exactly the same way when the balls flew, or when we chased through the woods together! Do tell me that this was all a jest—and also everything that people told me about you this morning. Evil jests—

MAX *enters from the right; remains standing, surprised.*

AURELIE Is it you? So early today?

ARDUIN *looks around, first sees him now.*

AURELIE Come closer. The gentlemen are not acquainted? Herr Max von Reisenberg, the Prince of Perosa.
Brief bowing on the part of the men.

MAX *kisses Aurelie's hand.*

ARDUIN Your fiancé, Aurelie?

AURELIE No, Arduin. Herr Max von Reisenberg is my lover.

ARDUIN *stiffens at first, then bows quickly and exits.*

Max, Aurelie

AURELIE At such an unaccustomed hour, Max? Oh, I'm glad you're here.—What a beautiful day. Now the clouds have dispersed completely. Why weren't you here yesterday— and the day before yesterday? I didn't see you for three days! Where were you?

MAX I was waiting for you to call me.

AURELIE I believe I did call;—you just didn't hear it.

MAX Maybe I did. . . . Am I not here?

AURELIE And you really did nothing but wait these three days?—Did nothing else? Thought nothing else? Embraced no other woman?

MAX Does it matter much to you? You smile while you ask.

AURELIE And you don't even answer. That's even worse than my smiling. *Pause* How is the beautiful Judith, my friend?

MAX Excellent. And how is Master Gysar?

AURELIE Not bad, I believe.—And how is the charming Fräulein Seraphine getting along?

MAX She's playing the violin, as usual.—And where did your cousin, Prince Arduin, come from all of a sudden?

AURELIE Indeed, where do they all come from? And where do they disappear to?—And were never here at all when all is said and done!

MAX The Prince made his presence pretty clearly noticeable. And the way you introduced me to him seemed not to have pleased him particularly.

AURELIE I really didn't consider whether it pleased him or not. But that my answer should have surprised you too! Strange! Shouldn't I have told him the truth, my lover? *Extraneously, with her eyes elsewhere.*

MAX Yes, if it had been the truth! But was it? The truth would have been: your one-time lover, your lover for a night, your—never your lover.

AURELIE *her hand in front of her eyes* I'm hurting.

MAX I suppose that happens between one happiness and the other.

AURELIE Is it really over, then?

MAX It never began.

AURELIE Weren't we blissful unto tears?

MAX The ones you wept in my arms were meant for another, not for me.

AURELIE Didn't I give you everything that I could give?

MAX Infinitely much;—only not yourself.—
Turns to go.

AURELIE You're leaving?

MAX May I still stay?

AURELIE I'm not sending you away.

MAX You're not holding me back.

AURELIE Who is waiting for you?

MAX Into whose arms will you fly?

AURELIE I will never forget you.

MAX I will never experience anything more beautiful.

AURELIE *takes his head in her hands, kisses him on the forehead* Farewell.

MAX *takes both her hands and kisses them* Thank you! *Exits.*

AURELIE *alone* I'm shivering.—And yet, it's good to be alone. Alone once again. . . between one happiness and the other. Between one pleasure and the other. Between one death and the other. . . .

Scene Two

At the Westerhaus residence.

President Westerhaus's workroom. To the left a fireplace, to the right a bookcase, in the center a large table with papers, letters, and so on, as well as a telephone. A smoking table and armchairs in front of the fireplace. On the wall to the right hangs a portrait of Julia which need not be clearly visible to the audience. Main entrance to the right. To the rear a door which is closed at the beginning of the scene. At the beginning of the scene the room is empty. The telephone rings. A servant enters from the right.

SERVANT *on the phone* This is Herr President Westerhaus's residence.—Who may I say is calling?—Right away.

He goes to the rear, opens the door, affording a view of the dining room. The following are sitting around the set table in the order given here: WESTERHAUS, *the* PRINCESS, SKODNY, JUDITH, RUDOLF VON HEYSKAL, JULIA, BRAUNIGL, AMBROS. *Lively conversation. The servant steps up to Westerhaus, who stands up, comes into the working room, and shuts the door behind him, while the servant remains in the dining room.*

WESTERHAUS *on the phone* Westerhaus here.—Yes, it's me.—Oh, good day, Herr Director.—I'm listening.—May I ask you simply to read it to me—with the proposed changes? *He takes notes while he listens* Good.—Oh, yes, I'm listening.—Oh—isn't that the brother of the—camel driver—? Very interesting.—By all means.—Tomorrow morning, then.—Thank you.—Certainly.—Until tomorrow, Herr Director.—
Hangs up.
JUDITH *comes out of the dining room, where some of the guests have gotten up. She closes the door and lights a cigarette.*
WESTERHAUS How many does that make today? It's not good for your voice. *Strokes her hair softly.*
JUDITH There's somebody calling every minute!
WESTERHAUS It happens.
JUDITH What is really the matter?
WESTERHAUS Nothing that could be of interest to little girls. *Turning aside, puts his notes in his pocket* You received a telegram this morning. May one ask?
JUDITH It said nothing that could interest great, big gentlemen.
WESTERHAUS *lightly* Perhaps it could—?
JUDITH *as if in passing* My room in South Kensington, at the Pension Dudley, is reserved. On Wednesday I have my first lesson with Jean de Reszke.
WESTERHAUS And when are you thinking of leaving Vienna?
JUDITH Just as we decided: tomorrow evening.
The telephone rings.
JUDITH *as if joking* Just let me listen.
WESTERHAUS *on the phone* President Westerhaus here. *Hands*

Judith the receiver Please.

JUDITH *listens with effort for a few seconds, then, shaking her head, returns the receiver to Westerhaus* I can't understand a single word. What have you got to do with camel drivers?

WESTERHAUS *on the phone* I'm sorry, there was a slight interruption.—Yes, of course. That's confirmed, then.—Well, yes. Thank you, Herr Matrei, I'll be in the office at five. *Hangs up.*

JUDITH What's the matter?

WESTERHAUS Dear child—*hesitating a little* I'm afraid nothing will come of Folkestone.

JUDITH Folkestone?

WESTERHAUS Or is it Brighton?—What was that town on the English coast where you wanted to meet Julia and me this summer?

JUDITH *with false harshness* Nothing would've come of that anyway. I have—made other arrangements for August.

WESTERHAUS *with light irony* Well, all the better. But as concerns London, too—I would wire a cancellation if I were you.

JUDITH But why?

WESTERHAUS Actually, it's hardly necessary.—In the Pension—

JUDITH Dudley.

WESTERHAUS They'll not likely be counting on your arrival.

JUDITH What do you mean?

WESTERHAUS I mean that it won't be another three days, —and the world will be in flames.

JUDITH War?

WESTERHAUS Yes.

JUDITH *after a short pause* Unbelievable what these camel drivers are capable of!

WESTERHAUS How clever you are.

JUDITH And that's why you're in such high spirits?

WESTERHAUS Why not? I don't have a son.

JUDITH But others—

WESTERHAUS *quickly* And it is not I who make the political decisions—or determine world history, even, as some people believe. I—only anticipate. I have every right to profit from this talent.

JUDITH You've also been mistaken at times.

WESTERHAUS This time—not.

JUDITH And if—this time too—you are lucky, will you then finally leave well enough alone?—

WESTERHAUS Enough of what?

JUDITH Of your—dangerous business transactions.

WESTERHAUS I could do without the transactions, perhaps, but the danger—? You're asking too much. The risk, that is the meaning of my life.

JUDITH Other people's risk too—?

WESTERHAUS People know that great opportunities also carry great cost.

JUDITH Not all of them think that far ahead.

WESTERHAUS Innocent people always have to suffer too.

JUDITH And you don't care about the innocent any more than about the guilty. Nor about your profits either—and not about the danger;—the meaning of your life is called Julia.

WESTERHAUS Didn't you mean to say—the curse?

JUDITH *remains silent.*

The PRINCESS *and* JULIA *come out of the dining room, followed informally by* AMBROS, SKODNY, RUDOLF VON HEYSKAL, BRAUNIGL.

PRINCESS My dear Frau von Westerhaus, it is a bit discourteous to run off so soon after dining, but—I still have to go to a reception. The daughter of the opera singer Fenz is getting married, the—the one who doesn't play the violin.

SERVANT *brings coffee and serves.*

JULIA Your Highness—please, a cup of coffee.

PRINCESS Thank you. *She helps herself* As it is, I wasn't at the ceremony, it would hurt his feelings, the old man,—a good thing he can't hear me—if I didn't at least go there to offer my congratulations. These former celebrities are particularly sensitive, naturally.

RUDOLF VON HEYSKAL Your Highness truly has a golden Viennese heart.

SKODNY I don't believe the opera singer Fenz considers

himself a has-been at all. He still has ambitions in a number
of areas.

AMBROS *coffee cup in hand, contemplates Julia's portrait, and
notices that Westerhaus is standing behind him* Wasn't this
picture hanging somewhere else before?

WESTERHAUS It has been hanging in the same place since
I've owned it, which is over three years.

AMBROS It's darkening a little, it seems to me.

WESTERHAUS Well, that is simply the fate of Gysar's portraits—of the official ones at least. The other one he made
of Julia, that one surely still shines just as brightly as on
the first day.

AMBROS What other one?

WESTERHAUS I do not have the privilege of knowing it, but
I have no doubt of its existence. Surely you don't either,
Herr Doehl? You must know that he paints each of his
lovers, well—more or less the way Correggio painted Io, as
the cloud descended upon her. And he is always the cloud.

AMBROS Legends always take shape around artists, Herr President.

WESTERHAUS Around beautiful women too. And these are
true most of the time. *He notices that the Princess is just
about to make her final farewells, looks at his watch* If Your
Highness will permit, I will escort Your Highness down the
stairs.

JULIA You're going already?

WESTERHAUS *surprised* I have to, unfortunately.

PRINCESS So, I wish everyone a very pleasant summer.

JULIA Your Highness is going to your estate?

PRINCESS I still have to put in my three weeks in Karlsbad,
like every year. But then it's right off to my beloved
wilderness in Ostrolszka.

RUDOLF VON HEYSKAL On the Russian-Polish border, Highness?

PRINCESS But why do you ask, Herr Councilor?

RUDOLF VON HEYSKAL Forgive me, Your Highness, but a
somewhat more securely located residence would be
advisable this summer. *The phone rings.*

WESTERHAUS *on the phone, makes a sign that the company*

should not allow itself to be disturbed.

PRINCESS   You really think it possible, Herr Councilor, that it will come to something?

RUDOLF VON HEYSKAL   One can not by any means characterize the political situation as absolutely clear.

SKODNY   To be sure, we've been through that a number of times in recent years.

BRAUNIGL   Which would make it all the more joyful to receive a clarification. A war would doubtless have a purifying effect, not only with regard to politics, but also ethically and morally, so to speak.

PRINCESS   This is very interesting, Herr District Attorney. Excellency Greising said the same thing, almost word for word, recently. A war would be a veritable fountain of youth for humanity, he said.

BRAUNIGL   That is my view as well.

WESTERHAUS *hanging up* It would seem that Your Highness can travel to Ostrolszka quite without worry. I just heard on the phone that the German Kaiser is going on his northern trip the day after tomorrow, as he does every year.

RUDOLF VON HEYSKAL   That doesn't prove anything, Herr President. Lord Grey is on vacation too. That proves very little in such times. Perhaps even the opposite of what it is intended to prove.

JULIA   And what do you think, Herr Captain?

SKODNY   I have to declare myself completely incompetent. I can only say that three or four years ago we were far closer to attacking. And nothing came of that either.

BRAUNIGL   Unfortunately.

SKODNY   Whether it was unfortunate, that I would not want to state with such certainty.

AMBROS   The gentlemen of the officers' corps seem fortunately to be somewhat more peace-loving than the Attorneys General.

PRINCESS *laughing* That's very good. Well, as always, I am not afraid. The Russians I've met, they were all eminently nice people.—So, Herr President, I'm ready.

Further brief leave-taking, the Princess and Westerhaus exit.

AMBROS *to Judith* I will say good-bye to you also, dear

Judith, for a long time, presumably.

JUDITH Why for a long time—? It's possible that I may—not yet be leaving tomorrow.

AMBROS But I will be in any event. I have to take advantage of my few weeks' vacation.

JUDITH *while Skodny and Rudolf von Heyskal are approaching her, to Ambros* I still have to speak with you for a moment.

BRAUNIGL *to Julia* It's certain that he's going directly to his office now?

JULIA Absolutely. Where else?

BRAUNIGL Wouldn't it be possible for him to take the next train—to Hamburg or to some other place?

JULIA He—leave me alone, when he doesn't have to. . . ?!

BRAUNIGL *looks at his watch* Four-fifteen. In one hour, my people will be in his office.

JULIA And I will be free?

BRAUNIGL Yes.

JULIA *takes a deep breath.*

BRAUNIGL Until eight o'clock in the evening. I am expecting you at eight.

JULIA That you can do in any case. Wait until nine or ten or twelve—I may very possibly show up.

BRAUNIGL Possibly.

JULIA Oh, there is no certainty at all in this world. Especially in—these things.

BRAUNIGL Julia, consider what I'm doing for you. I'm acting completely on my own responsibility. And I cannot guarantee that in around a week, or in three days he will not be released again.

JULIA Three days, that's a long time. How much can happen in three days! Are you developing scruples by any chance? All his speculations are directed towards war, and, you did hear, it is not going to come to war. He is ruined.

BRAUNIGL That remains to be seen.

JULIA And incidentally, didn't you say once that you would be capable of committing even a dishonorable deed for me. And perhaps now it will not even be one. I wonder if I'm still obligated, then, to keep my promise at all?

BRAUNIGL Julia!—

JULIA Four-twenty. Oh, how slowly the time passes. *Abruptly* I want to hear music. Herr Rittmeister, do play something for us.

SKODNY I, dear lady? You forget that I play only the flute.

JULIA Oh, yes, pardon me. Where then is—Max? *Calls* Judith!

JUDITH How should I know?

JULIA He's becoming discourteous, your friend Max. I invite him to lunch, he cancels at the last minute, then promises to be here for coffee afterwards—and now he doesn't come at all.

RUDOLF VON HEYSKAL With a groom, dear lady, one mustn't be so strict.

JULIA Groom of the Countess of Merkenstein's, you mean?

RUDOLF VON HEYSKAL It's no secret, after all. Just a few days ago I saw the two of them riding together in the Prater without a chaperone.

JULIA Certainly it's no secret. But no engagement either.

BRAUNIGL Are you speaking of the Countess Aurelie von Merkenstein? Isn't she engaged to the Baron of Falkenir then?

RUDOLF VON HEYSKAL Was, Herr District Attorney. But the engagement is said to have lasted only one evening. Then Herr Max von Reisenberg appeared and conquered, as he wished. And the spicy part, indeed, the sensation of the thing, as it were, is that as you will all surely remember, Aurelie's father, the Count Merkenstein, shot Reisenberg's father in a duel, for valid reasons.

BRAUNIGL Certainly I remember. I was the public prosecutor, after all. The Count was sentenced to a year in prison.

SKODNY And pardoned after a week.

RUDOLF VON HEYSKAL But the elder Reisenberg is said to have remained stone-dead nonetheless.

BRAUNIGL So, this young Herr von Reisenberg is to a certain extent predestined to be a seducer?

JULIA Seducer—?! Is there really such a thing?—I've yet to see one!

BRAUNIGL There are even seducers by profession. Or does Herr von Reisenberg have another?

AMBROS Why should he, Herr District Attorney? I find that

young people, like my friend Max, simply by dint of their existence, give the world's ambiance a friendlier and more gracious form. Why demand achievements from them too? Do you require achievements of a butterfly? of the spring wind?—You surely do not believe, Herr District Attorney, that a person such as Max von Reisenberg would have even the least bit to gain in either exterior or inner worth if he were to sell watches and rings on the Graben the way his father did. Or if he drilled recruits? Or if he sent criminals, and possibly also innocent people to prison? Or if he wrote documents in some office—from nine to four?

BRAUNIGL *in a superior tone* It may well be a prejudice on my part, Herr Doehl, but much as I would like to, I am incapable of summoning up any particular sympathy for even the most charming young people, if they don't at least make an attempt to become useful members of human society in some way.

JULIA —Until evenings, eight o'clock.

AMBROS Useful members of human society! Can there be a more useful occupation than to increase the total joy, to say nothing of happiness, in this earthly vale of tears?

BRAUNIGL That is a pretty paradox, Herr Doehl, but, forgive me, nothing more.—Just imagine such people, I don't want to name any names now, imagine them becoming older and gradually being obliged by the eternal laws of nature—to give up their profession of bringing joy and happiness. What will remain of all the splendor? What a sad or deplorable sight will these people present then!

AMBROS I'm willing to admit that without further ado, Herr District Attorney. But a retired postal official or even a pensioned-off General is not always a great delight to look at either.

MAX VON REISENBERG *enters from the right.*

JULIA There he is finally! What kind of behavior is this, to get here so late? We've been longing for your arrival.

MAX *somewhat amazed at the loud reception, kisses Julia's hand and greets the others.*

JULIA That is to say, we want to hear some music. You must sit down at the piano at once and play something delicious for us.

MAX Now?—At once?

JULIA Instantly.

MAX And if by chance I weren't in the right mood to play the piano today?

JULIA It will come. You may play whatever you like. Only music! Music! A waltz or a funeral march! Music!

SKODNY I recently heard a waltz with the curious title, "End of the World."

MAX Don't know it, but the title is suggestive,—maybe something will occur to me on it.

AMBROS Go on and play, Max! And if it's all right with you, we can leave together later. *In response to his glance* Surely you haven't forgotten? Wedding in the Fenz house.

MAX Certainly not. It was on my agenda.

SKODNY *has in the meantime gone through the dining room into the parlor and has struck a few chords on the piano.*

JULIA *takes Max by the arm* Come on, then, Max!
  Julia, Max exit. They are followed by Braunigl, Skodny, and Rudolf von Heyskal. The door remains open, the piano playing is audible.

AMBROS, JUDITH

AMBROS What's going on here, Judith? Something is not right today.

JUDITH Just today—you think so?—Nothing has been right here yet. What do I care? Tomorrow I'm going to England to Jean de Reszke. You don't believe it, Ambros? I have my ticket already. And I have some entirely different things planned too.

AMBROS I know—you have an engagement in Dresden, don't you?

JUDITH I had almost forgotten that. *She lights another cigarette* Perhaps I'll even begin my career with a breach of contract.

AMBROS It would be just like you to jeopardize your future

for the sake of some mood.

JUDITH But I won't be jeopardizing it. Rather, I will inaugurate it with proper brilliance. What will you bet? In one year I'll be the most famous cocotte in Europe.

AMBROS None of this comes from your heart, Judith.

JUDITH What do you know about my heart, Ambros? Most likely I don't even have one.

AMBROS Oh, you have one. You have a poor, wounded little heart, like a little seamstress.

JUDITH Ha, how well you know me! A wounded heart. . . . Unhappy love, what? For whom, then? For Max, maybe—? Wonderful!

AMBROS Max—No, no one need love him unhappily!

JUDITH Well, and you think—if I had set my mind to it— that I could not have won the President? Better he be ruined by Julia than by me. Others shall be ruined by me.

AMBROS Poor child.

JUDITH Save your pity, Ambros, I'm doing very well.

JULIA *comes quickly out from the dining room, nervously* Oh, you're still here, Ambros?—I thought I heard the telephone ring.

JUDITH *shakes her head.*

JULIA *absent-minded, to Ambros, in order to say something* So, you're leaving tomorrow too?

MAX *comes out of the dining room.*

JULIA *turns to him at once* Why did you stop playing, Max? *She goes towards the rear again at once.*

JUDITH Indeed, why did you stop, Max? It was such a beautiful accompaniment for our conversation, isn't that so, Ambros?

MAX I couldn't play any more. I sensed that you weren't there.

AMBROS Excuse me, Max—Won't you. . . with me, now—? Otherwise it could happen that the young couple will have left before we get there.

JUDITH *to Ambros* Oh, leave him to me for a few more minutes. I will send him away again right away. Farewell scenes mustn't last too long.

AMBROS *to Max* Well, so long, I'll see you at the Fenz's—. Good-bye, Judith.

JUDITH *pointedly* Until we meet again, Ambros. I'll see you.
AMBROS *exits.*

MAX, JUDITH

MAX Oh, Judith.—*He wants to take her hand.*
JUDITH Let that be for the time being. First of all I want to
know whether you finally withdrew your money from my
brother-in-law's bank?
MAX Just yesterday I took out another few thousand gulden—
for the near future—I really couldn't, all at once—It really
would have been an insult to the President.
JUDITH Are you really such a child? Or is this affectation
too?
MAX All right, I promise you: tomorrow I will take care of
whatever is necessary.
JUDITH Well—perhaps money really is no object for you any
more—
MAX How do you mean that?
JUDITH Why play at secrets? It's common knowledge that
you're marrying Aurelie. We were speaking of it before you
came.
MAX Where did you get that idea? Neither she—nor I have
ever thought of it.
JUDITH She was your lover. Don't deny it. The whole world
knows it—and your companion—are you keeping it a secret?
MAX I only know,—that we have said farewell to each other.
JUDITH Truly?
MAX Yes, it's over.
JUDITH *somewhat distrustfully* Since when?
MAX Yes, how long might it be? *Looks at his watch* A long
time. In less than ten minutes it will have been a century.
JUDITH I can't believe how affected you are, Max.
MAX *unperturbed* And yet, there is nothing more separating
that leave-taking from this—*looks at Judith*—homecoming,
than a stroll and a lunch. A somewhat sad stroll in the city
park among playing children, flirting nursery maids, retired
officers, and pairs of lovers—and a delicious, lonely lunch
in a dreamy corner with artificial lighting and half a bottle

of champagne.

JUDITH So it's really over? A pity, actually. Practical you're not, Max!—

MAX Couldn't you hear it in my piano playing that it's over? Didn't it sound very melancholy?

JUDITH Not excessively.

MAX Oh, it had to end. She is a wonderful, incomparable being. More wonderful than you, Judith. But so remote, so remote. It was beautiful, very beautiful—and yet, I confess it to you quite openly, sometimes it felt—unearthly in her presence.

JUDITH You can go ahead and say it, in her arms.

MAX If you wish.

JUDITH I understand this very well. I can very easily imagine that I might also feel weird—with someone—in someone's arms. I'll surely experience something of the kind too one day. You, Max, you are not the least bit unearthly to me.

MAX Thank God. Why should we be unearthly to each other? We come from the same stock, after all. Why, we belong together in a glorious and depraved way. Oh, Judith, don't you want to become mine?

JUDITH *again lighting a cigarette, exaggeratedly gay, as if she were singing* Tomorrow I'm going to England.

MAX Oh, that makes a delicious picture, traveling to England with you—or anywhere else too.

JUDITH No, Max, no. There is nothing between us two.

MAX But why, then?

JUDITH Can't be.

MAX Just between us two?

JUDITH Yes, just between you and me.

MAX This I do not understand.

JUDITH Just imagine, if it happened to me—to fall in love with you in earnest.

MAX Why, that would be wonderful.

JUDITH Yes, for you, but not for me. If there is one thing I fear—fear like death, it's the grand passion. And especially a passion for you, Max! You, who would never be capable of sacrificing anything for a woman, no happiness, oh, not even a pleasure that beckoned to you from somewhere else—

MAX   Judith, I swear to you—

JUDITH   Hush, Max, I will not accept any oath from you. Nothing remains for us, Max, but to bid each other farewell.

MAX   But surely not—for long, surely not *with real fear* forever?

JUDITH   Whether forever or not, that depends on you, Max.

MAX   On me? I don't understand.

JUDITH   If you want to see me one more time, then it must be for no longer than twenty-four hours, for one day *without emphasis* and one night.

MAX   Are you serious, Judith?

JUDITH   Absolutely. If you ever want to see me again, then you must swear to me, today—

MAX   I guess you are.

JUDITH   That you will not make the slightest attempt then to hold me any longer than I want. That you will disappear at my signal, without so much as turning around to the spot where I remain standing.

MAX   What are you asking of me, Judith?

JUDITH   I'm asking nothing at all. I'm only setting a condition. If it strikes you as too hard—

MAX   I accept it.

JUDITH   You swear?

MAX   Yes, I swear. So, when will I see you again?

JUDITH   Patience, my friend. Tomorrow I'm going to England. That is settled. I am disappearing from your life for a while.—I will call you when the time is right.

MAX   And when will that time be?

JUDITH   That depends on circumstances.

MAX   Days, weeks, months?

JUDITH   I don't know.

MAX   And how much—will have happened in the meantime?

JUDITH *smiling* In this regard you may rest quite easy, Max, absolutely easy.

MAX   Judith! *He takes her hand, is about to resume speaking.*

JUDITH   Well, not another word, Max. Surely you realize that you mustn't say another word now. Go.
The telephone rings.

JUDITH *starts* Go, Max. *She picks up the telephone.*

MAX *takes her free hand again, kisses it, and exits quickly.*

JUDITH *on the phone* This is President Westerhaus's residence.—You can not speak to Madame at the moment.—Important? *ever more hastily* We have company.—But who is this?—Oh, it's you, Herr Matrei?—Yes, it's me, Judith Asrael.—Well? And?—Better, that I?—Well, tell me—Yes.—Yes.—Do tell me everything, will you?—Yes.— Yes.—I hear you.—Yes.—*She groans slightly* Is a doctor. . . . What?—Too late. . . . Who is there?—And now—So.—No, I'll come myself.—Don't call again.—Yes.
She hangs up.

JULIA, BRAUNIGL, SKODNY, RUDOLF VON HEYSKAL *come in.*

JULIA *while still at the door, to Judith* For me?

JUDITH No, I would have called you. The gentlemen are leaving already?

RUDOLF VON HEYSKAL I do envy you so very much, Fräulein Judith. Give my regards to the Crystal Palace and the Thames.

JUDITH *controlled* I'll do that.
Julia and Braunigl stand to the side.

JULIA Past five. How come there's no news yet?

BRAUNIGL Your nervousness is attracting attention.

JULIA I will call the office myself.

BRAUNIGL Superfluous, dear lady. I will expect you at eight.

JULIA Do not speak to me as to an accomplice. I won't allow it.

BRAUNIGL At eight o'clock. *To the other men, who are already standing by the door* I'm coming with you, gentlemen. *To Judith* Once more, bon voyage, Fräulein.
Kisses Julia's hand; the three men exit.

JULIA Why did you leave the company, Judith? You had a little discussion—with Max—about Aurelie, right? Oh, I'm not forcing myself into your secrets. *Reflects, then suddenly* We could go to the opera tonight. I'll ask Westerhaus if he's in the mood. He must be in his office by now *Picks up the telephone* 7041. *To Judith* Don't you feel like it? *A Masked Ball? Rings again* Please, 7041, Fräulein. Ring up just once more, please. What? Thank you. *Hangs up; to Judith* The call isn't going through, that's really strange, don't you think?

JUDITH Yes.

JULIA But why should it be disconnected? There's something wrong here. With whom were you on the phone before, Judith? God, you're so pale. Who telephoned? You needn't spare my feelings or anything. . . . From the office?

JUDITH Yes.

JULIA Why didn't you call me to the phone? What's happened? Or did he ask only for you?

JUDITH Who?

JULIA Well, Westerhaus, of course. Won't you say something? Whatever your relationship with him, these are matters that concern me too. Especially me. In the end I'll find them out anyway. What's happened, Judith? Tell me the truth! Don't spare me! Were the police there?—Has he been arrested?

JUDITH How do you know that?

JULIA Has he been arrested? Yes or no?

JUDITH You knew?

JULIA Is it true or isn't it? Did I guess right?

JUDITH Yes, he has been arrested.

JULIA Are the police still there? Did the Police Commissioner telephone?

JUDITH Matrei telephoned. The office is officially sealed.

JULIA And where is Westerhaus?

JUDITH You knew that they would arrest him?

JULIA What are you talking about? I had a hunch. A foreboding. And you didn't? It had to come sometime. Should it perhaps surprise me? Does it surprise you? Now the time has come. Now he sits in jail. *Laughs maliciously* Oh, I was prepared for this.—By the way, perhaps they're only holding him for questioning. They will interrogate him, in three days he'll be free, in two weeks perhaps a rich man again, it all depends.

JUDITH Still, today he's in jail.

JULIA Yes, that he is. I don't imagine they'll let him out any more today. No, today, Judith, I am free. Yes, Judith, think, free, for the first time in seven years. I can do and leave undone whatever I want, can go wherever,—can sleep where I want and with whom I please. The choice is mine. You wouldn't believe from among how many.

JUDITH   Only the choice? No obligation?

JULIA   To whom? I'd like to see the man who dares to demand something of me. No one. No one. Ah, free, free! If I wanted to I could even go out in the street and bring back up a handsome lad—or stand at the window—and signal to one who strikes my fancy. But that wouldn't serve the purpose, really. He'd know nothing about it, after all,—and only then would I get my fun out of it,—if he were standing there—his hands and feet in chains.

JUDITH   You hate him that much?

JULIA   Yes, I hate him. You don't understand that?—Well, if you love him, why didn't you take him? I would have been so very happy. But you shall have him now. I leave him to you, I leave him to you entirely. Or do you think by any chance that I'm going to wait for him? And whether he comes out in three years or in three days, me he will not find here any more. I suppose it's more likely to be three years, don't you think? Oh, Judith, free, free. Oh, don't worry. I won't signal anyone to come up and I won't go to anyone. No, today no one. I shudder at all of them, who snatch at me with their greedy hands. No one, none. To sleep alone, alone—and no threatening eye looking over me! Ah, how beautiful that will be!

JUDITH   You're not yet glad enough, Julia. You still do not know everything. Rejoice, exult,—he is not coming back even in three years, any more than in an hour. He is dead.

JULIA   How? What? What are you saying?

JUDITH   At the very moment they were about to arrest him, he shot himself.

JULIA   That is not my fault.

JUDITH   You knew he would be arrested today.

JULIA   I knew nothing. I only had foresight. I could even see that he would shoot himself when it reached this point. But I am innocent. I warned him, a hundred times I warned him.

For the longest time. You know it!—Where is he?—I don't want him brought here. I don't want to sleep in the same house with a corpse.

JUDITH Have no fear, Judith, it will be taken care of—like everything else. Good-bye.

JULIA What do you want?—You want to leave?—What's the idea! Surely you'll not leave me alone now? Judith! We have a thousand things to talk over. And you mustn't go to England. You have to stay, Judith.—Judith! You're my sister. We belong together. And you need me too, after all!—And I won't abandon you. Just look *pointing to her pearl necklace* this belongs to me. Surely they can't take this away from me. And all this, too. *Pointing to the furniture and pictures* It's all in my name. Don't go away, Judith. I don't want to be alone tonight. And I have to talk to you. You're the more clever of us two, Judith. Do you think the police will come here too? Hadn't we *pointing to her pearl necklace* best put this in a safe place?

JUDITH *having listened unmoved* Good-bye!

JULIA Judith!

JUDITH I'll have my trunk picked up tomorrow morning. It's all packed.

JULIA You don't want to come back?—Not even for tonight?

JUDITH Do you really think that I will sleep under the same roof with you for even one more night?

JULIA Where will you go, Judith?

JUDITH There'll be a place for me near him for this one night.

JULIA What? You think I will allow—what presumption! I was his wife!

JUDITH If you dare come near this murdered man—you will be very sorry!
Exit.

JULIA *stands motionless for a while, then* Judith! *Goes to the door, then back again, looks about confusedly, then reaches for her pearl necklace.* He must keep it. Nobody will look for it at his house. *She rings, goes quickly to the door left, and calls in* My hat, my coat!
Exits.

Scene Three

At Seraphine's

In Eligius Fenz's house. A small parlor, furnished somewhat poorly but not without a certain comfortableness. Attached to it is a simple wood veranda from which a couple of steps lead down into the garden. The door stands open. Beyond the garden, houses in roughly Gersthofer cottage style. To the right, the main door, another door to the left. At left rear, a piano, half open, on the lid volumes of notes and notebooks. A music stand nearby. Right front, along the wall, a small desk, above it a small youthful portrait of the late Frau Fenz. To the left rear along the wall, an etagere filled with music. At the front left a small table with some chairs. In the corner, right, a composer's bust on a column. On the table, baked goods, bottles of liqueur, small plates, and so on. A vase with flowers on the piano, another on the etagere. On the walls, numerous small and larger photographs; above the etagere a portrait of Eligius Fenz in the role of Don Juan. In different places, red garland ribbons with gold lettering as well as two or three laurel garlands.

Late afternoon. Summery mood. The PRINCESS *comes out of the little garden, gradually crosses the veranda, and enters the room, escorted by* ELIGIUS FENZ, *followed by* ELISABETH, *still in her wedding dress (without bouquet, etc.),* LEINDORF *(in uniform),* SERAPHINE *and Elisabeth's two friends,* ALBINE *and* IDA. *Finally, the old singer* MEYERHOFER *and the retired opera singer* DEVONA. *They are both over eighty and old-fashioned, but very fastidiously dressed.*

ELIGIUS FENZ Once again, Your Highness, my very humblest thanks. This beautiful day has been properly consecrated only by Your Highness's gracious visit.

PRINCESS But what are you talking about, my dear Herr Fenz, it was an absolute necessity for me—my old, honored friend—*to Elisabeth* Well, my dear young woman, once more my warmest best wishes. And to you too, Herr Lieutenant,—and to you, Fräulein Seraphine, all the best on your tour. Well, and what will poor Papa do with himself now, all alone at home?

SERAPHINE Papa is traveling with me, Highness.

ELIGIUS FENZ Yes, Your Highness, I want to see the world again. Maybe an opportunity will present itself as well, to establish new contacts, to revive old ones. . . . One isn't tied down to this city, after all. These, again, are the advantages of my honorary membership in the opera.

PRINCESS There was truly no one who came after you, my dear Herr Fenz.

ELIGIUS FENZ You are too gracious, Highness.

They are at the door on the right.

PRINCESS But please,—don't let me disturb you—

ELIGIUS FENZ I hope Your Highness will allow me to accompany you to your car.

PRINCESS *greets the remaining people affably, exits right with Eligius Fenz.*

ALBINE *to Elisabeth* She really is a charming woman, the Princess.

IDA Without a trace of arrogance.

ALBINE And how young she still looks.

SERAPHINE *invites Meyerhofer and Mme. Devona to the table on the left* Please, dear lady. Please, Herr Meyerhofer. Won't you sit down and help yourself?

MEYERHOFER *and* MME. DEVONA *sit down at the table.*

SERAPHINE *pours some liqueur for them and places the baked goods before them.*

MEYERHOFER *serves Mme. Devona and pours some liqueur into a small glass for Seraphine.*

SERAPHINE *stops at the table with the two old people, clinks glasses with them, but takes only a sip. In the meantime*

ALBINE *to Elisabeth, while indicating Mme. Devona* Say, did she really sing Donna Anna once?

ELISABETH Yes. And old Meyerhofer Don Juan—even before father.

ALBINE You know what those two look like? Like Philemon and Baucis.

LEINDORF *Having stepped out on the veranda for a while, now approaches the group of Seraphine, Mme. Devona, and*

Meyerhofer.

ELISABETH They were even married to each other once. Only for one year! That was a long time ago. Papa says one had best not remind them of it.

SERAPHINE *without walking over, obviously at Leindorf's suggestion* Elisabeth, it's time for you to change.

ELISABETH *to Albine and Ida* Oh, yes, children, now it's getting serious.

ALBINE Are you really leaving today?

LEINDORF *goes to the rear onto the veranda, lights a cigarette.*

ELISABETH Of course, tomorrow morning we'll be in Venice.

IDA Felix and I, we've agreed not to leave until the following morning.

ELISABETH I would find that downright indecent.

IDA In a sleeping-car it's even more indecent; and uncomfortable besides.

ELISABETH You have a dirty mind.

SERAPHINE *comes up to them, more urgently* You must change, Elisabeth.

ELISABETH Well, farewell. Good-bye, Albine, good-bye, Ida! *She embraces both of them.* And just be sure you write me in Klagenfurt, diligently. I don't imagine there'll be much more entertainment there besides getting letters.
She exits left.

ALBINE We really have to be leaving now too, Seraphine.

ELIGIUS FENZ *comes from the right* Well, what do you say? A splendid woman, the Princess, don't you agree? In these circles, only in these, is there still a love of art. What, you want to go already? Well, children, we will not see each other for a long time.

SERAPHINE *goes over to Meyerhofer and Mme. Devona.*

ELIGIUS FENZ Both of you be sure to practice diligently during vacation, every day. In the morning, right after you get up, a half hour of scales. *Indicating Mme. Devona and Meyerhofer* Look at them, both of them, monuments of our old Opera. Mme. Devona there—la divina Devona—Her husband died during the night, in the morning, at seven o'clock, she was practicing her scales again.

IDA But wasn't Herr Meyerhofer her husband?

ELIGIUS FENZ Among others. She had another six or seven. How much she has lived through! I suppose one can say she was a slut, a divine slut! But from seven to seven-thirty in the morning, even after she had become world famous, she practiced her scales. So, take that for an example, you little rascals! Go kiss her hand, let her give you her blessing.

ALBINE *goes to Mme. Devona, says good-bye to her.*

ELIGIUS FENZ *to Ida* I hope you will bring me the finished Micaela.

IDA *also goes over to Mme. Devona.*

MEYERHOFER *and* MME. DEVONA *stand up.*

ELIGIUS FENZ *goes over to them* Oh, you must stay awhile longer, my dear friends! Do me the favor! I only want to escort the young ladies out.
    Exits right with Albine and Ida.

MEYERHOFER *and* MME. DEVONA *sit down again.*

LEINDORF *to Seraphine, front* Are you very angry, Seraphine, that I'm taking her away from you?

SERAPHINE Just make her happy, Herr. . . oh, but we're on a first-name basis now. Just make her happy, Karl.

LEINDORF It shall be my most sacred endeavor, Seraphine.

SERAPHINE What else have the two of you to do in this world besides making each other happy? So it can't be all that difficult in the end.

ELIGIUS FENZ *and* AMBROS *enter from the right.*

ELIGIUS FENZ Here I am, with another belated well-wisher.

AMBROS So where is the new bride?

ELIGIUS FENZ You'll not get to see her in her wedding dress anymore. She's just getting ready for her departure.

SERAPHINE We didn't expect you at all anymore, Ambros!—

AMBROS And I'm not the last one yet. There's someone else still coming.

SERAPHINE Anyone who keeps us waiting this long, he might just as well stay away altogether,—even if it should be Herr von Reisenberg.

LEINDORF *after briefly greeting Ambros, goes over to Meyerhofer and Mme. Devona.*

ELIGIUS FENZ   Right, Max! So what's keeping him? Do you know, Ambros, I have taken a great liking to that young man. An eminently musical nature. Seraphine is very much indebted to him.

SERAPHINE   Elisabeth had her head full of other things. I was absolutely dependent on him. And now he hasn't shown himself in three days.

ELIGIUS FENZ   And the day after tomorrow we have our first concert, in Marienbad.

AMBROS   Are you performing too, Herr Fenz?

ELIGIUS FENZ   No, but I'm traveling along. I had no other choice, in fact. The house is being closed up tomorrow morning.

AMBROS   Oh?

SERAPHINE   It's—sold.

AMBROS   Oh.

ELIGIUS FENZ   Yes—with all the furniture—Other people will be living here in a few days. A retired chief auditor and his family.

AMBROS   This dear little house, what a pity.

ELIGIUS FENZ   Why a pity? Elisabeth is married, she'll be moving from garrison to garrison as a soldier's wife—and Seraphine and I, we will travel. What do people like us need a home for? One only rusts. Oh, I'm delighted. Isn't that right, Seraphine, we are delighted beyond measure? Life will become glorious. *He takes a list out of his pocket* Every day somewhere else, practically. Thirty-five concerts!

AMBROS   Aren't you demanding too much of yourself, Seraphine?

SERAPHINE   One has to earn money, Ambros.

AMBROS *smiling*   Otherwise you would not play the violin at all.

SERAPHINE   Perhaps not for others.

AMBROS   Don't say that. The others are part of it. Even those who don't understand anything. It is with their response that art first begins.

ELIGIUS FENZ   That is very true. No audience, no art. You'll learn that in time, child. How did you put it, Ambros? Response. Yes, and it continues resounding in later years, in all sorts of forms. Do you know, Ambros Doehl, that even the Princess *in response to his glance*—there is only one Princess—was here personally to offer her congratulations? It may also be of some significance that my esteemed colleagues were conspicuous by their absence, apart from my beloved old friends, my dear Meyerhofer and my dear Devona.

He nods to them.

MEYERHOFER *lifts his liqueur glass in order to drink to him.*

ELIGIUS FENZ *goes over to them* Oh yes, enjoy it, my good old—your health! *He pours a small glass for himself too.*

MEYERHOFER *and* MME. DEVONA *stand up again, taking their leave.*

ELIGIUS FENZ *remains standing next to them.*

LEINDORF *is smoking on the veranda, sometimes disappearing into the garden.*

AMBROS *looks through the list in the meantime, speaks to himself* Langenschwalbach, Kissingen, Scheveningen.—What? you're getting to Holland too?

SERAPHINE And Denmark.

AMBROS Right. Copenhagen, Skodsborg—what, Gilleleije too?

SERAPHINE You know the place?

AMBROS Why, that's my secret enchanted beach. But I see it's all over with the secret now. That damned Director! I'll bet there'll be a casino there next year.

SERAPHINE It would be nice if you were still there.

AMBROS First of August? Well, let's hope I won't be called back prematurely. In any case, I will have the prettiest rooms reserved for you, with an ocean view.

In the meantime, Eligius Fenz has arrived at the door to the right with Mme. Devona and Meyerhofer.

ELIGIUS FENZ I am really sorry that you're leaving already.—

SERAPHINE *quickly goes over to them, also says good-bye to them. All four exit right, as Elisabeth enters wearing a traveling dress.*

ELISABETH Oh, Ambros! *Extends her hand to him.*

AMBROS *kisses her hand.*

LEINDORF *coming slowly towards the front, until he reaches them at the end of the following speech.*

ELISABETH *to Ambros* It's really nice to see you once more before I leave. And I thank you very much for the delicious marrons glacés. Imagine your remembering that I love them! And now I'm married to this dear young man. What do you say to that, Ambros?

SERAPHINE *has come in again.*

ELISABETH And that it would turn out to be a lieutenant, yet! He will soon be a first lieutenant, by the way, right, Karl?

LEINDORF Let's hope.

ELIGIUS FENZ *comes in again, goes right up to Leindorf.*

SERAPHINE *standing near them, purposely moves a little to the side, so that Ambros and Elisabeth stand alone.*

AMBROS Well, good luck, Elisabeth. Please don't forget me entirely.

ELISABETH I certainly will not.—Now there won't be any more poems, most likely.

AMBROS Who knows? None from me, of course.

ELISABETH I still have them all.

AMBROS *bows his head slightly.*

ELISABETH Do you know what I think sometimes, Ambros?

AMBROS *glances at her questioningly.*

ELISABETH That maybe we really were very foolish.

LEINDORF *in a softly warning tone* Elisabeth!

ELISABETH Yes, Karl.

LEINDORF *to Seraphine* Has the handbag been taken out to the car already?

SERAPHINE Everything is in order.

MAX *enters from the right with a large bunch of roses* I'm a little bit late. May I hope for forgiveness? *To Elisabeth* Will these modest flowers even be accepted, still?

ELISABETH *takes the flowers* How splendid!

MAX *greets the others.*

ELIGIUS FENZ You must have plundered a park, Herr von Reisenberg?

SERAPHINE That's his habit.

MAX *kisses her hand.*

LEINDORF You really can not take them all along.

ELISABETH Thank you very much, Max. You see, I'm putting this rose here in my belt, and this one—here. *Pins the rose on her breast* The rest, I'm afraid, will have to remain here.

SERAPHINE *takes the remaining flowers and distributes them among the vases in the room.*

ELISABETH   And now I must say farewell to you all. Good-bye, Ambros, good-bye, Herr von Reis—no, no,—Max. *Takes a look around the room* Isn't it strange that now I'm actually—

ELIGIUS FENZ   My child, my darling child! *He wants to embrace her.*

ELISABETH   Hush, father, we agreed, there'll be no crying. And you will not escort us outside either.

SERAPHINE   That, I'm afraid, you will have to put up with. *Elisabeth and Leindorf, escorted by Eligius Fenz and Seraphine, exit right.*

AMBROS, MAX

AMBROS   What a spendthrift you are, Max. Why, these flowers must have eaten up half your fortune.

MAX   Perhaps all of it. I don't know exactly. I have a yearly account with the flower seller.—Oh, what do you say, Ambros, isn't it beautiful here? This odd, somewhat taste-less parlor with its souvenirs of a bygone youth—moving, almost.

AMBROS   You, sentimental?

MAX   Certainly not. But is it not true,—one need only set foot in this room,—and he's embraced by an aroma that comes not only from the garden out there, a peacefulness—

AMBROS *sighs softly* Yes.—In any event, the atmosphere is more peaceful here than—back there, where we just came from.

MAX   Isn't it? And yet—*stares ahead an instant, then suddenly, in a cordial tone* Oh, Ambros, why do we see each other so seldom? I would so much like to chat with you again, as—

AMBROS   Let's simply say, as once. But you're so often busy of late, Max—

MAX   I think you have an entirely false picture of my life, Ambros. I assure you, I am one of the loneliest of men. No, don't laugh. Why don't we have dinner together very soon?

AMBROS   Today, dear Max, would be our last opportunity, since I'm leaving tomorrow morning.

MAX   You too? I don't believe how people are abandoning me. All right, this evening.

AMBROS   Don't take any obligation upon yourself, Max, that you may not be able to fulfill.

MAX *seriously*   I am free of all obligations, Ambros.

AMBROS   Oh.

MAX *almost as if speaking to himself*   That, what you mean, Ambros—that's over.

AMBROS   So quickly?

MAX   And—I want to tell you right away, Ambros, I'm a little concerned about Aurelie. I don't quite know what will become of her—because I barely know anything about her past. You know her better than I do. Yes, I feel it. And you are certainly the only human being with whom she has a spiritual, a friendly relationship. I noticed that in the way she spoke to me about you. Yes, about you she spoke, also of Prince Arduin; about Baron Falkenir never a word. You're the only one, Ambros, in spite of Falkenir, who could have any influence on her.

AMBROS *shaking his head*   It's too soon.

MAX   It could become too late.

AMBROS   She must follow her own path.

MAX   What do you know of the path she must follow?

AMBROS   Her fate is mirrored in my soul like the picture of a star in a dark pond. It follows its prescribed course; no mortal can meddle with it.

SERAPHINE *and* ELIGIUS FENZ *enter.*

ELIGIUS FENZ   Well, now they're gone. . . . Oh, children!. . . How empty the house has suddenly become. . . !

SERAPHINE *has gone out to the veranda in order to conceal how moved she is.*

ELIGIUS FENZ *goes out to her, softly strokes her hair. Pause.*

AMBROS *after exchanging a glance with Max*   I have to leave now, unfortunately. *Towards the veranda*   My revered Herr

Fenz,—dear Seraphine—well, we'll see each other again in a few weeks, I hope.

MAX I don't want to trouble you any longer either.

SERAPHINE Oh, Max, stay a while longer. The evening would be all too melancholy otherwise. Isn't that right, father? And besides, it would be a real consolation for me to go through my program with you one last time.

MAX I'd love to.

SERAPHINE *in a very lively tone* And let's begin right away, all right? Do stay here too, Ambros. And you, father, you sit down in the corner there, as usual, or on the veranda—and pay close attention—both of you.

ELIGIUS FENZ Yes, children, go on and play, play! I'll be glad to listen to you. But *somewhat embarrassed, laughs* but it'll be possible for me in spirit only, unfortunately. The fact is, I still have a pressing engagement, a very small farewell party with a few friends, much as I would have liked to, I couldn't refuse.

SERAPHINE You really want to go, father?

ELIGIUS FENZ Oh, I won't stay out very late.

SERAPHINE But we need an audience. *Pleading* Ambros!

AMBROS Don't be angry with me, Seraphine, my train leaves at seven tomorrow morning and I haven't even packed yet. Much as I would like—

ELIGIUS FENZ *having gone into the next room earlier, now comes back with his overcoat on his arm and his hat* You see, my child, I'm even taking my overcoat along, just in case it gets a little late.

MAX But Ambros, we did want. . . this evening—

AMBROS *resolutely* Much as I regret it, it won't be possible. I hardly know how I'll manage to take care of everything—

ELIGIUS FENZ We may as well go out together, Ambros.

AMBROS *to Max* Well, good-bye, I hope I'll see you in the fall. Have a good time, and drop me a line from time to time. Good-bye, Seraphine.

ELIGIUS FENZ *kisses Seraphine on the forehead, waves a friendly farewell to Max. Exits with Ambros Doehl.*

SERAPHINE, MAX

Pause. Twilight gradually increases.

SERAPHINE Isn't it strange?—I've known it for a long time beforehand, resigned myself to it—or at least imagined I had—and now that it has really happened—I can barely grasp it.

MAX —?

SERAPHINE That Elisabeth—is gone, I mean. Last night we still slept in the same room. Oh, how often we chatted until midnight—and longer; sometimes it got to be three in the morning. But if you were to ask me today what we actually had to talk about so long and so urgently, I couldn't tell you, even if I wanted to.—You know, we were never especially close;—she was more intimate with Albine, with Ida even, than with me. Yes, really. But—she was simply my sister and that means so much.—Do you have any brothers or sisters, Max?

MAX Depending how you take it. I have a married sister in Paris, I haven't seen her in five years, my brother went to America fifteen years ago, the last I heard from him was a year and a half or two years ago from some train station; a hasty greeting, I know neither where he was traveling nor whence he had come.

SERAPHINE *in front of the portrait of Frau Fenz* Don't you find that Elisabeth looks a lot like our mother? *Without waiting for a reply* Imagine what happened to me today. We were young girls when our mother died, you know—nine or ten. And today, during the ceremony, the thought suddenly struck me: I have to write mother how beautiful Elisabeth looked in her wedding gown. Isn't that remarkable? She's been dead ten years or more and—in some part of me I still don't know it—or at least don't want to believe it. *Looking towards the veranda* Actually, to tell you the truth, I would like to sit beneath the ash there, in the garden, and cry my eyes out. But that would be quite useless—and absurd besides;—and so the smartest thing, after all, will be for us to play together, aside from the fact that I really need the practice. My singing coach hasn't had time for me the last few days, unfortunately, and alone it gives me no real pleasure.

MAX *has been listening to her words with emotion and growing sympathy* Dear Seraphine. . . .

SERAPHINE Hush, you know very well that you have nothing to apologize for. Nor do I have any right to expect you. It's just that I had become so accustomed to your appearing every afternoon at four-thirty. It was also quite nice. Of course, you got up from the piano without fail at six-thirty—but that's none of my business. And actually, I'm reproaching myself that today I—you must surely have better ways of spending this fragrant summer evening. It's just that you have a good heart, that's why you're staying. You don't want me to sit under the ash and weep. The fact is, I would certainly not have cried, nor would I do so if you left now.

MAX Dearest Seraphine, would I conceal it from you if I would rather be somewhere else?—What shall we play? Program one, two, or three?

SERAPHINE I don't want to keep you any longer than absolutely necessary. You may disappear whenever you like. Even in the middle of a movement.

MAX I will certainly not disappear. I wouldn't know where to disappear to.

SERAPHINE Over?

MAX Yes.

SERAPHINE Oh—really. . . . So the moment may now be at hand—for you to cry your heart out on my bosom.

MAX I am absolutely not in the mood to cry.—I'm glad to be here, near you, Seraphine. And now let's play.

SERAPHINE Yes, I suppose that would be best. *She takes the violin from its case* So, what shall we play?

MAX That's for you to decide, Seraphine.
He is at the etagere, occupied with the sheet music.

SERAPHINE Well, then, Haydn E-Major, Mozart A-Major, and Beethoven's Spring Sonata.

MAX In a word, program one.
Selects the sheet music.

SERAPHINE *putting resin on her bow, in an incidental tone* And you've come from her just now—from Aurelie?

MAX No, not quite directly.—I would really find program two to be more important. The scherzo in Brahms left something to be desired the other day.

SERAPHINE We still have time for program two as well.

MAX Yes, then your father will still get to hear something too.

SERAPHINE Oh, by the time he gets back we can go through the entire violin literature. *She tunes* So, if you haven't come from Aurelie, then you've come—from another—from the other one?

MAX Yes, Seraphine, I came from Judith's.

SERAPHINE *after a slight start* You could have told me that right away too, my friend. If you're not open with me, then what's the sense of our entire friendship?

MAX Do you know she has an engagement in Dresden next fall?

SERAPHINE Of course I know. It's somewhat bold of her to risk going on stage next year already. Father is not all that delighted with her. He doesn't find her voice to be first rate by any means. Besides, it's a long time until fall.

MAX She's going to London tomorrow, to Jean de Reszke. Oh, yes, just think, this one too is running away from me.

SERAPHINE You don't say. You cannot possibly imagine how much that grieves me. But you're—an independent young man, you could follow her to England if you wanted to. You've probably made a date with her already.

MAX Oh, what you don't imagine, Seraphine. You have a completely false conception of my relationship to Judith. And of her as well, probably. She's a fairly enigmatic being.

SERAPHINE I would say that's more your fault, Max, that women strike you as so enigmatic.

MAX All women? Oh, no. You, for example, Seraphine, are not in the least enigmatic. With you everything is so clear, so deliciously clear.

SERAPHINE That's another thing you're just imagining.

MAX Oh, no. You're a wonderful person. Near you, Seraphine—

SERAPHINE You mustn't court me. That's not our style, Max. It's almost a little ridiculous.

MAX Don't speak to me like that, Seraphine. Today, don't be—don't ever be hard with me, Seraphine.

SERAPHINE Certainly—since you've already been abandoned

twice today—

MAX Oh, what does that matter? I've almost forgotten that already. The worst thing of all is that you are leaving me, Seraphine. That is altogether inconceivable. That's so horrible—
Having taken her hand, he now kisses it.

SERAPHINE *moved, looks down at him sitting at the piano, then she hastily takes her hand back, and says* We'll begin with the Haydn E-Major.

MAX Yes, we'll begin with the Haydn E-Major. *He opens the volume of music* Tell me, who is actually going to accompany you in your various concerts?

SERAPHINE A different person in each place, naturally. That simply can't be helped.

MAX It would be the most sensible thing, actually, Seraphine, if you engaged me as your accompanist.

SERAPHINE *factually* I doubt very much whether you'll do for public concerts.

MAX Haven't I made progress recently? Well, then. Do think it over for a while. I ask for no payment at all. We'll travel together and play our way through the entire world—

SERAPHINE Yes,—through the entire world. That would be something.—And in every place—a different one!

MAX *again taking her hand and pulling her towards him* No, Seraphine, in every place the same one.

SERAPHINE *very acidly* What's gotten into you? *She moves away from him. Pause* And what's more, be glad you don't need to, I mean, that you don't have to live from your little bit of talent, like—other people.

MAX Oh, God, one never knows. The times are so uncertain. . . .

SERAPHINE Well, when things reach that point, we'll talk about it.

MAX Perhaps they'll reach that point soon.

SERAPHINE What are you talking about?

MAX One has forebodings.

SERAPHINE You—and everyday worries! I have a difficult time picturing that.

MAX Will you write me, Seraphine? Will I always hear from

you?

SERAPHINE I can't promise you that. Nor do I want to.

MAX I shan't even hear from you?

SERAPHINE Let's not make any plans, Max. Everything will come in due course, as it must. For you and for me. Won't you turn on some lights, Max? *The room has grown dark; there is still twilight in the garden.*

MAX *turns on the lamp on the piano, a beam of which falls towards the veranda. He begins to play the piano, then stops suddenly* Won't you play by yourself first, Seraphine?

SERAPHINE By myself? Why by myself?

MAX As on that unforgettable evening I first met you.

SERAPHINE —And not only me.

MAX On which I presented a lilac branch to you.

SERAPHINE One of three.

MAX The one which smelled the sweetest and which is still blooming today.

SERAPHINE Are you quite sure of that?

MAX Oh, yes, that I know. . . .

SERAPHINE *stands in the doorway leading to the veranda and begins to play.*

MAX Beautiful. But somewhat melancholy.

SERAPHINE You think so? But I didn't intend it that way at all.

She begins anew.

MAX That does sound a bit more cheerful.

SERAPHINE Really? It's more cheerful? I didn't want that at all.

She begins over again.

MAX That's very original. A capriccio. How ever do you think of all these things?

SERAPHINE *abruptly stops again* That isn't what I meant either.

MAX Then what?

SERAPHINE *close to him, her violin in one hand, the bow in the other, kisses his hair* This—I believe.

MAX Oh, yes, Seraphine.

SERAPHINE *moves away from him again, stands with her back turned to him.*

MAX *stands up, softly grasps her arms* Seraphine!

SERAPHINE *slowly turns around.*

MAX We've known for a long time, you know.

SERAPHINE *somewhat acidly* What do we know? Nothing at all. Nothing, nothing, my dear, other than this is a beautiful evening,—which will never come again.

MAX *takes her head between both his hands, kisses her on the forehead.*

SERAPHINE *raises her head, both their lips find each other.*

Curtain

ACT THREE

Parklike grounds on the Danish coast. The sea is not visible. The park has a moderately tropical character, indicated by palm trees. The hotel may be thought to be far in the background, to the right. At the front left is a small hotel pavilion, villalike, with a small veranda, from which a few steps lead directly into the park. There are usable paths going past the pavilion in front and turning behind it. Approximately in the center of the stage is a flower arrangement on a lawn; further back but not far to the rear there is a modest rise which hides the view to the sea. Running over this rise is a path with a bench. At the right front small tables with chairs, belonging to the breakfast area of the hotel.

As the curtain goes up, the stage is empty.

Early morning, not yet completely light.

After a few seconds, MAX, *in a gray traveling suit, steps out of the pavilion onto the veranda, without closing the door behind him. He goes forward to the balustrade, looks around the park to all sides. After a while,* JUDITH *also comes out of the pavilion, wearing a morning dress. She goes up to Max. He turns to her, they look at one another, remain silent, and smile; suddenly she embraces him. Long kiss.*

JUDITH *freeing herself from the embrace* It's getting light already. Go.—They don't all have to know that you didn't sleep *indicating the hotel* over there.

MAX Whose business is it?

JUDITH No one's. But the truth isn't anyone's business either. Farewell, it's time.

MAX Judith. . . !

JUDITH *warding him off* I've kept my word; now you keep yours, *in response to his glance* to disappear as soon as I ask you to.

MAX Haven't you been cruel enough to suit yourself yet? How long did I have to wait in Vienna before your telegram called me to Sweden—to a spot whose name I'd never heard and which I've already forgotten again. I travel for a day and a night and another day, your beloved arms embrace me;—and the next morning you already wanted to run away from me?

JUDITH Yes, I wanted that! And it was against our agreement for you suddenly to be standing next to me on the deck as the ship departed. And in any case you should have felt obligated to continue on your way—to Copenhagen or wherever.

MAX I would have done so, Judith, absolutely—*smiling* had you let go of my hand when you got off.

JUDITH It was weakness on my part. Don't make me regret it. But now you have to be off at the first opportunity, train or boat.

MAX *shrugging his shoulders* Where to?

JUDITH Wherever you like.—It doesn't concern me.

MAX And you're staying here?

JUDITH Here or elsewhere.—It doesn't concern you—and must not concern you.

MAX An intolerable, deadly thought.

JUDITH No, Max, a delicious, heavenly thought. Oh, if only you felt it as I do. Weren't we happy? And won't this happiness always remain just as beautiful in our memories—as happiness without compulsion, without torment, without regret?—It will not wither or fade—become disgusting like any number of other things that may still lie ahead of us. Go, Max, go quickly—so that we may be eternally grateful to one another.

MAX How you talk, Judith!—It was a tender, innocent girl whom I took in my arms—and now you speak like a widely experienced woman.—Not like a woman after her wedding night;—no, like a woman who has long since known all the ugliness and all the misery of love.

JUDITH I'm an experienced woman, Max. I didn't need the night in your arms for that. I became experienced in the course of another night when, in a sad, bare vaulted room I kept a vigil over a bier—over the bier of a beloved man who had had no inkling of my love or didn't want to have any; in the dim light of two tall, flickering candles, in the silence and loneliness of a death chamber, I became experienced, like other girls on their first night of love. In that one night I lived through everything that can ever happen to me. All the wonder, all the horror of existence,—I believe—I already experienced my own death that night! And every-thing that is still to come will only be like the dream of an existence that's actually already behind me. You too were only a dream, Max. It's lasted too long already. Why are you still standing there? We've said good-bye to each other. Farewell. I want to go back to sleep.

MAX To encounter a new dream—a new day! A day—a life without me? I can't bear it.

JUDITH You'll bear it.

MAX *quickly* Perhaps I could bear it if you didn't want to slip away from me into such an impenetrable secret! If I knew what you're hoping—longing for—expecting—from your immediate future and beyond—or from this very day, perhaps—I want to know for what—for whom you're leaving me, me, in whose arms you were still obliviously happy a half hour ago. I will keep my word, yes, Judith, I will disappear, since you're asking me to;—but I want to know—

JUDITH You want—? Really—! Oh, the way you're already trying to put on airs as my master, because—I gave myself to you for two nights! Oh, how well I know you! How well I know you all!—*in a milder tone* Max. . . Max! Must it turn into a disappointment, even at the very last moment? Do you want to spoil an unblemished moment of happiness for us?—No questions—No concern!—We must be free—you and I. Over! Over! Over!—And everything—everything is possible again; everything—isn't that wonderful, Max? Possibly you'll sleep with a princess tonight, or with a water sprite—and I with a fisher lad or a prince—or alone—; but one thing is certain: not with you. Never, never again with you, Max. Because you, Max, you I almost loved.
Quickly goes into the pavilion and locks the door.

MAX *automatically follows her up to the door, remains on the veranda awhile, then goes slowly down the steps into the park. He looks all around; then he goes up on the rise, looks at the sea, comes down again towards the left, towards the pavilion, then back to the right. A SMALL BLACK MAN is setting the tables for breakfast, bows to Max by way of salutation.*

Max sits at one of the tables. The small black man looks at him inquiringly.

MAX   What? Oh, yes, you may bring me breakfast. *The small black man exits. Max remains seated, facing the villa.*

HANSEN *the hotel manager enters from the right, wearing a white suit. He is tall and slim, with a somewhat artistic carriage, and relatively long, blond hair with gray streaks. He casts a glance at the pavilion, then turns to Max* Good morning, Sir.

MAX *distant* Good morning.

HANSEN *introducing himself,* Hansen, the manager.

MAX *introduces himself* Reisenberg.

HANSEN   Oh, please, I know. Herr Max von Reisenberg from Vienna. You see, I'm the manager of this hotel.

MAX   My pleasure.

HANSEN   It's not obvious at first glance. For what would the gentleman have taken me, I wonder?

MAX *makes a polite gesture.*

HANSEN   People generally take me to be an artist. Not entirely without justice, if I may say so. I was an actor once. A fairly long time ago, now. Careers take strange turns, Herr von Reisenberg.

MAX   Without a doubt. Won't you sit down?

HANSEN *warding him off modestly, remains standing* A lovely morning.

MAX   Yes, wonderful.

HANSEN   May I call your attention to the unusual bird calls?

MAX   I've already noticed them.

HANSEN   Aren't they unusual, though? The fact is we even have exotic birds here that aren't found anywhere else in our country. It has to do with the climate—*the small black man brings breakfast for Max*—especially in the morning—the gentleman is an early riser?

MAX *pouring himself some tea* Not always. But since I intend to depart on the first ship—

HANSEN   Oh, that is most regrettable.

MAX   When does the first ship leave, Herr Manager?

HANSEN   At eight-thirty. I really am very sorry. The gentleman has had no opportunity to take a closer look at our beach yet.

MAX *buttering a piece of bread* You have some splendid, practically tropic vegetation here.

HANSEN And delicious aromatic air as well, like in the high mountains. *He takes a deep breath, as if in demonstration of his assertion.*

MAX *also takes a deep breath* Most refreshing.

HANSEN Perhaps it would be possible that the gentleman's stay—

MAX —Impossible, unfortunately. It would take an absolute miracle.

HANSEN Oh, if that's all there is to it—they frequently happen here.

MAX *looks all around* I can easily believe it.—Do you have an international clientele here?

HANSEN Pretty much. This year in particular the season began brilliantly. Of course, in the past few days—the alarming rumors—

MAX You mean the war rumors?

HANSEN And now things give every appearance of becoming serious.

MAX *absent-mindedly* I don't believe them.

HANSEN *gesturing towards the pavilion* This small chalet, for example, was already rented to a French couple. Yesterday they wired their cancellation. It would be available now.

MAX Unfortunately I can not take advantage of it.

HANSEN Pity. Perhaps the lady who happened to arrive with you on the same ship from Sweden would like to have it—?

MAX *coolly* I am not kept informed about the lady's plans.

GILDA *has appeared on the rise, looks out towards the sea.*

MAX *has noticed her* That little one up there looks somewhat exotic too.

HANSEN That's my daughter, Herr von Reisenberg. *Calls up* Good morning, Gilda.

GILDA Good morning, father.

HANSEN Won't you come down, Gilda?

GILDA Later, father. My hair's still wet. *She disappears again.*

HANSEN Her hair is wet because—she comes from the sea.

MAX Truly, your daughter looks like a water sprite.

HANSEN *earnestly* She may very well be something of the sort. Down there, on the beach, is her realm, if not in the depths themselves. Because it happens that she disappears without a trace for hours, for half a day at a time.

MAX And you're not afraid that she may be abducted sometime, by a triton or some other sea god?

HANSEN You're smiling, sir! If you had been through what I've been through, you wouldn't smile. *He has taken a seat at the table with Max after all.* Her mother too was such a creature, such a creature—of the flood. And she too disappeared occasionally for long periods, for days, for weeks—until one day she did not return at all. It's been seven years now, Herr von Reisenberg.—I can still see her, how she ran from this rise down to the shore, waved to me—with the exact same movement with which Gilda just waved to us—and that was—her good-bye forever. *Max looks at him.* Oh, if that had been the case, what you're thinking, Herr von Reisenberg,—we would've had to find her mortal remains. The ones who are of earthly origin, they're washed ashore by the waves.

GILDA *back up on the rise* Do look, father.

HANSEN What's the matter, Gilda?

GILDA A marvelous white ship is coming this way.

HANSEN Well, what else? Where's it coming from?

GILDA From the south, father.

HANSEN That'll be the "Öresund," I should think.

GILDA As if I didn't know the "Öresund." It is not the "Öresund" nor the "Neptune," and it is not the "Princess Dagmar" either. It's a ship that's never sailed past here before and looks splendid beyond all measure.

HANSEN You'll excuse me, sir. *Goes up the rise. Max looks at the pavilion again. The manager has reached Gilda.* A private yacht!—Oh, that can only be the ship that was launched in Copenhagen yesterday. It belongs to an Austrian prince. *Max becomes attentive* It's heading north.

GILDA No, father, it is heading for us. *Max stands up.* How it gleams!

HANSEN That's from the golden letters on the bow.

MAX *on the rise too* What do the letters say?

HANSEN *with his hand shading his eyes* The glitter of the gold is too blinding.

MAX I suppose it will dock here.

HANSEN No, that's impossible. Only our coastal steamers have a shallow enough draught. If the Prince wished to do us the honor of his visit, he would have to allow a boat to set him ashore. *He goes down towards the right. Max remains standing next to Gilda.*

GILDA *smiling at him* Good morning, sir.

MAX Good morning, Fräulein.

GILDA Do you like it here with us in Gilleleije, sir?

MAX Especially well, Fräulein.

GILDA Will you be staying with us for a longer time, sir?

MAX Not as long as I should like, Fräulein Gilda.

AMBROS *enters from the right, comes across the manager.*

HANSEN Good morning, Herr Doehl.

AMBROS Good morning, Herr Manager. The mail hasn't come yet?

HANSEN *looks at his watch* That would be quite impossible, Herr Doehl.

AMBROS *absent-mindedly* Anything new otherwise?

HANSEN A mysterious stranger who arrived from Sweden late last night and is staying here in the pavilion. And a countryman of yours, Herr Doehl, also arrived.

AMBROS Ah. *notices Max* Max! I had a feeling!

MAX My dear Ambros—*comes down from the rise.*

GILDA *waves to Ambros but stays on the rise.*

AMBROS *waves back; then, to the manager* Are the rooms ready? Both facing the sea?

HANSEN Of course, Herr Doehl.

AMBROS And the flowers have been taken care of?

HANSEN Yes, indeed. In fact, the arrangements would all be lovely if the sale of tickets didn't leave a lot to be desired.

MAX *has reached them. Ambros heartily shakes his hand. The small black man brings breakfast for Ambros. The manager has in the meantime gone back up the rise to Gilda.*

AMBROS *to Max* I'll sit at your table, if you don't mind. *Waves to the small black man, who places his breakfast on Max's table.*

MAX   What tickets was that ridiculous person talking about?

AMBROS *looks at him somewhat amazed* But Max?! Or are you trying to be discreet, perhaps? That would be—superfluous at the very least under these circumstances.

MAX   I have absolutely no idea what you're talking about, Ambros.

AMBROS *looking him in the eye* You of all people do not know that Seraphine Fenz is giving a concert here tonight?

MAX   Seraphine!—I swear to you Ambros, I had no idea—or rather, that I had completely forgotten.

AMBROS   And I would have sworn that you had been part of Seraphine's entire concert tour.

MAX I haven't seen her since her sister's wedding.—I've come directly from Vienna—

AMBROS   And directly to Gilleleije, just to shake hands with me?

MAX   That is practically true. Because—I'm obliged to go back again on the next ship, that is, even before Seraphine's concert.

AMBROS *almost laughing* Listen, Max. *Glances at the pavilion almost without intending to* Well, I won't ask any more questions. But at least tell me what you've been up to since we said good-bye to one another, since the day of Elisabeth's wedding and the catastrophe at the Westerhauses. How are Julia and Judith?

MAX   Judith is in London, I think,—and Julia is enjoying the freedom of her widowhood.

AMBROS   With District Attorney Braunigl?

MAX   That didn't last long. I don't know who her lover is now. And Braunigl has been suspended, as I'm sure you read. It turned out that no legal grounds existed for Westerhaus's arrest.

AMBROS   I hope they were able to salvage something from the debacle.

MAX   Not a whole lot. It'll be enough for half a year, I imagine.

AMBROS *regretfully* Oh! And what do they intend to do after that?

MAX   They had best give that some thought.

AMBROS Yes, they had best. . . . If circumstances don't save
them the trouble for the time being.

MAX —?

AMBROS I dare say we'll all be compelled to take part in the
same, somewhat difficult undertaking.

MAX You seriously think that we'll have war?

AMBROS I do indeed. Actually, I was already prepared this
morning to—Well, my trunks are packed.

HANSEN *on the rise, with field glasses, to Gilda* "Aurelie!"

MAX, AMBROS *together* What?

HANSEN The name is quite legible now. The name of the ship
is "Aurelie."

AMBROS What ship? *He stands up.*

MAX Prince Arduin's yacht, to all appearances, which was
launched in Copenhagen yesterday.

AMBROS *goes quickly to the top of the rise* And the ship is
standing still?

HANSEN A boat is being lowered. The Prince obviously in-
tends to come ashore here. *Goes down towards the right.*

MAX *standing next to Ambros* What does it signify, that he
calls his ship "Aurelie?"

AMBROS Perhaps an attempt to compel fate.

MAX You mean the Prince still thinks of that, that Aurelie—

AMBROS Why shouldn't he?

MAX After everything that happened?

AMBROS Certainly he thinks of that. His first priority may
be—to shoot you dead, dear Max.

SERAPHINE *and* ELIGIUS FENZ *enter from the right front, the
manager following behind them.*

ELIGIUS FENZ *going ahead, in a very lively tone* Good
morning, Herr Doehl! Ah, Max! This is what I call a
pleasant surprise. Look here, Seraphine,—Max!
*Ambros and Max have come down from the rise in the mean-
time.*

SERAPHINE *is visibly astounded by Max's presence.*

HANSEN Both rooms have a view of the sea.

AMBROS I've had the best ones reserved for you.

SERAPHINE *extends her hand to him* I thank you, Ambros. *To
Max, smiling* Welcome, Max. I'm glad to see you again.

MAX *moved, kisses her hand.*

ELIGIUS FENZ *to Ambros* We want to stop for a long rest here. We've earned it honestly. Six weeks on the road and almost every evening a concert.

AMBROS One could hardly tell the hard work the two of you've done by looking at you.

ELIGIUS FENZ Well, mine has been slight. But Seraphine— *he strokes her hair* she has celebrated some triumphs. Only yesterday in Skodsborg—

The small black man appears, prepared to receive any orders.

Another boy sees to Fenz's and Seraphine's hand luggage.

HANSEN Would the lady and gentlemen please to take breakfast here in the open?

ELIGIUS FENZ Breakfast we already had on the ship. It's charming here, Herr Manager. One could quite think one-self in the tropics. Aren't those palm trees over there,—date palms?

HANSEN An enchanted beach, Herr Fenz. That's common knowledge.

ELIGIUS FENZ Yes, it surely must be. An enchanted beach with sea sprites and the like. It even seems to me as if I'd already seen such a sea sprite.

AMBROS That wouldn't surprise me.

ELIGIUS FENZ A strange little creature like that was knocking about down on the beach. *Digressing* And how is the ticket sale going, Herr Manager?

HANSEN Let's hope it will improve by evening. It's been slow up to now, unfortunately. I'm sure it's because of the unset-tling news. A number of my guests have departed all of a sudden.

ELIGIUS FENZ Why would they do that? What is there to fear from a war on this enchanted shore?

A hotel employee steps up to the manager with a worried look on his face and whispers something to him.

HANSEN You will excuse me, madame, gentlemen. *Exits with the employee.*

Eligius Fenz and Ambros go up on the rise and sit down on the bench, with their backs to the audience.

MAX Seraphine!

SERAPHINE Max—?

MAX It would strike me as dishonest not to tell you, Seraphine. I am not here on your account. *Seraphine remains silent.* To tell you the truth—It hadn't even occurred to me, that your concert would take place here today of all days.

SERAPHINE It would also have been contrary to our agreement if you had come here on my account.

MAX *more securely* I had promised Ambros Doehl back in Vienna to visit him here.

SERAPHINE Really. . . .

MAX You don't believe me, perhaps?

SERAPHINE But of course. *Is about to go* So, I'll see you later.

MAX That's the problem, Seraphine! I might have to leave before your concert—this very morning.

SERAPHINE *harshly* Pity. Well, I'm sure we'll run into each other again. *Is about to go.*

MAX One never knows.

SERAPHINE Oh God,—when we last said good-bye to each other, we had no idea that we'd meet again so soon either.

MAX I had a feeling we would, Seraphine.

SERAPHINE You don't say.

MAX Yes, Seraphine. That morning I knew that no good-bye of ours could be for long, let alone forever. I just let you talk. It really couldn't be over!—Just think about it. Don't you remember anything anymore, Seraphine? I still remember everything. I still feel everything, I still see everything.

SERAPHINE *remains silent.*

MAX Oh, Seraphine,—how you ran through the garden under the stars, in your white dress, with your loose hair falling over your shoulders!—And your small room with the yellow wallpaper, with the mirror in its black frame and with the wobbly dresser—and the portrait of you as a child, with the two long braids—and the call of the blackbirds in the morning—and then how we sat in the parlor at dawn—I held you on my knees—and everything still looked so festive from the wedding.—And a little bit sad too. The half emptied glasses on the white tablecloth and the liqueur bottles—

SERAPHINE And there were still some baked goods too, fortunately, as many as Herr Meyerhofer and Frau Devona left over, that is.

MAX And breakfast out on the veranda—and the unforgettable fragrance from the garden—And what delicious coffee you made! And how we laughed. . . . Were you thinking of any farewell at that moment? I wasn't.

SERAPHINE But as you left we both knew it was one.

MAX No, Seraphine—

Eligius Fenz and Ambros Doehl come back down from the rise.

SERAPHINE *to Eligius Fenz* Isn't it time we looked at our rooms, father? I want to go up in any case to practice a little. So long, Ambros! Good-bye, Max! *Exits quickly.*

ELIGIUS FENZ Look at that child there! Even if the end of the world were scheduled for tonight, she wouldn't let it bother her. Every morning she practices her scales and her touch for two hours. Admirable. Well, let's let her practice. I want to look around the area a bit in the meantime. I always do that when I get to some new spot. One discovers the strangest things that way sometimes. The beach here looks very promising that way. Do come with me, gentlemen.

AMBROS *has received his mail from a servant boy during Fenz's speech, looks through it quickly, opens just one of the letters and reads it.*

ELIGIUS FENZ Oh, you're busy, Herr Doehl. You come with me, Max. Surely you know your way around here quite well already.

MAX I only arrived here late last night.

ELIGIUS FENZ Well, so let us reconnoitre together.

AMBROS Max, your steamship leaves at eight-thirty.

MAX Mine?—That is by no means certain.

ELIGIUS FENZ Good-bye, Ambros. Come, Max.

Grasps him under the arm; both exit.

AMBROS *looks after them, shaking his head, then he busies himself with his mail again, quickly and seriously.*

HANSEN *enters hastily, carrying newspapers* Three more departures! And now, when they say—*pointing to one of the papers*—that a court of arbitration is to convene.

AMBROS That news is out of date. I may well have to leave before the day is out too. It depends on one more telegram that has to be here any minute.

HANSEN And if I may ask—the Countess will in that case also—

ARDUIN *enters hastily from the right. A hotel employee has shown him the way and disappears immediately. Arduin steps up to Ambros, who only now sees him* Good morning, Ambros Doehl.

AMBROS Greetings, Your Highness.

HANSEN *introducing himself, with a deep bow* Manager Hansen—*About to continue.*

ARDUIN *curtly but politely* Pleasure. I require nothing for the time being. *Hansen exits.*

ARDUIN, AMBROS

ARDUIN Well, here we are. I'm glad to still find you here after all. You have postponed your departure then?

AMBROS Unfortunately not for long, Highness. Perhaps for only a few hours. In any event, welcome. Your yacht was deservedly admired from shore already. It glitters splendidly from a distance.

ARDUIN And if only you had an inkling of what glitter it contains within. I hope you will do me the pleasure, Ambros, of having lunch with me on board.

AMBROS *hesitating* I'm afraid there will not be any more time for that. I may have to leave as early as noon. Indeed, who knows whether it will be possible by tonight to get across the border without difficulty.

ARDUIN Ah, have people been driven mad here too? I can vouch for it: there is at present no reason to be overhasty in your departure.

AMBROS My sources of information say otherwise, Your Highness.

ARDUIN Since when do poets have sources of information?

AMBROS Not poets, but journalists.

ARDUIN What? You're a journalist?—You've kept this a secret from me until now.

AMBROS   I have no reason to keep it a secret from you anymore, Your Highness,—since you've joined the diplomatic ranks.

ARDUIN   Oh, so that is known? Even though I only traveled on secret missions?

AMBROS   The whole world is talking about your secret missions!

ARDUIN *smiling* Yes, my diplomatic talents have been discovered at Court. Or, more precisely, they remembered my family connections with most of the ruling and deposed royal houses of Europe, and so I've gotten around quite a bit in the past three months. I assume you've spent your time in a more amusing and useful way and have given the world some new immortal tercets.

AMBROS   They were sonnets this time, Highness.

ARDUIN   You must read them to me soon.

AMBROS   And when does Your Highness command me to appear? After lunch, perhaps? For dessert?

ARDUIN   Best of all at night, under a blue starry sky. In fact, you should come with us.

AMBROS   —?

ARDUIN   The fact is I have a rendezvous with a lady, which is the reason I stopped off here,—in spite of your having refused me in so unmistakable a manner.

AMBROS   You made a rendezvous for here in Gilleleije? Here of all places?

ARDUIN   Yes, in your honor. It's a rather romantic affair. That is to say, I don't for the time being know who the lady is. I have only spoken to her once, and she was wearing a mask then. It was on the same night—I'm sure you still remember, Ambros,—that we took part in a fairy tale.

AMBROS   So, Highness, then you had your adventure after all?

ARDUIN   It's only about to turn into one now.

AMBROS   And are you also quite certain that the mysterious lady will keep the rendezvous?

ARDUIN   Things which are of little importance to a person always prosper.

AMBROS   Then I imagine she would have to be here in

Gilleleije by now.

ARDUIN We may assume she is. And perhaps you've seen her
already.

AMBROS Among the female beings who are staying here at
this beach, I'd hardly know one whom I could picture—
Unless a young lady who is said to have arrived from
Sweden late last night and is sleeping *indicating the pavilion*
behind those shuttered windows—

ARDUIN She may very well be the one. That's how I picture
her, more or less.—To have a quiet night's sleep before
setting out on a journey into the unknown—that would be
just like her—insofar as I can judge. I mean, our entire
acquaintance was of a quarter hour's duration. Our conversation began with my proposing to her that she spend the
night with me in my palace, which still belonged to me till
morning, which she declined to do; and it ended with my
inviting her to accompany me on my journey, which she accepted. Since then I have neither heard from nor seen her.
Shouldn't one knock?

AMBROS But we can't be totally sure, that just this woman—

ARDUIN Well, then it'll just be a different one. But I'm
convinced it's her. Of course, we can also wait until she
wakes up, and chat until then.—It is beautiful here. And the
fragrance—of the kind I know only from southern coasts.

AMBROS And you are seriously considering setting out on a
journey now, Your Highness?

ARDUIN Yes. And I will repeat my question again, quite in
earnest this time, would you like to accompany me? Duration—and destination unknown. Surely that must tempt the
journalist in you, if not the poet!

AMBROS Unfortunately, Your Highness, I must decline on
account of another, more pressing matter. And, if I may be
permitted to make an observation—*Arduin makes a gesture
indicating, please, speak your mind*—I'm afraid, not without
valid reasons, that it will not be all that easy to complete
any pleasure cruises on an enchanted yacht in the near
future,—least of all for a major general in the Austro-
Hungarian army.

ARDUIN I am that, it's true. But I also carry the title of Major

in a French cavalry regiment. And my mother lives in the
castle of Rodegna, thirty miles from Florence; Italian,
English, probably some Slavic blood too flows in my
veins—

AMBROS Now you'll be faced with the necessity of deciding
on one direction or another.

ARDUIN But why? Since the Grand Duchy of Perosa no longer
exists, I can no longer afford the luxury of a patriotism
limited to one specific country. Never has this become
clearer to me than in the course of the past few months. I'd
have to found a principality by myself somewhere, I suppose, in order to know with any certainty where I belonged,
even if it were only on a deserted island in the ocean.

AMBROS In order to conquer the world from there.

ARDUIN That shouldn't be all that difficult, Ambros Doehl.
When one has had a close-up look at the people who
determine world history—
*The door to the veranda opens, Judith comes out, wearing a
traveling dress.*

JUDITH, ARDUIN, AMBROS

JUDITH Greetings, Prince Arduin! Good morning, Ambros.

AMBROS So it's you, Judith!—I could almost have guessed.

ARDUIN Judith! Now I know why Julia was so careful to hide
you from me. *He goes closer to her and kisses her hand* I'm
glad that it's you—and that you're here.

JUDITH Did you doubt it? *To Ambros* How wonderful that I
still get to see you before I set out on my journey.

ARDUIN Did you come from Sweden, Judith?

JUDITH I don't believe it concerns either one of us any longer
where we're coming from, Prince Arduin, but only where
we're going.

ARDUIN Excellent, Judith. We're going to understand each
other. My boat is waiting at the dock; it will bring us to my
ship in a few minutes. Herr Ambros Doehl is giving us the
pleasure of his company for lunch.

AMBROS Forgive me, my Prince—

ARDUIN May I ask for your arm, Judith?

JUDITH You are in a hurry, Prince.

AMBROS I advise you be likewise, Judith. If you're eager to go on a cruise to South America or Ceylon, or wherever, then don't hesitate. Some news may arrive at any moment which would prevent the Prince from undertaking this trip.

ARDUIN Whatever news may come, Judith—we are sailing.

JUDITH Then I beg Your Highness only for as much time as I need to lock up my trunks and have them taken to the beach. In a quarter of an hour I'll be at your disposal. *Exits into the pavilion.*

ARDUIN Honestly, I have never encountered such a being. She's taking all this as if it were the most natural thing in the world.

AMBROS Why should a beautiful woman find it unusual for a young prince to be taking her on a trip? There will be any number of things yet that she won't find unusual. In any event, you will have a charming traveling companion in her, provided that she gets ready in time—which we hope she will.

ARDUIN One might almost think that my speedy departure is of some importance to you—And your letter, telling me I'd no longer find you here? Very strange!—Why didn't you want me here? What's behind all this? Be honest with me, Ambros. Is there an assassination attempt being planned, perhaps?

AMBROS Your career has not reached quite that high yet, Highness. No danger of any kind threatens you. My only wish was for a certain meeting not to take place, and now it will be unavoidable after all.

ARDUIN What meeting?

AMBROS Between you, Prince Arduin, and Aurelie.

ARDUIN What are you saying, Ambros? Aurelie is here?—with you?

AMBROS *hastily* Along with me. Along with a friend. Understand me, Prince Arduin.

ARDUIN And that's why you didn't want me to come here?

AMBROS At any rate, I want to make you aware that Aurelie finds herself in such a state of mind that any emotional shock—most especially careless allusions to the most recent past—could have serious consequences. *Arduin smiles. Ambros, in response to the smile, continues* And it would be irresponsible to disturb with so much as a single word the peace of mind this distracted soul has so laboriously achieved.

ARDUIN   With all due respect, Ambros, to your gallantry;—but—forgive me,—when one comes from Herr Gysar's gardens she has forfeited the right to play hard to get.

AMBROS   That would be only one person's business. The Countess is under my protection for the time being—until that moment when she is taken from my hands by the man who has the power as well as the responsibility to save her soul from its confusion, for which he is probably to blame; —the Baron von Falkenir.

ARDUIN   He knows that she's here? You've notified him?

AMBROS   Yes. Unfortunately not until yesterday. But I have no doubt that he set out at once in order to come for Aurelie.

ARDUIN   I don't know, Ambros, whether your right to meddle in Aurelie's destiny is any more legitimate than mine. Anyway, I have a different view of how Aurelie could be saved than you. In any case, the most foolish thing, it seems to me, would be to deliver her up again to this Falkenir. I will do my part to preserve her from this fate.

AMBROS   I see her coming, Prince. I beg you again to consider—

ARDUIN   I want to try a different remedy to cure her depression, *with a glance at the approaching but not yet visible Aurelie* in which, by the way, I refuse to believe until I've spoken to her myself.
Aurelie enters from the left, not from the rise, wearing dark clothes. In the beginning she acts calm, superior, ladylike; only her glance occasionally gives expression to her strange forlornness.

AURELIE, ARDUIN, AMBROS

AURELIE   Greetings, Arduin. I saw your yacht, it looks most splendid. It's too great an honor that it bears my name. What brings you here?

ARDUIN A short stop on the way into the unknown. I had no idea you were here, Aurelie.

AURELIE Why not? When two people fly through the world the way you and I do, they may easily run into each other somewhere. *Only now turning to Ambros* A delicious morning. I lay on the beach and the waves washed over my feet. I even slept a little, I believe. It was very late when we returned from the sea last night, Ambros. *She sits down.*

ARDUIN *lightly, not maliciously* I imagine there was moonlight too?

AURELIE The moon only came out as we reached the shore. It must have been after midnight, right, Ambros?

ARDUIN And when you stay out on the water so late at night, do you then usually sleep on the beach in the morning, Aurelie?

AURELIE Slumber and dream. Today I even happened to see someone in a dream whom I once knew well, and who—I could tell from the expression on his face—imagined that he was real.

ARDUIN And was he quite, in the end—

AURELIE No more than you, Arduin—than all of you.

ARDUIN And even had a name, like us others?

AURELIE A beautiful name. I once spoke it with pleasure— Max.

ARDUIN *with a glance at Ambros* Herr von Reisenberg?

AMBROS *to Aurelie* You've spoken to him?

AURELIE He wasn't alone. Who do you think was with him? Our sprite. *To Arduin* Have you seen our sprite yet, Arduin? And they were being followed by a sea-god once named Eligius Fenz. *Smiling* You do know that this is a fairy-tale beach, don't you Arduin?

ARDUIN And I imagine our friend Ambros Doehl is the author and manager of this entire fairy-tale farce.

AMBROS If that were the case I would not have allowed you to appear in it. I'm only a participant—in a single episode.

ARDUIN *to Aurelie* So Herr von Reisenberg is here too. He's pursuing you, I suppose? If you should have any order for me, perhaps, of whatever sort—

AURELIE *smiles* An order? I suppose you want to challenge him to a duel? Oh, yes, you're very substantial, Arduin. It hurts one's soul to see how substantial all of you are. That's why I've decided only to dream you from now on. It's more convenient and merrier. If only you weren't so noisy and violent time and again and put one in danger of waking up.

ARDUIN *in a new tone* You have no further reason to dream, Aurelie. I want to create a reality for you that will be more beautiful than any dream. My ship is out there, Aurelie, you've seen it. For you it was built and made ready to sail, I've always known it. It bears your name and, if you like, it is yours—the same as everything I own. Come with me!

AURELIE Where's this journey supposed to take us?

ARDUIN Wherever you want. And wherever it goes, with you it will have a purpose and a goal. Let the world fade away in the fog behind us or go up in flames, we will find a new and better one for ourselves somewhere.

AMBROS *having become uneasy, but still not sharply* Your Highness!

AURELIE Do be still, Ambros. If a poet sometimes acts the pedant, why shouldn't a prince for once string words together like a poet?—It's a pleasure listening to you, Arduin, continue.

ARDUIN What is there for me to add if you understand me? *Without pathos* Come! Is there something or someone holding you back? Have you sworn to be faithful to any person, whoever he may be? And—if you had belonged to another last night and promised yourself with the most sacred of oaths to a different one for tomorrow—are such commitments valid for you or me?

AMBROS Prince Arduin!

AURELIE Do leave him alone, Ambros. Isn't he making sense, basically? An adventure, yes, one adventure more for him and for me. It's worth considering.

ARDUIN Take it that way, if you prefer. It'll satisfy me for a start. What is to come of it beyond that is up to the gods.

AURELIE What is to come of it? My beautiful, daring prince, not much, I'm afraid. Not even an adventure. Nothing. This time, nothing. But you mustn't therefore give up hope. One must never do that with women like me. Perhaps we will meet one day on a different beach, in a happier hour. And, who knows . . . .

ARDUIN   I have no intention of ever landing on a European shore again. And if you persevere in your refusal, Aurelie, then my decision will be firmer than ever. If you do not come with me now, at this moment, Aurelie—then we will never see each other again.

AURELIE   I would be sorry. But I can't change things, Arduin.

ARDUIN   Why do you scorn me, Aurelie? Am I not worthy of you? I, of all people, not worthy of you?

AURELIE   Whether worthy or not surely doesn't matter. *In a louder voice but without pathos* But no man on the face of this earth, even if I'd sold or given myself to a different man every night, will ever touch so much as the tip of my finger if I do not wish it. So—farewell, Arduin, and the best of luck on your voyage.
Pause.

ARDUIN   I thank you, Aurelie, for your good wishes. But before we part forever, may I venture one last, modest request at least?

AURELIE   —?

ARDUIN   That you do me the honor of drinking a glass of wine to my auspicious departure on board the ship that bears your name. *With a glance at Ambros* Oh, I don't intend to abduct her, and there'll be no love potion in the champagne. I swear it. It will be a somewhat melancholy but entirely harmless lunch.

AMBROS   I can readily believe that. And if I'm not mistaken, another lady is also invited.

ARDUIN   Imagine, Ambros, I had almost forgotten.

AMBROS   Then I may perhaps remind Your Highness that you also invited the lady I just mentioned to be your guest for dinner, and, if I remember correctly, for the entire journey —into the unknown.

ARDUIN   This is all true, actually, Aurelie. And the young lady would have made a good lady's maid for you.

AURELIE   What truly princely whims you have, Arduin. And if in the middle of the journey it had suddenly occurred to you to have us exchange roles—?

ARDUIN That could never have happened. You would have been the absolute mistress of my ship. And you will remain its guardian angel in any event. More than that. Its patron saint. Every morning, every evening, I'll say my prayers before your picture, with greater faith and longing than I've ever knelt before any altar.

AURELIE Before my picture? What picture are you talking about? There is no picture of me that could be in your possession.

ARDUIN There is, Aurelie. An incomparable one, splendid and infamous. Painted by a great artist who is a great scoundrel besides.

AURELIE You have Gysar's picture? By what means did you pry it from him?

ARDUIN By the most customary in the world.

AURELIE He sold it to you?

ARDUIN I was looking for you, for you yourself. I thought he was keeping you hidden. I offered him money, a great deal of money, he couldn't have gotten a better price for you in person. I had to be satisfied with your picture. Now it's mine, all mine, no person will ever lay eyes upon it except me. The room in which it hangs will never be entered by any unauthorized person. I've locked it up in a silver chest which no one but I can open.

AURELIE What gives you the rights over this picture, Arduin? Gysar may have sold it to you a thousand times over—and you may have paid him for it with a principality;—the picture is mine, and I am laying claim to it.

ARDUIN Come with me, Aurelie, and I will throw it into the sea before your eyes.

AURELIE Into the sea—my picture?! that picture! Oh, how little you know me. Do all you men really allow yourselves to be deceived again and again by this clear forehead, these bright eyes, this chastely flowing dress? Don't you know anything? Have you no inkling of the blazing memories behind this brow? of the flaring yearning in these eyes, of the burning nakedness under this dress? I'm going to fetch the picture from your ship before you leave, and I'm going to travel around the entire world with it, and stand next to it

everywhere I go, so that people will be able to compare us
at leisure and decide whether the scoundrel or the artist was
the greater. But this I am telling you all, in my nakedness
and in my sinfulness I belong to myself alone. No one took
anything from me and no one can give me anything. What
have I to do with shame, since no one really knows me?

FALKENIR *enters from the right,* AURELIE, ARDUIN,
AMBROS

FALKENIR *not quite close to them yet* Aurelie!
AURELIE *sees him, remains motionless, makes a barely notice-
able movement as if to flee.*
FALKENIR *a step closer* Aurelie!
AURELIE *strokes her temples, as if gradually waking up.*
FALKENIR *drawing closer to her* Aurelie!
AURELIE *seems about to faint.*
FALKENIR *catches her; there is no embrace, only a fleeting
contact which is broken at once.*
ARDUIN *goes towards Falkenir.*
AMBROS *lays a hand on Arduin's arm, as if to hold him back.*
AURELIE Leave me alone with him. *Arduin and Ambros exit.*
AURELIE *in control* Why have you come, Falkenir? By what
right do you stand in my way?
FALKENIR I'm not here to stand in your way; I'm here to
meet you and to extend my hand to you. It's up to you
whether you will take it or not.
AURELIE Your hand, what for? Do you long to raise me up?
Leave me where I am, I'm quite all right.
FALKENIR To raise you up, you up to me. . . ?! I don't feel
like one who stands above you. If anyone is to blame here,
then it is I alone.
AURELIE You speak of blame? Why? You showed me the way
that was predetermined for me; and I have taken it. There is
no blame for me to absolve you of;—no, it is for me to
thank you, for recognizing me in good time for what I am
and what I was, even before I knew it myself.
FALKENIR And even if I did recognize you;—it was all too
easy to be satisfied with that. First, and more important than

any recognition, comes what gives purpose to any human relationship—responsibility.

AURELIE   Where did you get this new bit of wisdom? And what makes you think that it's any better than the old?

FALKENIR   I got it from a hundred lonely days and nights, and it is better than all wisdom—it's called love.

AURELIE   Ah, do I understand you correctly, Falkenir? Has it come so far with me now, that a lover could bed himself calmly down in my arms without fear? Have I gone through enough pleasure and pain now, that the gracious rescuer, assured of my weariness, may sleep at my side in blissful confidence? That could be a mistake, Falkenir.

FALKENIR   If I were standing here making any claims upon you, I would deserve your scorn, Aurelie. Because I know I have no right to demand anything of you. But what you cannot keep me from doing is—to confess to you. Whether your path suits you well, only you can tell. But this is certain: I was the reason you walked upon it to begin with. And that is why I'm responsible for every injury and for every hardship that you encountered on your way, or may yet encounter. And that is why, Aurelie, I'm offering you today what I may, and must, and wish to offer you: security, shelter, and my name.

AURELIE   *not hard*   Do you really think that anything like that would really matter to me? Or do you believe you have anything to make up to me? And if it were so—could it be done with everything you're offering me? No, Falkenir, I do not need your name or any protective hand. And no one has to answer for me but I myself.

FALKENIR   You still misunderstand my coming here. No one is compelling me to undertake this responsibility.—Listen to me, Aurelie. Uncertain times are upon us. I don't know whether there's any person alive at this moment under whose protection you would or could place yourself in any eventuality and without any reservation. And sooner than you, than we both suspect, you could feel the need for such protection. That is why I want you to be assured of a home, come what may—wherever you may be coming from—for whatever distant place you may be leaving it again—a home whose peace no one may disturb: my house.

AURELIE *fending him off with a motion of her hand.*

FALKENIR *quickly* Even if you allowed me to, even—if you demanded it—it would not be possible for me to stay near you in the immediate future. I will be granted nothing more—if you accept my proposal—than to bring you home from here. Because I myself have been entrusted with a mission which calls me abroad immediately.

AURELIE Is that why you left Rome?

FALKENIR It was the overt reason. But before setting out on a very long journey of indeterminate duration and not entirely certain outcome, I felt—as I am sure you'll understand—I felt an irresistible urge in my heart to see you, to speak with you, to tell you what thoughts took shape in my mind and formed themselves to a decision during these weeks I've stayed in Rome. I didn't find you in Vienna, where I was obliged to spend a few days in any event. No one could tell me, either in Vienna or in Merkenstein, where you had gone to—or fled to.

AURELIE *quickly* And how is it you've come here? *Without awaiting his reply* It was Ambros who summoned you.

FALKENIR No, Aurelie. I had no word of any kind from him these last three months, as little as from Prince Arduin; notwithstanding, call it a hunch, call it a luck, it wasn't difficult for me to discover your trail.

AURELIE And—you find me here with the two of them—and don't ask me anything more?

FALKENIR I have cause and the right to ask only the one question, whether you want to come with me or not. Whatever has happened since we last saw each other, Aurelie, does not concern me. Would I have come otherwise?—And if, foolish and proud, I disdained my good fortune,—only because its permanence was not at the same time guaranteed —are you, therefore, in this moment of decision—because that's what it is, Aurelie—going to refuse something that—even though, naturally, it wouldn't be apparent yet today—may become sometime in the future—good fortune— for you, too?!

AURELIE Never, Falkenir, never can there be any happiness,

any happiness common to you and me.

FALKENIR   That is entirely up to you.

AURELIE   How wrong you are, Falkenir! You, a man so very shaken by possibilities, by distant possibilities, that he thought he had to flee from me—you believe yourself strong enough to resist past realities?

FALKENIR   Possibilities are uncannier specters than past realities. They hover around us, thousandfold, incomprehensible, nameless; as desires and dreams,—as uninvited guests, they sit down at our table and drain the drink of life from our cups, and we watch them, with dry, hot lips, dying of thirst.

AURELIE   I wonder if memories would be more welcome guests for you?

FALKENIR   Whatever we've been through, and were it most horrible, is settled. In the light of day, Aurelie, of our day, the ghosts of the past will fade into nothingness.

AURELIE   Can there be a day bright enough for you, so that they could fade away?

FALKENIR   That day is here, Aurelie—if only you wish it.

AURELIE   Do you really believe that, Falkenir? And if they suddenly stood before you, face to face, these ghosts of the past—do you mean to say they wouldn't make you shudder?

FALKENIR   What's the point of your question, Aurelie? We will never conjure them up.

AURELIE   If you're not afraid of them, why not—?

FALKENIR   Because—it would be an outrage, against you and me.

AURELIE   And if they required no conjuring? If they—some time—met you—here or there—it really could happen— Falkenir—met you as the realities they were—and are—?

FALKENIR   What are you saying, Aurelie—?

HANSEN *enters quickly from the right* Have I the honor to be speaking to the Herr Baron Falkenir?

FALKENIR   I am the Baron.

HANSEN   A telegram, Herr Baron.

FALKENIR *takes it from Hansen* Forwarded from Copenhagen. *Opens it* Nothing I didn't already know. *To the manager* When does the ship to Copenhagen leave?

HANSEN   According to the schedule, at two o'clock, Herr
Baron. But under the present circumstances we may count on
a considerable delay. The official notification of the
declaration of war has just been posted in the hotel. *A hotel
employee comes quickly up to the manager from the right,
speaks to him briefly in a low voice.*
AMBROS *enters from the left; he has seen the manager, Falkenir,
and Aurelie standing together*   Pardon me, Baron Falkenir.
The manager and the hotel employee exit.   The ship to
Copenhagen will be full. I just want to let you know that I
reserved a motorboat yesterday that will take us from here
to the capital in two hours. It has enough room for all of us.
May I invite you to join me?
FALKENIR   I thank you, Herr Doehl. At what time—*Glances at
Aurelie.*
AMBROS   The sooner the better. The evening express leaves
Copenhagen after seven.—How soon can you be ready,
Aurelie?
AURELIE *remains silent.*
AMBROS   Starting tomorrow it may not be as easy to get over
the border. I would also advise you against traveling alone.
ARDUIN *enters from the right; to Ambros*   I have to admit de-
feat. Your information was right. I'm not sure we'll ever
see each other again; so, I suppose the time has come to bid
each other farewell. I want to say good-bye to you, Aurelie.
Shakes hands with her   And to you too, Baron Falkenir. *They
shake hands as well*   Keep a fond place for me in all your
memories. Good-bye, Ambros.
AMBROS   I imagine Your Highness will be giving up the
planned cruise?
ARDUIN   I wouldn't dream of it. This war is breaking out not
only counter to my prediction, but also against all human
reason. I will not have anything to do with it, either on one
side or the other. I needn't fear that people might interpret
my decision as showing a lack of courage. But—this is
certain, I have no further business with these developments.
JUDITH *coming from the veranda, having changed her dress*
Forgive me, Prince Arduin, for making you wait.
ARDUIN *goes up to her, kisses her hand; then to the others*

Permit me to introduce you to the kind young lady who will do me the honor of accompanying me on my cruise.

JUDITH *comes down from the veranda, up to Aurelie* My name is Judith Asrael.

AURELIE You're Judith?

ARDUIN *to Ambros* I'm very sorry to be deprived of your company, Ambros. There may be all sorts of interesting things to experience on my cruise too, perhaps even more interesting than what might lie in store for you.

AMBROS Unfortunately I have only one fatherland, Highness.

ARDUIN *smiles and extends his hand to Ambros, then to Judith* Your arm, Judith. *To the others* Once more, good-bye!

AURELIE Arduin?!

ARDUIN *stops, remains standing.*

AURELIE *lightly* Have you forgotten that you invited us to your ship for lunch?

ARDUIN Not at all, Aurelie, but *smiling* it seems to me you didn't accept my invitation.

AURELIE Then you misunderstood me.

AMBROS We have to be in Copenhagen before evening, Aurelie.

AURELIE There's plenty of time till then. And we have our motorboat. I'm coming, Arduin! We are all coming;— Falkenir too.

FALKENIR *about to say something.*

ARDUIN *very quickly* That the invitation includes you too, Baron von Falkenir, goes without saying. I'm very happy to be able to welcome all of you on my ship, and ask only for a short time to give my crew the necessary instructions. I'll pick you all up in half an hour at the latest, if I may.

AURELIE But you mustn't—in honor of your guests, perhaps, make any changes on your ship. Everything must remain the way it is. And I'm counting on it that you'll conduct us through all the rooms of your enchanted yacht, and show us everything there is to see there. Will you promise me that, Arduin?

ARDUIN *after hesitating unnoticeably* You have my word, Aurelie. In half an hour, then. So long! *Exits quickly.*

AMBROS *takes two steps as if to follow him, then stops.*

JUDITH *goes up to him and looks at him questioningly.*

FALKENIR *to Aurelie* What is the meaning of this, Aurelie?

AURELIE It means, Falkenir, that it's now up to you whether you want to come face to face with the ghosts—or not.

FALKENIR *with a movement of his hand towards the sea* Ghosts?—there. . . .

AURELIE There or elsewhere. There and elsewhere.

FALKENIR What do you intend to do? Doesn't it tell you enough that I'm here to take you home?

AURELIE No, Falkenir. Until you have stood before the ghosts, face to face, head to head, you will know nothing about me or about yourself. Still, if you lack the courage—to take this upon yourself, then let's rather part. I won't hold you to be weak-spirited as a result. Indeed, I'm telling you, Falkenir, it's better that you go, that you go at once, instead of fleeing in horror and revulsion before sunset.

FALKENIR *looks all around.*

AURELIE Well, Falkenir? . . .

FALKENIR I'm staying.

AURELIE Let's stroll around the park a little then. You really should see something of this wonderful beach before you leave again. And now—you must tell me about Rome, all right? *She greets the two others amiably, very much the lady of the world, and exits with Falkenir right.*

AMBROS *quickly, to Judith* You must at all costs prevent the Prince from coming back here.

JUDITH How should I, how can I do that?

AMBROS You must follow him out to his ship immediately and there—give free rein to all your seductive powers.

JUDITH What are you asking of me, Ambros?

AMBROS Now or never is the time to prove your feminine genius. More depends on it than just your destiny alone.

JUDITH So it seems, at any rate. But—

AMBROS Considerable harm could result if this lunch were actually to take place. Deviltries, perhaps crimes. It mustn't be, under any conditions. Come Judith, I'll bring you down to the shore myself—

Max and Gilda enter from the left.

GILDA Look, Herr Ambros Doehl, what wonderful shells we've

found. It's not every day that the sea brings this kind.

JUDITH You're not gone yet?

MAX *to Judith* We were evidently destined, once more—

AMBROS *quickly* Gilda, you will do me the favor of taking this young lady out to the white ship with the golden letters right away, on the swiftest boat.

GILDA To the enchanted ship?

AMBROS Yes, you'll do so right away. Judith, please!

GILDA Oh, gladly.

MAX Best wishes on your journey, Judith.

JUDITH And to you on yours. *Embraces him.*

AMBROS The fastest boat, Gilda.

GILDA *to Ambros* Oh, I'll take care of that, that she disappear from here again as quickly as possible. If you please, Fräulein.

JUDITH *tears herself away from Max* Farewell! Good-bye, Ambros. In half an hour I'll be on the high seas or—you will have been right—and I'll become a seamstress. *Exits with Gilda.*

MAX, AMBROS

A short pause.

MAX *shaking his head* May I be allowed to observe, Ambros, that you're playing a somewhat strange role towards me? You conceal from me that Aurelie is here—with you, in your company. You send Judith to Prince Arduin's ship before my very eyes—

AMBROS You shall have the explanations you want at the appropriate time. For my part, I only wonder why you didn't leave at eight-thirty.

MAX Oh, as to that—I'm even considering whether it wouldn't be the smartest thing to stay here, at least for me.

AMBROS That might present some difficulties, Max. You are a reserve officer, if I'm not mistaken?

MAX You overestimate my military talents, Ambros. I only made it as far as cadet-sergeant.

AMBROS Well—however, if you don't report to your detachment immediately, then I dare say you'll be forced to give up any thought of returning to your fatherland for a long time.

MAX I could get used to the possibility.—Fräulein Gilda has suggested I take over part of her father's responsibilities, as the manager's deputy so to speak.—Well, yes, why not? I have polished manners, as people judge these things, I know languages, and I have legible handwriting—

AMBROS I assure you Max, this is no time for jokes.

MAX *playing with some small shells which he has taken out of his jacket pocket* For what, then, if I may ask?

AMBROS For this: to prepare in greatest haste for the trip home.

MAX There is a motorboat down there that you're said to have rented. Why then don't you invite me to come along, Ambros?

AMBROS Because Aurelie will probably be coming along.

MAX Well—and? We didn't part as enemies. As I passed by her this morning—although she acted as if she hadn't noticed—she smiled very kindly. She would certainly have nothing against my coming along.

AMBROS But the Baron von Falkenir is part of the company as well.

MAX What—? Falkenir is here? What is that supposed to mean?

AMBROS Nothing too difficult to understand, I think. And you will understand in any case, Max, that I'm unfortunately not in a position to invite you on my boat, but rather would like to advise you urgently—

MAX Well, what—? To hide from Herr von Falkenir, perhaps, like the lover in the farce?

AMBROS That happens in the life of every Don Juan. Or maybe it didn't happen to your famous ancestor? Just think how comically he acted in all his affairs. He sneaks up to Dona Anna in disguise, he runs away from Elvira, towards Zerlina he behaves like a fool; only the idea of inviting a dead governor to dinner saves him, at the last moment, from being ridiculous. And that ends badly enough for him, as you know.

MAX Fortunately, my governor is still alive.

AMBROS   What is that supposed to mean? Has your personal bravery been called into question? I'm not warning you to be careful, Max, but to be considerate. To jeopardize the hard-earned happiness of two human beings for the sake of a conventional pose, that would be somewhat too costly a jest.

MAX   It could also turn out differently.

AMBROS   —?

MAX   Perhaps I've decided to fall, a sacrifice to Aurelie's happiness.

AMBROS *bursts out laughing.*

MAX *hurt, turns away from him.*

AMBROS   Don't be deceived about the role you've been given to play in Aurelie's life, and be satisfied that it has been a splendid one.

MAX   Too cheap for my taste. And it may not be over yet.

AMBROS   How you misunderstand. And if suddenly you should feel a need to do tragedy,—well, there'll probably be another opportunity to satisfy it very soon now.

MAX   And you would find such a pose less conventional, Ambros?

FALKENIR *and* AURELIE *enter from the right, still in conversation.*

FALKENIR *suddenly notices Max, casts a quick glance at Aurelie which says, so that's it, you knew.*

AURELIE *goes towards Max.*

MAX *takes a step towards her.*

AURELIE *extends her hand to him.*

MAX *kisses her hand.*

AURELIE   We saw each other very fleetingly this morning. Could it be you didn't even recognize me?

MAX   I thought you didn't notice me. *He greets Falkenir by means of a slight bow.*

FALKENIR *steps closer, shakes hands with Max* Have you been here long, Herr von Reisenberg?

MAX   Arrived yesterday and here for the first time. But I want to make it clear right away, Herr Baron, that you will find me no less ready for any kind of conversation that you may wish to pursue than for one about the scenery or the weather. *Pause.*

FALKENIR I see no reason to have the kind of conversation you mean, Herr von Reisenberg;—unless you yourself thought you had to insist on it for some reason. *Max remaining silent, he continues* As for me, I assure you that I harbor no hostile feelings towards you whatsoever. *Pause.*

MAX *bows and exits.*

FALKENIR, AURELIE, AMBROS

FALKENIR This ghost struck me as somewhat harmless, Aurelie.

AURELIE You controlled yourself excellently in any case— Isn't that right, Ambros? Or perhaps you didn't notice how his fingers were twitching as he stood face to face with Max?

AMBROS I don't rightly know what you mean, Aurelie.

FALKENIR *lightly* Can't you see, Ambros, that the fairy tale has begun again? I have tests to undergo, before I am considered worthy to—take the princess home. Isn't that so, Aurelie?

AURELIE *in earnest* Not whether you are worthy, Falkenir:— but whether you'll still feel like—associating with me. But how to determine whether you have passed a test or not? You won't know for sure—and maybe I won't either. *After a short pause* You, Ambros, shall be the judge.

AMBROS Is now the right time for such—strange trifles? Truly, no fairy-tale wind blows in this world any more, Aurelie. *In a different tone* I'm somewhat concerned about our boat. There were other applicants for it too, a family from The Hague—I'd be in favor of our departing without further delay.

AURELIE Impossible. We've been invited to a luncheon. Arduin will be here any minute to pick us up.

AMBROS The Prince will surely not take it amiss if we don't await his coming.

AURELIE I'm of a different opinion, Ambros. I think he'll take it very much amiss.

AMBROS *goes towards the rise.*

AURELIE Is there still no boat coming from the yacht?

AMBROS No.

FALKENIR Perhaps we could go meet the Prince along the shore.

AMBROS However, it seems to me,—the yacht itself is beginning to move.

AURELIE What? Is it coming closer?

AMBROS No. It couldn't do that anyway. There are dangerous rocks along the shore here. The yacht is heading out towards the open sea.

AURELIE What are you saying, Ambros?

AMBROS Without a doubt, it's moving ever further from land.

AURELIE *goes up the rise to Ambros.*

FALKENIR Strange.

AURELIE This is your doing, Ambros. You spoke with Judith.—Why have you done this?

FALKENIR *as if he believed he could guess, with a movement of his hand towards the sea* Gysar—? *To Aurelie* You think a meeting with him would've touched me more deeply than the meeting with that other one did? *To Ambros* It was an excess of consideration, Ambros, for you to want to spare me this test.

AURELIE You're mistaken, Falkenir,—Gysar is not on the ship.

FALKENIR *turns with a questioning expression, first to Aurelie, then to Ambros.*

AURELIE Let's say farewell to each other, Falkenir.

FALKENIR What are you talking about, Aurelie?

AURELIE This ship's sailing away,—take it as a sign of fate. Now you will never know who I am. I'm sailing away from you there, with that ship.

FALKENIR *after a short hesitation* You speak—of a picture— of your picture, that Gysar painted?—How has this picture come into Arduin's possession?

AURELIE In the most natural way in the world.

FALKENIR Gysar sold the picture to the Prince?

AURELIE He would have sold me, too, if he had been offered enough. And how much longer—I suppose I'd have let myself be sold at that.

FALKENIR Aurelie—

AURELIE Why not? Once we begin to slide, do we know where we'll stop?

FALKENIR You're saying things you yourself do not believe, Aurelie.

AURELIE You don't know me, Falkenir. The person you see here before you, this is not Aurelie. This face, these eyes, this forehead, these are all deceptive. God created only my mask, another created me the way I really am. I myself didn't know myself before. He didn't allow me to see the picture before it was finished. And when I saw it for the first time, I struck him who had painted it in the face as I would a liar, and wanted only to run away.

FALKENIR And stayed—?

AURELIE He swore he would destroy the picture if I stayed. That night he gave a party. Haven't you ever heard about Gysar's parties?—A black, star-filled sky was above me, lawns blazed red and green in the torchlight. There were women there and young men, beautiful, strangers, God knows where they came from. I wandered about between light and darkness, alone, pursued; I pulled myself from the grasp of greedy hands and searched for Gysar. Why? To embrace him or to kill him? I don't know. Couples glided past me, all around me the night was alive with the lamentation and singing of violins and flutes. All around me gliding and sliding, shouts of joy, a sinking down, and dying away. Wasn't I among those who sang and shouted and glided along? Not I, who lay on the lawn, forehead smothered in flowers, darkly glowing eyes above me, embraced by inescapable arms? Were they Gysar's eyes or someone else's? Did it last for minutes or hours? Was it a dream or was I awake? I don't know. The flutes and violins sounded farther away, the voices echoed farther, shapes faded in the distance. The sky was extinguished above me, and I stared, alone, up into the flickering grayness. And then I experienced it—all of a sudden I was not myself any more. I was the picture Gysar had painted. I felt myself, felt the limbs I'd surrendered, my quivering breasts, my fading glance, all as I'd seen them in Gysar's painting—and knew then: this painting did not lie; this painting expressed a truth of which I'd had no idea and of which I still had no idea. That picture is Aurelie—but I myself, as you see me here, am only a picture. I am a mask and a lie. What I say, what I look like, what I do—this is all the pale shadow of my real self. There, on that ship, I am sailing away; and what remains behind here, that's nothing but an apparition which you're allowing to make a fool of you. *Pause.*

FALKENIR   I carry within me a thousand pictures of you, Aurelie. What does that one signify? A thousand paintings can not portray you any more than a thousand words could. You're here, and I love you. That is more than all paintings and words. Let's go home, Aurelie.

AMBROS   We mustn't delay any longer. The boat is ready.

AURELIE *does not move.*

FALKENIR   Come, Aurelie. . . . Well—?

AURELIE   I don't know yet whether you'll want to ride in the same boat with Ambros and me.

FALKENIR *surprised, looks at both of them; then*   What do you mean, Aurelie?—One more test?

AURELIE   Won't you confess that you summoned Falkenir, Ambros?

FALKENIR   What is that supposed to mean, Aurelie? I've never received a letter from Ambros.

AMBROS   It couldn't have reached you yet, Falkenir, since I only sent it yesterday, and to Rome.

AURELIE *smiles and nods.*

FALKENIR   And what did your letter say?

AMBROS   I asked you to come here to take Aurelie home. Since you are here of your own accord, all the better.

AURELIE   And if you had not sent this letter?

FALKENIR   What's the point of your question, Aurelie? The letter was written by a friend, that much is certain.

AURELIE   Yes, he is your friend. You have no idea how much.

AMBROS   And yours, Aurelie.

AURELIE   I know. If I hadn't sensed that—would I have fled to you, Ambros? How I breathed again when I landed on this shore! How well and free I felt when I saw you again.

You didn't ask—and still, you knew everything. I told you nothing—and still, I felt as if I had poured my heart out to you. How I rested in your company—and awoke every morning pure as a maiden. Oh, if only you had come yesterday, Falkenir!—We rode out to sea in the evening, and not for the first time. There was peace all around us, peace in our souls. We were friends, Ambros, weren't we? *Pause* And from one moment to the next we weren't any-more. In the wink of an eye, without so much as our fingertips having touched, without our glances melting into each other, without either of us saying a word, we had stopped being friends. Didn't I suddenly open my arms to you? You saw it, even if I didn't do it. I did it, even if you didn't notice it. Then you reached for the oars; and with heavy strokes you steered the boat back to shore again. There we stood, now, in the middle of the night. You and I,—in the middle of the night, alone. You had only to take my hand, to whisper a single word, and I would have followed you wherever you wanted. But you walked back here with me in silence, without so much as touching my hand—and disappeared before the door to my room was closed. It stood open the entire night, but you didn't come. It's only today that I understand. *To Falkenir* He had summoned you and did not want to betray you. It was only because of him that I didn't belong to another the night before your arrival;—I was ready.

FALKENIR I had no right of any kind to you and—have none. If it has become clear to you that you love Ambros,—why did you hesitate to tell me? I couldn't have found a worthier companion for you myself.

AURELIE I do not love him, Falkenir. I have never loved him. It was a mood, nothing more. . . a mood that will not recur, not this one, any more than last night's boat will ever move through the same waters again.

AMBROS You know Aurelie is telling the truth, Falkenir. She has never loved another besides you.

AURELIE That's how it is, Falkenir. Never another besides you. Nevertheless, the eternal currents to which you opened my ears flow unruly through my heart. Torchlight, flutes, and violins, the nocturnal rush of the waves, a flattering voice, the fragrance of lilacs—and your Aurelie glides into the arms of a seducer, of a friend, of a stranger who knows how to seize the moment.

FALKENIR   You didn't know, Aurelie, that I would come back —or how. And even if you had known—you were free.

AURELIE   And now that you've come, have I become a different woman? And if I promised you to be faithful—and—if I could do it—would the eternal currents cease to exist therefore? And do you think, today, that I could ever belong to you as completely as you believe yourself condemned to demand? That you could ever possess me as completely—as no man can possess a woman, nor any woman a man, as no human being ever can possess another —or may?

FALKENIR   No, Aurelie, I don't think that, I think it less than ever. However, I also no longer believe that the meaning of love is to enjoy its possession in peace. Loving means worrying, struggling, courting—loving is having to win anew the thing one loves every hour; being ready to renounce it if fate wills it; and signifying home, time and again, home, no matter where the beloved is returning from—nor for what distant place she longs.

AURELIE *remains silent.*

AMBROS   If ever there were tests imposed, be they in fairy tales or in actuality—this time they've been passed.

AURELIE *looks at him.*

AMBROS   My judgeship is at an end. I find for our departure. So long!

AURELIE, FALKENIR   *remain silent.*

FALKENIR   Give me your hands, Aurelie.

AURELIE *extends them to him with a forlorn look.*

FALKENIR   Why don't you say something, Aurelie?

AURELIE   What do you want want me to tell you, Falkenir?

FALKENIR   Whether you finally realize that I laugh at all the ghosts you've allowed me to encounter.

AURELIE   Today you laugh at them, Falkenir.

FALKENIR   Aurelie!

AURELIE   It was longing that changed you. Won't fulfillment do so again?—Don't answer, Falkenir, you can't know. You have not yet kissed my lips, have never yet, while resting on my breast, heard the rush of the eternal currents. You don't know whether one morning, whether on the first morning you awake in my arms, the ghosts will not be standing around our bed and prove themselves more powerful than today.

FALKENIR *about to reply.*

AURELIE   You can't know it. And if it happens,—where, Falkenir, where would we have to flee from one another then, in order not to dissolve in shame and despair?

FALKENIR   No such morning will come.

AURELIE   You can't be sure, Falkenir.

FALKENIR *after hesitating* And if it were to come—

AURELIE   —?

FALKENIR   Then it would be—the last morning for me.

AURELIE   The last morning—for both of us, Falkenir.

FALKENIR *looks at her a long time* For both of us.

AURELIE   Will you swear that to me?

FALKENIR   I swear.

AURELIE   Then embrace your bride for the first time.

FALKENIR *kneels before her, kisses her hands.*

AURELIE *raises him to her, embraces him, then frees herself from the embrace; they are both silent.*
Ambros and the manager enter.

HANSEN   The matter had already grown somewhat dangerous.

AMBROS *to Falkenir* Imagine, that Dutch family was just going to appropriate our boat.

HANSEN   But nothing more can happen now, I've put a small crew aboard.

AURELIE   How long will it take this boat to get to Copenhagen?

HANSEN   No more than two and a half hours. And the express train doesn't leave until seven-thirty. If the lady and gentlemen would still like to take lunch on the terrace, perhaps—

AURELIE   Only two and a half hours? Then it's not even necessary for us to leave our beautiful beach in such haste.

HANSEN   As far as the boat is concerned, I will assume all responsibility now. And you will have it continuously in view from the terrace.

FALKENIR *to Aurelie* Well, then let's have lunch there, if it's all right with you.

HANSEN *exits.*

AURELIE Thank you, Falkenir. *To Ambros* And don't you sail away on us, Ambros. *To Falkenir* You will answer to me for him. *In response to his somewhat suprised look* The two of you will have to allow me a few more minutes. This dark dress isn't suitable for the brilliant sky or—for anything else. Just be patient a while and I'll come back—in white— as befits a bride. *Goes slowly towards the right, looks back smiling once.*

AMBROS, FALKENIR

FALKENIR *after a pause* Do you have anything else to tell me, Ambros?—Perhaps there were things in your letter that you couldn't or didn't want to say in Aurelie's presence?

AMBROS *in a not entirely convincing tone* Everything is in order now, Falkenir, and my letter has become superfluous in any case.

FALKENIR Still, since I am going to read it—did it contain nothing but your summons for me to come here and—take Aurelie home?

AMBROS A few words concerning Aurelie's state of mind which will no longer be news to you. Since your arrival, Falkenir, the spiritual bewilderment that's held her captive for these three months—although her intellectual powers remained completely unclouded—has begun gradually to dissipate. That she's hardly equal to any further shocks—you know that as well as I do.

FALKENIR That sounds almost like a warning, Ambros.

AMBROS It's a statement of fact. It lies in your power alone to give Aurelie back her existence as a fully recovered person. You sensed this even without having received my letter. And thus, everything will be all right.

FALKENIR Let's hope so, Ambros.

AMBROS I'm convinced of it.

FALKENIR I'm only asking myself one thing. I wonder if what you refer to as morbid bewilderment isn't perhaps expressive of Aurelie's true nature. And if what struck you—*hastily* and me too as a gradual awakening, as the beginning of a new clearness, if just this state doesn't signify a kind of involuntary, I mean—unconscious—dissimulation—

AMBROS And doubt of this sort is agitating you now?

FALKENIR I don't want to call it doubt. But am I not in fact obligated to consider—even so remote a possibility? Neither my feelings nor my conduct towards Aurelie can be influenced in the least by such considerations. I am and will remain aware of the full extent of my responsiblity.

AMBROS You frighten me to the core, Falkenir.

FALKENIR There's no reason for that.

AMBROS If at this moment you're already beginning to play this dangerous game of possibilities all over again, then it would seem best to me—forgive my frankness—that you leave before Aurelie comes back.

GILDA *who has already appeared on the rise earlier and sat down on the bench, now waves in the direction of the sea.*

AMBROS *who had already noticed her earlier* To whom are you waving, Gilda?

GILDA I'm waving to the Countess. She's waving back.

AMBROS From the terrace?

GILDA No. From her boat.

AMBROS What are you saying? *Rushes up* Really—Aurelie.

FALKENIR *likewise up on the rise* In her white dress.—She's rowing towards the terrace, I imagine.

AMBROS That's not the impression I get.

FALKENIR *turns towards Ambros with a questioning look.*

AMBROS *calls out* Aurelie!

FALKENIR *smiling, unsure of himself* She couldn't be thinking of following Prince Arduin's ship?

GILDA Now she's putting down the oars.

AMBROS Let's bring her back.

GILDA *to Ambros* Doesn't the Countess often go for a boat-ride this time of day?

AMBROS We're going after her. You'll row us, Gilda.

GILDA *notices their agitation* I'll untie a boat right away.

We'll catch up to her in ten strokes. *Goes down.*

FALKENIR *to Ambros, anxiously* Do you think, Ambros—?

AMBROS   I wonder, could she possibly imagine—that you didn't pass the tests.

Both men hurry down the rise and disappear.

ELIGIUS FENZ and HANSEN *enter from the right.*

ELIGIUS FENZ   But I assure you, Herr Manager, just now I saw some people intently reading the posters about the concert. It was premature to suspend the sale of tickets.

MAX *enters from the left, wearing a traveling coat* Far and wide, no sight of any coastal steamer, Herr Manager.

HANSEN   It's running two hours late. You will make the express train for sure, Herr von Reisenberg, it will wait for the steamer, of course.

SERAPHINE *enters from the right* You haven't left yet, Max?

ELIGIUS FENZ   Oh, my poor child, it really has come to nothing with the concert tonight.

HANSEN   Unfortunately.

SERAPHINE   I read the telegram in the lounge. So, it's war. Poor Elisabeth.

MAX And have you figured out what you're going to do now?

SERAPHINE   I imagine we'll stay here for the time being, as we intended.

ELIGIUS FENZ   Of course. We have nothing better to do. You'll have a wonderful rest. She is a little pale, don't you think?

HANSEN   The air here works wonders.

ELIGIUS FENZ   At what time is lunch served here, Herr Manager?

HANSEN   From twelve-thirty on.

ELIGIUS FENZ   In that case I'm going to have a vermouth first. *Exits slowly to the right with the manager.*

SERAPHINE *apparently about to follow them.*

SERAPHINE, MAX

MAX   Seraphine.

SERAPHINE *stops.*

MAX Why have you kept from me, Seraphine?

SERAPHINE I really didn't know you were still here. And besides, I was practicing.

MAX Even today! As if there were nothing more important in the world.

SERAPHINE For me, hardly.

MAX By the way, it sounded very beautiful. Insofar as I can judge—I happened to walk past your window a couple of times—your tone has become softer, fuller, warmer.

SERAPHINE Don't you think so? Yes, I have made some progress.

A short pause.

MAX Do you know, Seraphine, that I—to all appearances, will have to go along too—?

SERAPHINE Along? Oh, that. *After a short pause* The uniform will suit you quite well.

MAX Why are you talking like this, Seraphine? It's downright painful to me.

SERAPHINE But why? We ran into each other by chance; so let's behave accordingly.

MAX Since it's become doubtful whether we'll ever see each other again, our meeting no longer strikes me as all that fortuitous.—And I scarcely know whether I should wish to return.

SERAPHINE But how can a person talk that way, Max?

MAX The fact of the matter is this, Seraphine, that I am, as the saying goes, ruined.

SERAPHINE You mean, that you have no more money? That isn't so bad, really. You will simply work.

MAX Yes, but at what? *As if the idea suddenly struck him* Wouldn't you like to engage me as your accompanist in the event I should return. Well—we did play up to each other so well, and you wouldn't have to depend on strangers, on a different one in every place.

SERAPHINE That's not so bad. There were some quite talented, nice young people among them.

MAX You're smiling, Seraphine, as if all this were only a joke. If you had any idea how serious I am. If you knew everything I've been through since we last saw each other—what only today—Oh, Seraphine, what a fool I've been. My life was so very senseless, so empty;—only you, you—

SERAPHINE *quickly* You're being ungrateful—to your life, Max.

MAX *repeating* Only you, Seraphine! That, at any rate, would be reason enough to be grateful.

SERAPHINE *smiles.*

MAX *almost shyly* Won't you take me for your husband, Seraphine, if I should return?

SERAPHINE *almost frightened* You—for my husband— *determined* no.

MAX Your no sounds almost as if you—were angry with me.

SERAPHINE Angry? What gave you that idea?

MAX How different, Seraphine, how calm—how downright happy would I leave—if you would at least leave me a faint hope, that—

SERAPHINE *quickly* It can't be.

MAX —Seraphine—

SERAPHINE *more determined* You should not tie yourself to me. You must not tie yourself to me. Nor I to you.

MAX Why, Seraphine?

SERAPHINE Because you are not the man—because I can't expect you to—*with a sudden resolve* because you shouldn't marry a girl—who has a child.

MAX What are you saying, Seraphine? What—child are you talking about?

SERAPHINE *almost laughing* But Max!

MAX Seraphine! You're going to have a child? We're having a child? And you're telling me only now?

SERAPHINE If you didn't have to go to war, you wouldn't have found out for a long time—or never.

MAX *joyfully* Is it true, Seraphine—we're having a child?

SERAPHINE I am, Max. For the time being it belongs entirely to me.

MAX That is pure nonsense, Seraphine. It goes without saying that you'll return to Vienna now—with me, and you will become my wife before I enlist.

SERAPHINE But Max! Why, you're not nearly grown up

enough for marriage.

MAX It really is the only sensible, the only possible thing. What would you do otherwise? After all, it's not such a simple matter that lies ahead of you, especially under these circumstances. You don't even have a home.

SERAPHINE Would I have one then?

MAX *is unable to respond.*

SERAPHINE And by the way, the entire matter is much simpler than you picture it. For the time being, I'm going to stay with Elisabeth. Where else would I go? Leindorf has to go to war too, after all, so this will actually work out quite well, for Elisabeth too.

MAX They'll be difficult days for you, Seraphine. Just think—

SERAPHINE Difficult days? But why? Would they be any easier if I were married to you? No, Max, they'll be beautiful days. I'm very happy to be having the child. Believe me. And also that it will, in a certain sense, be yours at the same time.

MAX *smiling involuntarily* In a certain sense—

SERAPHINE Well, yes—*strokes his hair gently.*

MAX —of a person whom you actually did not love at all.

SERAPHINE Not loved! Oh, Max, if only you understood me! If only men ever understood! They're always astonished, but they understand nothing. Everything between us had to happen the way it did. Don't you know that? I knew it when I threw the three roses in your path. And when you gave me the lilac branch, wasn't I already yours then?—Oh, it really was so beautiful, Max! All the evenings, from the first to the last, and the last, the one night—how beautiful. But that it was only the one night, and that it can never come again, and that we knew it then—that really was the most beautiful part of it all.

MAX Seraphine!

GILDA *who has been visible on the rise, now rushes down and calls* Father!

MAX What's wrong, Gilda?

GILDA I'm looking for father.

MAX What's the matter? What's happened?

GILDA There he is.

HANSEN *enters hastily from the left* Did you call me, Gilda?

GILDA There's been a terible accident. The Countess—*she is unable to continue.*

MAX Aurelie? What about her?

GILDA She's thrown herself into the sea. And with her the gentleman who arrived here today.

MAX Falkenir?

GILDA They both threw themselves into the sea and are drowned.

HANSEN *as if he were about to go.*

GILDA It's too late, father.

MAX But for heaven's sake, how ever did this happen?

GILDA The Countess rowed out to sea, I saw her from the rise. She waved in greeting, then she let the oars sink. It was so strange. I thought right away that this wasn't the usual boat ride. The two gentlemen too.

MAX What gentlemen?

GILDA Herr Ambros Doehl and the gentleman who arrived only today.

MAX Falkenir.

ELIGIUS FENZ *enters.*

GILDA We rowed out after her. Oh, she wasn't far out yet. We would've certainly caught up to her in a few more seconds. Because her boat was standing still. She was smiling, she was smiling the whole time. One would've thought the whole thing was a joke. But we all knew it wasn't. And when we were only a few oarstrokes away, she suddenly stood up straight in her boat and waved again. Yes, really, as if in greeting—and still she smiled. And before we could grasp it, she swung herself over the edge of her boat. At first she seemed suspended in air. And in that very instant Herr Falkenir was already swinging himself over the edge of our boat. Herr Doehl wanted to follow too, but I held on to his arm. Herr Falkenir reached the Countess at once. She had sunk, but he grabbed her body below the surface and carried her back up. We thought they were saved, both of them, and both their heads were above the water for a few seconds. It almost looked as if they kissed each other. And the Countess was still smiling; not with her lips, but with her eyes. They smiled quite blissfully. We were barely an oarstroke away from both of them. I thought they would take hold of the edge of our boat. But neither of them reached out, neither he nor she, and then, quite suddenly, they both sank at the same time, inconceivably quickly, as if the sea had swallowed them.

MAX   It wasn't possible to save them?

GILDA   They sank so quickly, so deep—no one could go after them. I had to hold Herr Doehl back with all my strength. One could see from the circles in the water how fast they sank. Of course, we still called for help, God knows why I did it, and a few boats did set out.

HANSEN *goes up the rise.*

MAX   Where have you left Ambros Doehl, Gilda?

GILDA   He must still be standing along the shore, I think. I rowed back right away. What more could we have done out there? In the end he'd have thrown himself in after them.

AMBROS *appears above with the manager, who has taken a few steps towards him.*

MAX *goes towards him as well.*

HANSEN   I am disconsolate, Herr Doehl. But as Gilda says, every attempt to save them would have been in vain.

ELIGIUS FENZ *strokes Seraphine's hair.*

AMBROS   There will be all sorts of things to put in order now, Herr Manager, unfortunately I have no more time—

HANSEN *matter-of-factly*   The late Countess's rooms will of course remain locked until the authorities are informed. Herr Baron Falkenir, to my knowledge, took a room in Copenhagen; he had a telegram forwarded from the Hotel d'Angleterre barely an hour ago.

AMBROS   I hope no effort will be spared to recover the bodies.

GILDA   That isn't necessary. By tonight the sea will have washed both of them up on the beach.

SERAPHINE   Is that certain?

GILDA *nods.*

AMBROS *to Max*   There would be a place free in my boat now—and more than one too, Max.

MAX *to Seraphine*   Seraphine! Won't you come away from here with us after all?

SERAPHINE *shakes her head* Someone has to stay here—for when the bodies drift to shore tonight.

GILDA *above* The magic ship—it's sailing ever further out to sea.

MAX Is it still visible?

GILDA The golden name is gleaming ever so brightly.

MAX *to Seraphine, in explanation* It's named Aurelie—and on that ship, Judith is sailing away with Prince Arduin.

SERAPHINE *merely looks at him.*

MAX Come with us, Seraphine, you won't find so easy a way to leave later on.

SERAPHINE Oh, don't worry, Max. If I ever want to leave, I'll get through all right.

AMBROS *leaving the manager and going towards Max* No more long good-byes, now. Farewell, Herr Fenz. Good-bye, little Gilda. Good-bye, Seraphine. Let's get to our boat, Max.

MAX Farewell, Seraphine.

SERAPHINE *takes his head in her hands, kisses him on the lips, and exits quickly to the left.*
Ambros and Max exit, accompanied by the Director.

ELIGIUS FENZ, GILDA

GILDA *her glance follows Max.*

ELIGIUS FENZ You mustn't be sad, little water sprite.

GILDA Sad—? Yes, that's it. I was so curious to know what it's like to be sad. I think I know now.

ELIGIUS FENZ Are you sorry the handsome young man left again?

GILDA I was barely thinking of him just now. . . I was thinking only of the two—I wonder why they did that? They really were so beautiful, and still young.

ELIGIUS FENZ Yes. And they didn't know that life becomes ever more precious the less of it remains.

GILDA *looks at him, laughs softly, and runs up the rise.*

ELIGIUS FENZ *glances after her.*

GILDA *above* Now it has disappeared completely—the magic ship. Now I can't see it at all anymore.

ELIGIUS FENZ *begins once again softly to sing the champagne*

aria, then goes slowly up the rise to Gilda.
GILDA *waits for him, smiling.*

Curtain

THE WAY TO THE POND

.

CHARACTERS

ALBRECHT BARON VON MAYENAU, *former Chancellor*
ANSELMA, *his unmarried sister*
LEONILDA, *his daughter*
SYLVESTER THORN
KONRAD VON URSENBECK, *The Marshal's son*
ANDREAS UNGNAD, *the Baron's secretary*
DOMINIK, *Servant of the Baron's*
A GROOM *of Konrad von Ursenbeck's*
TWO MAIDSERVANTS

    The action takes place around the middle of the eighteenth century, in the Baron's castle, a few hours' journey from the seat of government.
    The third act takes place a few hours after the second, the fourth approximately 36 hours after the third.

FIRST ACT

Great hall in the Baron von Mayenau's castle. A door to the right serves as the main entrance. A door to the left. A gallery runs above and all around the hall, a staircase leading up to it from the front left. Family portraits on the walls. To the right a high fireplace, a table and chairs before it. Chairs also against the walls. In the center background, a spacious bay with three tall bow windows. View to the rear over sunken gardens to a riverine landscape. Haze-shrouded hills in the distance. Within the bay, a large desk, in front of it a chair. Books and papers on the table.

A late morning in May. ANDREAS UNGNAD, the Secretary, enters from the left, a tall, lean, middle-aged individual whose clear eyes are generally wide open, as if staring into space. He carries a leather portfolio under his arm, enters the bay, and opens one of the bow windows. He opens the portfolio, takes out several sheets of paper with writing on them, places them on the desk, then takes some sheets of white paper from a drawer and arranges them on the desk, after which he begins to sharpen a quill. DOMINIK, the 50-year-old servant enters from the right, carrying letters.

DOMINIK The mail, Herr Secretary.
SECRETARY   I'll make room.
    Give it here.
DOMINIK   It isn't much. How different—
SECRETARY *interrupting him*
    When your lord was still Chancellor,—yes, I know.
DOMINIK Day in, day out, twenty, thirty petitions,
    Secret reports, missives from ambassadors
    And princes, imperial notes, hand-written,
    When His Majesty did not deign to appear
    In person for weighty consultation.
SECRETARY *pointing to the mail*
    This seems mail sufficient, truly, for one
    Who lives so isolated as your lord.
DOMINIK But of substance, nothing. None of these seals
    Protects a diplomatic confidence.

Takes one of the letters, looks at it
A begging letter. *Lets it fall, takes another.*
           This from a woman
Of humble station. *Taking a third letter.*
           This from a lady.
SECRETARY A penetrating glance!
DOMINIK   One learns in time
To see behind unbroken seals as well.
SECRETARY Tell your lord—if he is awake as yet—
That I'm ready.
DOMINIK   You may well think he slept
This lovely morning away. Before dawn—
The house lay yet in sleep—he took to horse
And speeds now across the meadows which escort
The river's course for miles throughout this land.
SECRETARY I can see the country for the first time,
Free of haze now, up to the farthest hills.
A well-situated residence. Looking
Down upon the extensive, sun-drenched plain.
Athwart the towering, shady mountain forest—
Turns to Dominik
It's good to linger here.
DOMINIK   It was good, once;—
When we came here to rest from time to time—
No more than that—perhaps in springtime,
When peach blossoms bloomed—or in October
For the hunt—in short, escaping the toils
Of state affairs. Yet to be bound here—six years—

ANSELMA, *the Baron's sister, over forty, still beautiful, enters
from the left. At the same time, TWO MAIDSERVANTS enter
from the right with a large quantity of lilac branches.*

ANSELMA What do you have there?
FIRST MAID   The lilacs, gracious Miss,
For the tower suite.
ANSELMA   Still more new branches?
SECOND MAID Yesterday's are no longer fresh enough.
ANSELMA *smiling* Thinks Leonilda.—Well, if our guest

Lets us wait much longer, and the lilacs
Meant to welcome him wilt every night,
Our park will soon appear no different
Than if a storm had raged through all the shrubs.
But run along, adorn both rooms and hall,
As the young lady bade.
The two maids go up the stairs to the gallery, then disappear
to the left through the door to the tower apartment.
ANSELMA *to the secretary* My brother makes
  You wait, Secretary.
SECRETARY   For the first time.
ANSELMA Surely the lovely morn keeps him outdoors.
  Well, you knew enough vexation in bygone
  Gloomy days. When our guest arrives at last
  And makes himself at home here for a while,
  You'll have more leisure then, I imagine.
  With a friendly greeting, exits right.

SECRETARY, DOMINIK

SECRETARY Whom does this flowery decor bid welcome?
DOMINIK A friend of the Baron's, who, as I hear,
  Was deemed vanished if not, in fact, deceased.
  No man of rank, his name is plainly—Thorn.
SECRETARY Sylvester Thorn?
DOMINIK   Sylvester, yes. You know him?
SECRETARY Only by name. You by sight, I suppose?
DOMINIK Perhaps, but then, perhaps not. How should I
  Recall everyone, both highborn and low,
  Who all these years—I've been in the Baron's
  Service a total now of seventeen—
  Has stepped across the threshold of his house,
  The more so when it was the Chancellor's house?
  Or how remember a thousand faces
  Fleetingly seen and then not seen for years
  Till scarce an echo of a name remains?
  Ah, what times were those, Secretary! My head
  Still spins when I think back. The anteroom
  Never bare of people. Every day filled—

Reception, audience, secret counsel, feasts—
His house was the very center of the world.
Now, deplorably, we exist at its edge.
SECRETARY Still, your Lord adapted excellently well.
DOMINIK You think so? You're mistaken. Whatever
The Baron does, he does only from boredom,
Whether he buries himself in his books
Alone, rushes his steed through the meadow,
Dictates from morning to night (no scrivener
Has yet endured but you, hence you are called
Secretary), or whether he—it's known
By everyone, else I'd not breathe a word—
Loses himself upon most secret paths—
His real purpose is only to kill time.
It's boredom, restlessness, perhaps despair.

The BARON ALBRECHT VON MAYENAU *enters with*
ANSELMA *from the right. He is a handsome man of fifty, with
a high forehead and a penetrating glance; he is wearing a
riding suit.*

BARON It's uncivil—
ANSELMA   His carriage lost a wheel
Perhaps.
BARON   And he could find no messenger!
ANSELMA
And if it were a whim. . . .
BARON *has stepped into the bay, lets the letters slip through
his hands as he glances at them*
                              From him, nothing.
DOMINIK *has helped the Baron take off his doublet and now
exits with it.*
*The two maidservants come down from the gallery carrying
wilted lilac branches.*
BARON *to Anselma* What are they carrying?
ANSELMA   Wilted lilacs,
Meant to bid your guest welcome yesterday.
His rooms have just been adorned with fresh ones
Again—Leonilda desired it thus.

BARON   Where is the child?
ANSELMA   She is already gone.
BARON   Into the garden?
ANSELMA   No.
BARON   I wonder, then—
   Could she have strolled out to meet our guest?
   The maidservants have exited to the left.
DOMINIK *enters from the left with a silk robe for the Baron.*
ANSELMA   As if we knew what road he's coming on.
BARON *lightly, to Anselma, while putting on the robe with
Dominik's help*
   Must Leonilda know? I have more faith
   In her intuition than in others'
   Certain knowledge.
DOMINIK *has exited.*
BARON *to the Secretary*   Ready?
ANSELMA   Brother, grant me
   One word before you begin.
BARON *a little surprised; then, to the Secretary*
                           Leave us alone.
   The Secretary exits.

BARON, ANSELMA

BARON   Anselma!—Well?—You're silent? You seem moved.
   He takes her hands.
   Sylvester?—His delay? His being near?—
   Is that it? *Suddenly* If he were coming for your sake—?!
ANSELMA   You're making me laugh, brother! I, and he. . . .
   How long ago that was—if it ever was!
   Do look at me. It often seems to me
   That only for you am I the little
   Sister still who has to be protected
   From all manner of perils, whether from
   Princes or from poets threatening me.
BARON   Anselma! Had I only not done so!
ANSELMA   You did right. I thank you for it. Enough.
   It's all so distant. Now others are young—
   Protecting those others may now be meet.

BARON What do you mean—others?—Leonilda!?—
ANSELMA Yes.
BARON   You believe—you find it possible—!
  But—just think, when Leonilda saw him last
  She was a child. The man whom she awaits
  In joyful anticipation, for whom
  She adorns both rooms and hall with lilac,
  Is surely not her groom of girlish dreams;
  No, he is her father's friend,—the first guest
  To step across the threshold of our house,
  Since her return home from the convent school.
ANSELMA That's just it. Whomever we awaited,
  She would adorn this house, adorn herself
  For him—and offer her young soul to him
  As welcome gift. Thus I wonder how smart
  It really was to take from the peaceful,
  Protective shelter of the convent, a child—
BARON Of nineteen—
ANSELMA   Precisely why I ask if
  You were smart to set her in an open
  World—riddles and temptations all around—
  Before a proper son-in-law was found.
BARON I'm not anxious about Leonilda.
  Her senses lie spread out to heaven itself,
  In childish clarity and piety.
ANSELMA You think her pious?
BARON   As I take it, sure.
  In the convent she was pious after
  The convent's fashion; differently here.
  Here is no need for confession or fast,
  Nor even for prayer upon one's knees.
  Look in her eyes, reflecting vast distances,
  When she comes home from her walk. Just listen
  To her voice's timbre, cheerfully light,
  When she tells what adventures befell her
  On her way: meetings with beetles, butterflies,
  A village chat, a talk with peasant children,—
  Watch her at play, listen to her questions,
  While she reads, observe her brow and take note

How wonderfully, smiling and serious,
Her young soul unfolds itself to the world—
Then judge whether her existence must not
Itself be deemed heavenly devotion.
ANSELMA But hardly the devotion of a child,
It seems to me, who yesterday was praying
Still in customary ways, ashiver
With the fervor of her imploration
To a great, exalted, faraway God.
I do not think a child breaks her habit
Of practicing this sort of piety
From one day to the next, nor dares approach
The eternal, incomprehensible
Deity far away from any altar.
BARON *ever more surprised*
Your words, Anselma—what have they to do
With Leonilda, with my child? Tell me
Everything you know.
ANSELMA *after a slight hesitation* What I saw last night—
And what I am convinced did not occur
For the first time last night—I can only
Describe as having spied Leonilda
At a divine service, albeit one
That did not seem altogether Christian.
I'd almost call it pagan; still, I have
No doubt—because I'd shudder even more
At any other interpretation—
That the secret sense of all her actions
Was devotional.
BARON   What was it you saw?
ANSELMA That often in sweltering summer nights,
She left her bed and room, on her balcony
To refresh herself in the nighttime breezes;
That sometimes she ran down the winding stairs
As well, into the garden, there to stroll
About alone in darkness and fragrance.
A light sleeper, I have long known all this.
But last night—say it was curiosity
That compelled me to follow her last night—

BARON *impatiently*
   Follow her where?
ANSELMA   Through the garden at first,
   Then through a small gate that shrub-entwined, near
   Invisible, opens out to the wood—
BARON What? She left the garden? Did you see right?—
ANSELMA
   Her white nightgown shimmered forth as she rushed
   Further along an unknown trail until
   She reached a secluded pond. I have not
   Found my way back there since I was a child
   And often thought I'd merely dreamt of it—
BARON Dreamt? Of what? Of that pool in the forest?
ANSELMA Of a green, iridescent giant's eye
   That from earth's bosom stares up to heaven
   As in eternal, painful wakefulness.
   There—
BARON There—?
ANSELMA Leonilda hastens away
   From me, glides off, vanishes from my sight
   In shadowy banks, until a short time
   Later, played upon by the evening wind
   And illuminated by the bright ring
   Of golden hair all around, her pale face
   Reappears in the middle of the pond.
   Then darkness swallows her up once again,
   And the waves' song, her hushed accompanist,
   Alone betrays her drawing nigh or far.
   Now dying away, now rushing up again—
   And then, gliding up, as if borne aloft,
   She is standing there, silvery upon
   A narrow strip of meadow, motionless
   In the moonlight. The blue drops run slowly
   Down along her body's length, a cool breath
   Of air caresses her, she feels it not.
   No muscle moves, marble her head and limbs
   For several minutes, till gradually
   One arm frees itself from her side and then
   The other, she lifts them, spreads them—a smile

Plays around her mouth; alien, full of pain,
It plays around her mouth,—her eyes, sightless
And vacant not a moment ago, find
A focus, an unwieldy block beneath
An oaken canopy, by moss overgrown,
Erected as a sacrificial stone
In primitive times—

BARON   If not set there by chance!
I see it still, a stone like thousands others—

ANSELMA To us, perhaps, but not to Leonilda.
For in the way she strides up to the block,
Her arms uplifted, her face ecstatic,
It's clear she thinks the stone a sacred relic.
And then, first slowly, then quick and quicker
Still, hair aflutter, she spins in whirling
Circles around the stone.

BARON *smiling*   Around the idol.

ANSELMA *serious* I nearly said so. Because as she lets
Herself sink down at last, stretches her limbs
On the grass, breathing free, like one redeemed—
It seems to me there flashed between the gray
And green—it was no trembling moonbeam's lie—
As if there flashed behind moss and stone—
She hesitates

BARON What flashed?

ANSELMA It was no human visage that I saw.
Still, whatever it was, it made itself known.
And if it was no eye, no human eye,
Still, I saw it shine through the ritual night
Like a glance that with ironic pity
Embraced a lovely, naked human child
Who blinking sleepily, flamed with foreboding,
Gave herself to the glance of the god.

BARON   Well—
And?

ANSELMA Is it not enough? If you had seen
How lovely she was and how she knew it,
And how intoxicated by that knowledge,
And doubly drunk because a god saw her—

BARON *quickly* Let Leonilda relish her beauty,
   And the gods be made glad by their looking,
   They are immortal, mute, and used to it—
   And thus is Leonilda thrice cleansed of sin.
   No other saw her. No one knows the gate,
   No one the trail on which you followed her,
   And there's no second way leads to the pond.
ANSELMA She is your child.
BARON   She is my daughter, yes.
   And grows to womanhood, like other maids.
   Let us not forget that. The bonds of blood
   Too easily cloud our sight.
   Warning   Don't ever
   Rouse up her mind from its innocent state.
   And let her never learn, swear this to me,
   That her secret is known to both of us.
ANSELMA Nor let us speak another word of it.
BARON What else is there to say? That I know it,
   Is good. I thank you.
ANSELMA *after an almost imperceptible hesitation*
                Good luck with your work. *Exits.*
The Secretary enters immediately upon Anselma's departure,
as if he had merely been waiting for it. He enters the bay,
ready to work; the Baron has remained standing, lost in
thought. The Secretary then makes his presence known by a
slight clearing of his throat.
BARON Where did we stop?
SECRETARY   How Your Grace's late father—
BARON *interrupting* Yes, I know. How father took me, a boy
   Of ten, to Court for the first time. Read aloud
   To me so I can find the context again.
SECRETARY *reads* "Thus I stood before the Imperial Prince.
   His boyish brow, in flowing blond hair framed—
   Pale and serious—all too serious almost
   For his years—he counted but twelve, as I—
   Welcomed me—for the first time so near him—
   With the brilliance of inborn majesty.
   And as he, gracious, not without a smile,
   Yet with princely gesture, offered me his hand

To kiss, and I bowed to brush it softly
With my lips, my heart swelled—and not alone
With love for my lord's son, this handsome lad
Whose school- and playmate I was ordained to be,
No, with humility too. . ."
BARON *interrupts him*   Humility?!
I said that?
SECRETARY *continues reading*
". . . before the wonderful child
Whom my destiny. . ."
BARON *interrupts him, lightly*
                              Write "God," it's all one.
SECRETARY *continues reading*
"Selected as my future Emperor."
BARON Humility?—The word rings false. Father
Never taught me that. Mayenau Castle
Towered proudly upon this spot, the same
As Ursenbeck's on the river bank across
The way, before, nine hundred years ago,
The ancestor of my Imperial Lord
Wandered from his wild mountainous country
Abode down to the sun-drenched plain below.
He holds the pages in his hand, thinking.
This too must be written, it seems to me—
As well as a number of other things
Which took place along the banks of this stream
During the course of these nine hundred years.
But it almost appears that to reveal
The hidden meaning of my life's story
I would have to start at the world's first day
And conclude there, where my world fell apart.
Pulling himself together
But it has not done so yet. Continue!
SECRETARY *reading* "And thus, myself a boy as yet, I took
A vow in this hour—to serve this boy
Who would one day wear the crown of this realm,
With body and soul, being and estate,
In good times and bad, with truest devotion."
BARON And kept the vow, if not as a courtier,

Then as a man.
To the Secretary Don't write. I want to tell
The tale, and not be lawyer, plaintiff, judge.
Should I begin to sound like one—I know
You're clever enough to tell if I do—
Leave your pen at rest.

The door to the right opens, LEONILDA *appears carrying a large bunch of wildflowers, and, seeing her father at work, is about to disappear again right away.*

BARON	What news?
LEONILDA	Forgive me,

I didn't know—
BARON   Do come closer, my child,
   As long as you're here, I'll have to suffer it.
   To the Secretary
   We'll stop for today.
   The Secretary quickly orders the papers on the desk and exits.
                    From where—? But I see. . . .
   Pointing to the flowers
   These grow only out on the hunter's plain.
LEONILDA I picked them on my way back, but I was
   In the village first.
BARON   With your little friends?
LEONILDA And who might they be?—
BARON   Well, the teacher's
   blond sons,
   The meadow-keeper's girls, Catherine, Marie,
   The forester's Ulrich—
LEONILDA *smiling*   You know all the names?
BARON Naturally! They are your playfellows.
LEONILDA There was no occasion for play today.
   I spoke to the meadow-keeper himself,
   And to the teacher, too—
BARON   Isn't he keeping school?
LEONILDA Nobody in the village is attending
   To his business today. The people stand
   Together, old and young, before their doors,

Depressed, excited.

BARON What happened?

LEONILDA You don't
Know as yet?—At break of day a courier
From court rode full speed through the village—

BARON And?

LEONILDA A courier with orders for the Marshal.

BARON Surely that's normal, since Marshal Ursenbeck
Is at the border with an advance troop.

LEONILDA But this time the order is to attack!

BARON You don't say! And from where do you know this?

LEONILDA Everyone is saying so. A rumor
Arrived here from the capital last night.

BARON Who brought it?

LEONILDA A rider in black who drank
A mug of wine at the meadow-keeper's,
Remounted quickly, and was gone again.

BARON I believe the rider, and the mug of wine.

LEONILDA And not the courier from court?

BARON The order,
Even, although I assume it was sealed.
How, then, is one to know what it contained?

LEONILDA What else can it be but the decision?

BARON The decision—war?

LEONILDA Don't you yourself think so?

BARON *reflecting* The order to attack?—Possibly—all
The more since the right moment has been missed.
Because the Emperor's resolve vacillates,
Blown along, helpless, by each passing whiff
Of air, between too early and too late.
So it was, and is, and will ever be.

LEONILDA And what, if he asked you at this moment,
Would you advise?

BARON I don't know, nor have I
Any further cause to think about it.

LEONILDA Is it not the fate of your fatherland
That is at stake here?

BARON The fate of his realm.

LEONILDA Is it not the same, fatherland and realm?

BARON It could be. It should be. It's that whereby
　A sovereign's greatness makes itself known:
　If a feeling for both takes shape within
　His subjects' hearts, and a concept of both
　Takes shape in their minds. Enough of that, now.
　Breaking off, quickly
　And these flowers—you picked them for our guest?
LEONILDA Am I not right? Was not Sylvester Thorn
　The dearest to you among all your friends?
BARON *after reflecting briefly*
　I esteemed him.—Yet that was long ago.
　I am surprised that you still think of him,
　And that you can still recall his features.
LEONILDA Recollection? How little that would be—
　He lives in me.
BARON　　　　　　Your face is all aglow—
　What ails you, child?—When I see you like this
　I almost fear for you.
　In response to her glance
　　　　　　　　That he who comes
　May be a different man from the one
　You are expecting; and that you be kept
　By pride from realizing it at once.
LEONILDA The same returns who left ten years ago.
BARON A man in the last splendor of youth left.
　But evening already casts the early
　Shadows of decline on him who returns.
LEONILDA The man I speak of, father, does not age
　Any more than youth ever beamed forth from him.
　For just as the wisdom of the ancients
　Glimmered deep in his eyes back then—as if
　He had already lived a hundred lives—
　So today—even in his aged glance,
　That glad smile of youth will be clearly written
　Which brightened my heart through these many years
　Since the evening he departed.
BARON　　　　　　　　　　You think
　Of that evening still?
LEONILDA　　　　　Your farewells floated

Like steam in the room and fell on your words'
Otherwise so free-flying give-and-take
As on swords clashing muffled in the fog.
And as out of a fog echoed the song
Which his best beloved, playing soft upon
The spinnet, sang in her dark voice.
BARON   You still
Think of her too?
LEONILDA   She was very lovely,
Yet her smile was hard, and angry her glance.
BARON Did you see her so? I found her eye clear,
Her smile as pleasing as the world demands
Of women who upon the stage display
The gift of their talents, in song or dance,
And offer it to the masses for gain.
LEONILDA I wonder if he'll bring her.
BARON   Ha! The idea!
Her name still resounds loudly through the world,
While his own is long since in stillness wrapped.
And you will sooner find hate and love, life
And death walking down the street together
Than these two: obsolescence and renown.
He comes alone—has been so all these years
And wished to be—alone and far from home.
LEONILDA Unhappy lot!
BARON   By him chosen. Never
Was he banished.
LEONILDA   Persecuted—?
BARON   He was
Never threatened by any serious dangers,
And he had friends of sufficient power
To turn them all away in any case.
LEONILDA People hurt him.
BARON   The world just paid him back
In somewhat coarser form the bold derision
With which he vexed it.
LEONILDA   From a noble heart.
BARON Indeed, but one made dark by bitterness.
If not by hate.

LEONILDA *shaking her head* He hated—?
BARON   This country,
  Which, of course, scarce understood him as he
  Deserved.
LEONILDA And yet he never wished it ill.
BARON *smiling* This too you know?
LEONILDA   I feel it. He was misjudged
  If not by a prince, yet by a people.

KONRAD VON URSENBECK, *twenty-one years old, a captain
in field uniform, enters from the right.* LEONILDA, BARON

KONRAD Forgive me for entering unannounced.
BARON *amazed* Konrad von Ursenbeck?
KONRAD   Himself, Herr Chancellor.
  My mission's urgency must plead for me.
BARON I'm no Chancellor, as you know.
KONRAD   Colonel, then.
BARON And that still less. Your cousin, if you wish,
  Since we are kin through our great-grandmothers.
KONRAD Uncle, then—
BARON   Good, as befits my gray hair.
KONRAD So I'll greet Leonilda as cousin.
LEONILDA Welcome, cousin.
KONRAD   You've become a young lady
  Since we set our colored feather balls flying,
  And pretty too.
LEONILDA *teasing* Your mission is that urgent?
KONRAD *smiling* That was by the by.
BARON   You come from the army?
KONRAD From the Marshal, my father.
BARON   And headed?
KONRAD To court. But with orders to deliver
  A message from my father on the way.
  Gives him the letter.
BARON *astonished* From the Marshal—for me?
LEONILDA *turning to leave*   See you later.
KONRAD Perhaps.
LEONILDA   At table, surely.

KONRAD   I must be off.
  Still, I'll stop on my way back if I can,
  My pretty cousin, to fetch your blessing.
LEONILDA It would have little power. Bon voyage.
  Exits left.

BARON, KONRAD

BARON *having read the letter, after brief reflection*
  So, to the Emperor?
KONRAD   Yes, the third time
  In seven weeks and with the same message.
BARON Do you know what this letter says?
KONRAD   Insofar,
  Uncle—
  interrupts himself, continues with spirit
       Allow me, please, to call you Colonel,
  Since you were one.
BARON   That's long ago.
KONRAD   And fought—
  Father told me the tale often enough—
  Alongside His Majesty on that day—
BARON *warding him off* A day far back.
KONRAD *noticing the Baron's gesture, as if to himself*
            I suppose it must be.
  A short pause.
BARON Your road was long, be seated!
  Offers him a seat.
KONRAD *sits down*   A short rest.
  Three hours of hard riding lie ahead
  If I would reach the city in good time.
DOMINIK *enters.*
BARON Bring wine!
DOMINIK *exits.*
KONRAD   Only if you join me, Uncle,
  Come with me to court, as my father hopes,
  May I allow myself such a delay.
  Pause.
BARON *walks back and forth in thought, then*

How long have you been at the border now?

KONRAD Should one count according to weeks, or days,
To whom the minutes are eternities?

BARON You're setting your watch by your impatience.

KONRAD You would do the same in my position.
We marched southward on a roadway frozen
Solid. Now the country is in blossom.
And had not—inconceivably!—our steps
Been halted by the Emperor's command,
We would have, months ago, boldly passing
Our neighbor's barely guarded posts—stood so wide
Upon his springtime plain that he'd have heard
Our victor's fanfare all around—even
Before he'd gathered his host to resist.

BARON *calmly* It would have been a sneak attack, and theft.

DOMINIK *has brought wine, the Baron pours, Dominik exits
again.*

BARON *drinks to Konrad.*

KONRAD *pledges to the Baron*
Theft, you say? Theft, Uncle, of a country
That after all was ours thirty years ago—?

BARON And eighty years ago, theirs.

KONRAD   And whose, then,
Three-hundred years ago, or a thousand?
And for whom was it determined by God?

BARON You'll fast reach the end of all questions thus.

KONRAD Of you I ask but one. Will you come with me?

BARON What should I. . .there?

KONRAD *indicating the letter which the Baron is still holding
in his hand*   It's written there.

BARON *with growing agitation, but controlled* I think
Your father has slept the past seven years
Away, because that, almost to the day,
Is how long it has been—don't you know that?—
Since I've had no more to do with Emperor,
Court, and realm than any other persons,
Be they resident in castles or huts.

KONRAD Nonetheless, for twenty years you were Chancellor
Of the realm and Emperor's friend.

BARON   That office—
  As the Marshal too well knows—is today
  Managed by another man—by the third
  As I'm told, since my leaving.
KONRAD   The Chancellor's
  Office—but the friend's—
BARON   Were that an office,—
  Where lives the Prince rich enough to pay it?
KONRAD No office, but yet a mission.
BARON   Well said.
  And if it was one, I have fulfilled it.
KONRAD Not to the end.
BARON   Above and beyond it—!
  For much earlier, shyly at first, and then
  Purposely, the King shut his mind to me—
  As if memories of oft and gladly
  Followed advice tortured him like unpaid
  Debts, or as if he were ashamed of words
  That had flowed from heart to heart, soul to soul;
  Or rued his gift of princely confidence
  Which I received as freely as he offered
  It to me ever since our youthful days.
  And yet, the more mute he grew towards me,
  The deeper bored my eye into the core
  Of his being. I saw how somber haste
  Masked itself as urge to action, the lack
  Of resolution as judicious forethought,
  Weakness as benevolence, exhausted,
  Enervated hatred as righteousness.
  And what the world saw fit to praise as love
  Of fellow man, was in the pained, scornful
  Smile about his mouth and his dark glances
  Revealed to me as scarce controlled disgust.
  Still, I grew only more deeply attached
  To him for his troubled heart's sake; but he—
  As if I'd pried a secret from him—turned
  Away from me ungraciously, a stranger.
  And because, by envious courtiers flattered,
  The mood of even a noble prince learns

Soon to assume the lineaments of just wrath,
There came the day—and an occasion too—
Your grandchildren shall read it chronicled,
I've forgotten it myself—came the day
On which the King showed his Chancellor, the lord
His servant, one friend the other, the door.

KONRAD You know he regrets it.

BARON   I have no doubt.

KONRAD Your place has been unfilled since you left court—
Despite three chancellors—and His Majesty,
Lonely, peevish, weak, listening to all men,
All men mistrusting, despising everyone
Together with, it seems at times, himself.
You are—everyone agrees—strong enough,
You, the only man to save the realm—and him.

BARON And if—as I fear—what you, the Marshal,
And the army long for as salvation
Strikes me as unconducive to the nation's
Health?—
In response to a movement from Konrad
            And believe me: had I stayed at court,
Your father, instead of swinging his rusty
Sword again in battle, a gray-haired man,
Would in the gladness of former triumphs
Look calmly down from his castle, over
The peacefully blossoming countryside
Where free from care and looming misery
The farmer works for him, for us, for all.

KONRAD That is the peasant's charge—ours, to watch
That our hostile neighbor not disturb him.

BARON Nothing could have been further from his mind.
In this neighbor you have awakened now
The enemy from sleep of many years.
Who bid you approach his border threatening?

KONRAD The Emperor, as you know.

BARON   But who was
It tricked the order from His Majesty?
Your party, for whom war endows the world
With meaning, because only in war can

You find your self-fulfillment; not so much
Your father, as those around him who lust
Still after untasted glories, no matter
If thousands of others, lacking glory,
Unrewarded, guiltless, must also pay.
You, Konrad, I mean you too.
KONRAD   I hope so.
But I was not admitted to those councils
Where either war or peace are decided.
And it may very well be true—my judgment
Is not certain on the point—that our
March south this winter was precipitate
And ordered without justification.
But I am sure that hesitation now,
Though it cannot make just an unjust act,
Will, however, turn our heroic show
Of arms to empty threats of children's fists.
BARON They—on the other side—hesitate too.
KONRAD They are only waiting until the sun
Calls the sinister fever spirits up
From out of the green swamps of their country
As confederates against our forces.
BARON The spirits lie asleep.
KONRAD   Their breath, however,
Has arrived, exhausting body and soul.
BARON Yours, I see, have both remained uninjured.
KONRAD Only since I rode away do I know
Myself again, but there were times—and not
For me alone—when we felt the poison
Creep gradually into our veins. Every
Effort—riding to horse, officially
Or for pleasure, drinking or casting dice—
Took place as in a dream. We did not live—
We lingered merely. Our weapons' flashing,
Else the brilliant welcome of longed-for battle,
Was an empty light show; their clanging—else
Most precious music to us—senseless noise.
And our hate, born of red hot flame, fizzles
Out to ashen sparks of faint mockery

When blown by winds from the enemy's tents.
A coarse jest comes back from the other side.
Laughing applause resounds in our ranks—
From theirs, bright singing arises—our men
Listen—begin to hum—then sing along—
Until finally—as if not deadly
Foes, armed to the teeth, lay across from each
Other, but variously uniformed men
Of one host awaiting gladsome war games—
A joint song resounds up to heaven.

BARON So, what you call the spirit of fever
Shows its might on the other side as well.

KONRAD But they're accustomed to its hellish breath.
It would not take many more nights like that
For their advantage to grow measureless.
And since we tarry and leave them the choice,
They will know how to use it against us
At the right moment, in terrible ways.

BARON I don't believe in spirits.

KONRAD   So call them
Something else. I know what happened to me.

BARON I'm sure you didn't sing along.

KONRAD   What I did
Was far worse than to join in the singing.

BARON *teasing* What—worse still?

KONRAD   Only now I realize
How far out of my mind I was. You know
That between our two countries runs a brook,
A temporary border, dividing
The two camps, wide in spring, but towards summer
Daily thinner in its narrowing bed.
And there, where I stand watch with my company,
The sand swallows it up so that both banks,
Drawing ever nearer, are banks no more
But rather neighboring paths through the reeds;
And as I wander up and down one evening,
It happens that across the way a youth
Strolls about—on his watch or to enjoy
The solitude merely, and the quiet—

Of my age and rank, but in his country's
Colors, naturally. Now, heaven knows,
Or maybe hell, which one of us two first
Inclined his head in greeting, or uttered
A word; but nonetheless, with that first word—
Perhaps I spoke it—as a flock, released
From bondage, breathing free at last, pours through
The gate left open by its drunken keeper,
So a forceful stream of delivered words
Broke forth through my lips and his. And since then,
In many an hour, both day and night,
As we wander through the reeds during watch,
Greetings, questions, and answers go flying
Back and forth, and our conversation
Spins itself out with no hesitation,
Trusting and cheerful above the dry stream
That fabricates a border at our feet.

BARON And what sorts of things do you talk about?

KONRAD As young people do—of hunting, women—

BARON *smiling* No state secrets, exactly.

KONRAD   Of boys' games.

BARON They do not lie all that far in your past.

KONRAD Of home, parents—his mother is still alive.

BARON *somewhat surprised* Does he know that you are the
 Marshal's son?

KONRAD What do you think!? I never told my name
 Nor he his.

BARON   Needless precaution, almost.
 No war has been declared. And no one keeps
 The chancellors or ambassadors of both
 Countries from conversing in neighborly
 Friendship as you did.

KONRAD *as with resolve*

                     So let me finish:
 As I bid him farewell before departing,
 My father's letter safe in my doublet—
 What could have come over me! I opened
 Wide my arms—pulled him to my heart—and we
 Held each other close, like friends—like brothers.

BARON As nobles should, even before a joust.
KONRAD Well said, dear Uncle. Your words have calmed
   me,
   Even if that was not your intention.
   His trick is spent. And I don't wish to meet
   Him face to face again until—to atone
   For my disgrace in blood—I may and must
   Do so with drawn sword. Help me to do it!
   It's not a matter of this sword, merely
   One of a thousand, just as my voice speaks
   For a thousand others whom you don't hear.
   And if you mistrust them and mistrust me,
   As one who may be too young and foolish,
   Who is tempted by danger and adventure—
   Speaks not this letter loud enough? My father—
   You know him—no fool, a youth no longer,
   Has had his fill of glory and battle,
   And knows as I and thousands others do,
   That with every day or hour we delay
   A bad outcome for us grows more certain.
BARON I read the Marshal's reasons and doubt not
   That he stated them even more clearly
   In that other letter for the Emperor
   You carry in your belt than in the one
   To me. And even if all his reasons
   Struck me as being beyond argument,
   Yet could I only echo them dimly.
KONRAD Come with me anyway, and speak, and spare
   Me thus the need to lay before the court
   My father's letter—*hesitating*
                  in which, should he fail
   For yet a third time to receive orders
   For prompt attack, his office he resigns.
BARON *perplexed* And—then?
KONRAD   We will see.
BARON   Say it.
KONRAD   The army
   Is my father's, if he wants it.
BARON *almost threatening*   You mean?

KONRAD But he doesn't. You've heard of his attempts
  To remain his Emperor's true servant.
BARON He threatens him.
KONRAD   No, he gives him a choice.
BARON And if the Emperor decide against him?
KONRAD The army will decide for the Marshal.
BARON Revolt?
KONRAD Obedience. But to the right Lord.
BARON The Emperor is Lord.
KONRAD   If he give commands.
BARON That he will do.
KONRAD   God willing, the right one.
  Herr Chancellor, help in it, and come with me!
DOMINIK *opens the door right in which Sylvester Thorn
  appears.*

    Curtain—which goes up again immediately.

SECOND ACT

BARON, KONRAD. SYLVESTER THORN *enters.*

THORN Am I still welcome?
BARON *joyfully*　　　　　You're here, finally!
THORN My friend!
BARON　　　　　Heartfelt welcome to Mayenau!
　They shake hands heartily, but do not embrace.
BARON *introducing* Konrad von Ursenbeck.
THORN　　　　　　　　　Is it possible?—
　The Marshal's son?
　Extending his hand to him
　I am Sylvester Thorn.
KONRAD *a bit puzzled*
　You are—?
BARON *laughing*
　　　　I will vouch for it.
KONRAD　　　　　　Pardon me—
　I didn't know that he—you, were still alive.
BARON *to Thorn* A doubt that we all shared with him until
　The morning three days past when your message
　Informed us of your early arrival.
　Already so near—and still you delayed?!
THORN Forgive me. Instead of the fast coach, which
　Though speedy, always moved me to impatience,
　I chose to saunter hither through the spring,
　Lazily crossing the paths of my youth.
BARON Quick, Dominik, another glass!
DOMINIK *exits.*
THORN　　　　　　　　　　Thank you.
　I'm scarcely thirsty. The shade in your woods
　Is moist and cool as ever. And your meadows
　Still give off the fragrance of dew-drenched flowers.
　And sharp as ever blows the wind of home.
　My home's meadow and wood and wind as well.
DOMINIK *who has brought the extra glass, exits.*
BARON Well, then, to your homecoming this first glass!

To Konrad
Clink glasses with us in your father's name,
Who oft caroused with us in younger days,
Bring him the news, Thorn has come home.
KONRAD   Nothing else?
BARON Yes: a friend's greeting.
KONRAD   For my father.—But
For the Marshal?
BARON *hesitating slightly* Nothing more. . . .
KONRAD *formally* Farewell, Uncle!
Excuse me, Herr Thorn.
THORN   I fear my arrival
Interrupted your talk.
KONRAD   It had ended.
Urgent business calls me to the city.
BARON You still have time to drink your wine with us.
THORN The city lies near. How often I rode
From Mayenau along the river's course.
With a glance outside.
I sense it there, in the gray distant haze—
With gloomy streets, encircled by bastions,
And somewhere, there, what used to be my house—
KONRAD You once had a house in the capital?
THORN I did, until they drove the stranger out.
KONRAD *astonished*
As a stranger?—You?—Out of your own house?
THORN *with bitter contempt*
Merely what I deserved, since my mother's
Great-grandfather moved here from a foreign
Country.
KONRAD From an—enemy?
THORN   In the course
Of centuries, at times an enemy.
Foreign, at any rate. And if the people
Wish, as you well know, foreign means hated,
Vulgar, base.
KONRAD   Your mother's great-grandfather?
THORN *with a bitter laugh*
Great-great-grandfather. Still, once a foreigner,

Always a foreigner.
KONRAD   Is there a law
That an established, a deserving man,
With no cause save that his mother's ancestor—
BARON *interrupting, to Sylvester*
Do not bewilder this young man's clear mind.
No one drove you out. And had anyone
But tried something of the sort, both the law
And all your friends as well were strong enough
To protect you.
THORN   I asked for no help.
BARON *teasing lightly*   No,
Of course not. It is well known you preferred
Once, when the mob marched past, to fling open
Your window and so to expose yourself
To their howling.
THORN   I still hear it today.
BARON And it had stopped even before the watch
Appeared.
THORN   Yes it had, until the next time,
For which I had no desire to wait;—
For ugly shrieks of fury as little
As for gentle calls of consolation,
For hostile fists clenched in anger no more
Than for friendly arms raised to rescue me.
I almost think I was in greater haste
To escape my supporters, who flattered
Me without understanding, than those dull,
Blameless haters. But be that as it may,
I threw off with pleasure the laughable
Tinsel of fame, deceitfully woven
Of equal parts of honor and abuse.
Only one thing enticed me: to escape
Both friend and foe in twilight of oblivion.
BARON Much as you succeeded in expunging
All living traces of yourself—you know,
You remained in the thoughts of many.
THORN   Yes,
As dead, and so I was.—Having escaped

Myself, I wandered, through a cool, clear world—
One unclouded by demands—a new man.
Landscapes in their essential fruitfulness
Bloomed and faded around me as I passed,
Yet none assailed my heart obtrusively.
I met people in this new world as well,
Under circumstances immensely varied,
Unusual and common—men and women,
With a childlike seriousness acting out
The eternal plays of life for their cheerful,
Undisturbed minds—yet not one demanded:
Poet, create imitations of us
And explain what he who created us
Before you did wanted with us. And thus
I glided over foreign soil, not held
Fast anywhere by strength of roots, a guest
Yet free.
BARON   And were you happier than here?
THORN   Wishless, and obligated to myself
   Alone, I was well.
BARON   I seem to recall,
   In the old days, your being, if not richer,
   Yet surely more prodigal.
THORN   Like a fool.
BARON   Who in his foolishness was dear to me.
THORN   So prepare yourself to love me anew.
   He who returns remains the fool of yore.
BARON   Free and wise only in a foreign land?
   I must ask you, then, if you consider
   The cost of your return so excessive,
   Why've you come back?
THORN   Don't I ask myself that?
   Did I not, for ten years, inhale the sharp
   Foreign air more lightly than I ever
   Breathed my homeland's? Did I ever look back?
   Or wish to surface from the oblivion
   Into which I had so happily sunk?
   When, then, did I first hear that word—stranger—
   That I wanted never to hear again?

Or feel the peril which would not apply
To me, threatening stormlike overhead?
What could malicious jabber mean to me
There, in a land, where rootless and unknown,
I dwelt now in this place, now in that;
What could curses and hostility mean,
Directed against a neighboring country,
One like many others, with mountains, streams,
With fields, pastures, towns, villages and marts,
With people, good and bad, beasts tame and wild,
And different from all others only
In the fact that my cradle stood there once?
Whence came it that the soil beneath my feet,
Where I had passed ten years unmolested—
Soil everywhere familiar to my step—
Should all of a sudden become foreign?
What was it that drove me like one expelled
And persecuted out of a region
I had thought safe, onward, ever further,
To where, through valleys and over mountains,
The border, that grand creation of man,
Cuts across God's good earth, invisible,
But nonetheless with bloody pen engraved?
Still, when after my secret, hurried trek—
For mistrust watched over here the same as there—
I stood breathing free like one who has reached
His destination—I felt the foreignness
In my heart again, nothing else, as if
The fatherland had no desire to greet
The returnee with even the humblest
Of welcomes. Yes, for a number of days
Yet, I wandered thus, through an alien world,
No less alien than the one whence I came,
Engulfed by noises I could not make out,
Echoing from distant, colorless streets—
Till gradually, from that riotous sound
Voices close by, ever closer, broke free,
And the grayish overcast all around
Brightened to ever livelier colors;

Then I knew—as if a fog had been torn
Suddenly asunder—that only now
Had I crossed the truly valid border—
Not the transitory one which the luck
Of battle or the mere whim of a prince
Measures boldly out in space—no, the one
Indelible for all eternity
That has burned its brand in my longing heart.
Because this was home, now, no fatherland,
Nor a prince's chance realm which tomorrow
May be as decayed as it was yesterday.
Now it was first my home surrounding me,
This little bit of earth belonging to me,
As I to it, no matter who its prince.
And if all the people living here from
Earliest days screamed curses in my face—
And even if they erected a stake
To burn me, neither their threats nor their hate
Could ever again confound this feeling.
You, earth, know I grew from you; you, heaven,
That you shine down on my home. And I am
No depraved soul who draws breath between you.
He stands in the bay looking out at the landscape. Pause.
BARON *approaches him, softly puts his hand on Thorn's*
shoulder, smiling.
No stake burns in this country now—surely
Not for you.
THORN *still without turning around*
     Please forgive me, I was moved.
Turns to Konrad
You too—forgive me—
KONRAD *somewhat embarrassed*
       I have to thank you.
So exalted a flow of words—believe me—
We never hear that around our campfires. *Pause.*
But now—I have to go.
BARON   Konrad—
KONRAD   Uncle—
Have you anything else to say to me?

BARON I hope that if you come back tomorrow,
  You will stop to rest in my house again.
KONRAD Thank you, but the road along the river
  Leads quickest to the army. I must take it. *Exits.*

BARON, THORN

THORN Surely, I arrived at a bad time.
BARON   Quite
  The right time; now let me embrace you at last.
THORN The lad who just left, it appears, is one
  In front of whom our greeting thus would seem
  Improper. Still, I liked him.
BARON   Let's let him
  Be on his way.
DOMINIK *enters with a small traveling bag.*
BARON *to Dominik*
                     To the tower with that;—
  And also with whatever else there is—
THORN There is nothing else. All my other things
  I left at home.
DOMINIK *exits.*
BARON *suprised* At home?
THORN   Let me explain.
  There is a house, which I left this morning,
  Standing in a quiet, wood-ringed meadow,
  Where by happy chance I came upon it—
  Of late my home, soon my property.
BARON   What—?
  So quickly back to solitude again!
THORN I spoke of quiet, not of solitude.
BARON So you are not alone?—Yes, if I read
  Your smile aright—married even?
THORN   I'm not
  That far just yet. But soon.
BARON   So, home has snared
  You right away with its strongest magic?
  Right? Or did you bring a foreign woman?
THORN Neither. You know the woman I've chosen.

Alberta will be my wife.
BARON   What? Alberta?
  To whom you said farewell before my eyes?
  Farewell forever, as it seemed?
THORN   Forever—
  But not for the last time. From year to year,
  Emerging from this adventure or that,
  Untouched by pain inflicted or suffered,
  We found each other again with renewed
  Longing after old and new tenderness
  And torture, fate's predetermined couple,
  Always, after an interval of bliss,
  To part anew.
BARON   You know that so well
  And still seriously consider marriage?
THORN   The storms, and youth, are past. A year ago,
  When after a longer separation
  Than any before, I found her again,
  It happened that the applause of her rapt
  Listeners for her singing had resounded
  For the final time. The fact that I, led
  By chance alone to that very city,
  Was in the audience on that very day—
  We both received it as a sign from fate.
  She stepped freely, from unfaded splendor,
  Into the long-yearned for obscurity,
  Threw herself into my arms—like a bride—
  Redeemed; we enjoyed the peace we had not
  Had before—heart to heart, and soul to soul.
  And now, our later union was granted
  What we never prayed for in the fullness
  Of youth. I've made a home in my homeland
  Not just for her and me, but for the child
  We expect before the new moon as well.
BARON   Be thrice welcome, then, here in this country.
  Only now, moved that you have found your way
  To your old friend at such a time, can I
  Forgive you for not wanting to stay long.
THORN   You know how gladly I came. But let me

Confess at once that it was not longing
To see my friend alone that drew me here.
BARON   Others here in this house as well, rejoice
 At your arrival. But, loath to disturb
 Our talk, they keep, modestly albeit
 Impatiently, to their rooms. I'll call them.
THORN   Not yet. I feel the need, before greeting them,
 To tell you the reason for my coming.
 In response to the Baron's look of astonishment
 The—other reason, I mean—which may seem
 Strange to you at first glance. *Explaining*
        Before leaving,
 I handed to you what I, in the course
 Of many years, had daily recorded
 In a secret book—In the deep slumber
 Of half-forgotten words my youth reposes
 Safely here in this castle. I have come
 To hold a dialogue with it—at last.
BARON *cool*
 You have come for that? The book is sealed shut.
 I would have sent it to you by safe courier.
THORN   I've come not to fetch—but—to destroy it.
 In response to the Baron's surprised look
 Today, for one last time, I'll conjure up
 My youth, from sleep-entwined pages, harrow
 It out of my mind's eye to stand in the light.
 And, having served its purpose, page for page,
 It shall be turned to ash, lest so dangerous
 A game tempt me again.
BARON   Will memory
 Stop glowing just because the word is burned?
THORN   What is memory?—An intangible
 Shapelessness between nothing and something;
 And like sand on the beach, under constant
 Threat from waves and new life-floods.—However,
 As the sculptor's hand holds fast and shapes dust
 Which else would blow away, the word likewise,
 With its magical dexterity joins
 What is past and passing into one, and,

If it came from a fulfilled soul, transforms
Them to overwhelming reality.
BARON   And your book contains such overwhelming
Reality?
THORN That may very well be.
My question is, what if I am tempted
In the future, as I am now, to measure
Who I am by who I was—and the past,
As mirrored in the youthful clarity
Of my words, prove more alive than the present?
That is what worries me.
BARON   And if this game
Seem so perilous to you, why risk it?
THORN   Today I'm still assured of victory,
But will I be next year? Or tomorrow?
Therefore, let it be read today—and burned.
BARON   Well, since you're in such a rush to perform
Your exorcism, let both sacrifice
And altar be prepared immediately.
Anselma has kept your book. She'll place
It in your hands at once. In the meantime,
To help your weighty words of foreboding
Turn more quickly to lighter truth—I'll see
That the stake is readied.
THORN   Go on, tease me.
BARON   I know you, my friend—until you've obeyed
The dark compulsion hanging over you
You will be lost to us other mortals.
Therefore, let the unavoidable task
Be performed first, that we may all savor
Gladly our friend's company, and he ours.

LEONILDA *enters, carrying lilac branches.*   BARON, THORN

LEONILDA   Not I, but the blossoms grew impatient.
Many waited for you and had to wither—
These chose for themselves a happier fate.
THORN   Anselma?
BARON   Does the magic start before

The book is unsealed? Yes, had Anselma
Traversed so many years against the flow
Ordained for humankind as Leonilda
Passed according to the unhappy law,
They might well look like twin sisters today.
THORN Is it possible—your daughter?
BARON *to Leonilda*   Look at him—
He's barely thought of us for many years,
And should you think that now he's here, with us—
Then you'd be wrong. That will take a while yet.
Just don't flatter yourself that you exist. *He exits.*

LEONILDA, THORN

LEONILDA How puzzling.—What did father mean to say?
THORN No puzzle, simply a jest. I'm here now.
You've grown very pretty, Leonilda.
LEONILDA I have already been told that today.
You say it differently.
THORN   Well, then, I see
You've remained pretty, Leonilda.
LEONILDA And remained the same otherwise as well.
THORN You were a child when I saw you last.
LEONILDA And
Look forward today to the fairy tales
That you will tell me, as you did back then.
THORN I told you fairy tales?
LEONILDA   Have you forgotten?
THORN *shaking his head*
No, no—fairy tales were never my thing.
LEONILDA *disappointed*
You don't remember? We strolled hand in hand
In the sultry summer shade of garden
Walks, the fragrance of burning flower beds
All around. *Glances out through the bay*
            The others slept in the cool house—
The day slept—the world—we two were awake.
I listened. You told.
THORN *remembering*

                    Fairy tales, yes, which
I recalled because you wished to hear them—
Where are they gone now?!
LEONILDA   I still know them all—
Not in words, yet much better than in words.
They go on dreaming mutely in my soul.
How else would I ever have known, Sylvester,
Who you are?
THORN *smiling* I suppose they spoke of me
In this house occasionally?
LEONILDA   Of you?—
Of one whose name had been Sylvester Thorn—
And of his works. Still, when I took them out
Of my father's bookcase to read, I soon
Realized that he who had conceived them
Was a different man than you. It would have
Hurt me to believe that one who wasted
His heart thus, with mere earthly love and hate,
Who, devoid of will, gave and lost himself
In temporal stuff, could be the same man
Who giving me his wondrous hand to hold,
Softly led me through a fairy-tale land,
On which eternity shone far and wide.
THORN Whether it hurts or not, that's how it is,
That I'm—the other one.
LEONILDA   You never were.
You had put on a mask and were so used
To it that finally, because it was
Reflected in every mirror held up
To you, you mistook it for your own face.
But I, I know your real face, Sylvester.
And if you look in my eyes long enough,
You'll see for yourself, through the deceitful
Mask, the face well known to me, your true face;—
And will tell me your lovely fairy tales
Once more in the shade of garden walks.
THORN They
Were not lovely—only in your pure soul
Did memory transform them so happily.

Thus they're yours;—they never belonged to me.
LEONILDA You've been gone too long. But see how quickly
    You'll become yourself again; then you will
    Give me a new, still more beautiful tale.
    And since none knows how to listen to it
    Like I do, it shall belong to us two—
    As a child belongs to both its parents.

ANSELMA *and the* BARON *enter.* LEONILDA, THORN

BARON *is carrying a sealed book in his hand.*
THORN *moved, kisses Anselma's hand.*
ANSELMA We're very glad to see you here again.
    Indicating the book
    We bring you the book we must thank for it.
THORN *indicating the Baron*
    I hope you don't believe him. He wishes
    Quite to misunderstand me.
BARON   Do you hear
    It crackling up there? Logs burning. Lead him,
    Sister, to the place of execution.
THORN Truly, your jests will induce me to throw
    All these pages unread into the fire.
BARON May God prevent it! Would you have the ghosts
    Of your youth, unredeemed from the ashes
    Rising, afflict your sleep?!—
    To Anselma   Show him the way!
ANSELMA Sylvester, would you please to follow me?
THORN *hesitating*
    Since you won't have it otherwise—
BARON *with no change in tone*   It's high time.
    The pages begin to burn already
    In your hands.
THORN *as above* In that case, I'll take my leave.
BARON It is granted.
ANSELMA   Until the dinner hour.
BARON The dinner bell may ring too soon for him.
THORN Do you want to bar me from the table
    As punishment? I'll be ready—I know

One dines at Mayenau not only well
But punctually.
BARON *laughing* That he did not forget.
ANSELMA *goes ahead.*
THORN *with the book, follows her up the stairs to the gallery.*
He looks around once more from the steps. One can still see
how Anselma opens the door to his room for him and then
exits to the left.

LEONILDA, BARON

LEONILDA The ghosts of his youth? What kind of secrets
Is there between the two of you? What book
Is that with which he disappeared just now?
BARON His diary. We kept it here for him.
He wants to read it one last time—and then—
Burn it.
LEONILDA Today? Right away?
BARON   So he must,
Since he's leaving us soon.
LEONILDA   Not tomorrow?
BARON Perhaps by tomorrow.
LEONILDA   Why the hurry?
BARON Didn't he tell you?—
LEONILDA   I didn't ask.—Do you
Know why?
BARON   Of course.—Because his beloved,—
His bride awaits him.
LEONILDA *surprised, but not deeply stirred*
                                  He is engaged?—And
To whom?
BARON   To one who came up earlier
In conversation. The same one you saw
Right here many years ago—saw and heard.
LEONILDA The singer with whom. . . back then? That can't
be.
BARON But it is.
LEONILDA You said yourself—remember—,
Not an hour ago you said they had

Long since left each other.
BARON   And so they had;
  Still, they found each other again, it seems.
LEONILDA They—found each other—? I can imagine
  How that happened—if it happened! She felt
  Her beauty fade, her youth, and so snared him,
  The kindest of men, all over again.
BARON She's not old. Younger than Sylvester—and—
  Still lovely, I suppose. . . .
LEONILDA   I don't believe it.
  People who are bad, like her, age early.
BARON My all too clever child—let your father
  Counter one bit of wisdom with another:
  Women becoming mothers, become good.
  Leonilda now shows real emotion for the first time, but says
  nothing. The Baron takes her head tenderly between his hands
  and kisses her on the forehead.
  And now you understand what draws him home.
LEONILDA And he kept—that—from me?
BARON   No, he forgot.

ANSELMA *enters.* LEONILDA, BARON

ANSELMA The book is unsealed. And the ghosts hover
  Around him. He barely heard the door close
  Behind me.
BARON   This magic won't last long either.
  And then it will be our turn to rise.
ANSELMA True, but also as nothing more than ghosts.
BARON For him, yes. But we know that we exist.
SECRETARY *has entered carrying papers, goes into the bay,*
  where he appears to straighten out the desk in preparation
  for working.
BARON It's good you have come. Let us put the time
  Before dinner to good use.
ANSELMA   At the risk
  That our guest won't join us, I'll see the meal
  Prepared as best I can. *Exits.*
LEONILDA   And when it's ready,

I'll fetch him—
Anselma, who has still heard these words, turns around to
Leonilda with a smile. Leonilda, facing her father, continues
        And I know, in spite of all
The ghosts, past and future—he'll follow me.
BARON *smiling* To the table!
LEONILDA *cheerfully, almost confidently*
              And anywhere I please.
She exits.
BARON *moved, looks after her.*

BARON, SECRETARY

SECRETARY *after a pause*
What is your Grace's pleasure?
BARON   Read the sentence
At which my daughter interrupted us.
SECRETARY *reads*
"His boyish brow, in flowing blond hair framed
Pale and serious—"
BARON *interrupts*   No, we had gone further.
SECRETARY *reads*
". . . With my lips, my heart swelled—and not alone
With love for my lord's son, this handsome lad
Whose school- and playmate I was ordained to be. . ."
BARON *interrupts* I'm in no mood to continue today.
And besides, what compels me to follow
Events chronologically? I will please
Myself, and choose one day, one more alive
To my mind today than all the others.
Walks back and forth in the room, his face becoming clearer;
he indicates to Andreas by means of a gesture that he is to
stand ready, and begins to dictate
The sky was burning down through yellow clouds
Upon our ride. Side by side—as often
Before our stallions' daily morning
Romp bore us across the blazing meadows—
So we rode full speed, this overcast day—
The young emperor and his adjutant—

Through uprooted fields towards the livid haze,
Which, resembling first a wall, opened up
Exactly like hell's jaws—
Suddenly interrupts himself
                              No, not like that.—
Just how did that singular day begin?
Dictating
Stirred to wakefulness by the first glimmer
Of light let in by the tent flap's being
Blown aside by the early morning wind,
I stole quietly from my bed—as not
To wake my companion—and stepped outside
Into the grayness of the enormous field,
From which—like the sigh of one single breast—
The anxious breath of a thousand sleeping men
Lost itself in mute-indifferent space.
That extensive field was our homeland,
The thousand thralls of sleep its protectors,
The young man who slept in the tent, its prince,
And I one of those thousand, and—his friend;
The glimmer that woke me, the first greeting
Of the day on which our country's destiny
Should be determined for all time—and was
Determined for thirty years,—of the day
On which I rode into battle's bloody
Grimness at the side of my friend and prince
For the first time, as formerly to play,
To hunt, or to adventure bound,—of the day
On which a bond between all men, never
To be torn, should have been woven—and tore
When all was said, like every human bond.
He stops, moved
Oh day of fraud, senseless like no other—
And full of profoundest truth like none since.
But who understood that?—
                              Strike that and write.
He begins in a dry tone
Following a two-week long cease-fire,
Of which the two sides took full advantage,

The armies faced each other, battle-ready.
It was before dawn, on the tenth of May—
He stops suddenly
What time is it?
SECRETARY   The clock in the village
Just struck twelve.
BARON   It vibrates still in the air. . . .
Now Konrad is riding through the city gate—
Quite moved, to himself
And stands before him at this very hour—
SECRETARY   *as if he were waiting, repeats*
It was on the tenth of May, before dawn—
BARON   It was!—Enough. Let me alone—
The Secretary stands up.   Today's
No day for looking back.
The Secretary leaves the bay.
                              The time's aglow
With the future.—And the world smells of youth!
He stands in the bay and looks out into the distance.
The Secretary has exited.

The curtain falls.

THIRD ACT

The park belonging to the castle at Mayenau. Very late evening, almost night. At first, darkness; then, in the course of the act, increasingly bright moonlight. An open space with flower-beds, lanes to the left and right. In the background, fairly distant, the silhouette of the castle.

SYLVESTER THORN *enters from the castle, crosses a part of the stage, and then remains standing.*

THORN   Shall I wait for morning?—Why? Better for me
    To go,—without seeing anybody.
    What I was obligated to do here,
    Is done. The ghosts of past times, conjured up
    Into the light, are banished to perpetual
    Silence in the tinder of my diary;
    And now I almost have to ask myself
    Why I came! Was it worth the effort
    To so much as lift the hand that let fall
    One page after another into the flames?
    Had not what became ashes today turned
    To dust long ago? Where have you gone, days
    Aglow with bliss, and rich as these, you days
    Of cruel sorrow? You gray mornings, heavy
    With dark questions, you mild redemptive dawns,
    And nights, unfathomable and inventive
    Of pleasure and pain; you cheerful-drunken
    Feasts, with conversation light and earnest
    In the circle of friends,—you springtime strolls
    Beneath green canopies, and noon respites
    On meadows at the forest's edge, amid
    The buzz of butterflies, beneath the blue
    Of heaven; you autumnal solitudes,
    Cold as glacial snow and pure, and lastly,
    You hours, sacred to the works given
    Me to strive after—if not to complete—

Where have you all gone? How shall I hold you?
What would I be holding if I held you?
You lived once, after all! And I fancied
You kept alive forever beneath my seal.
Alas, I did not keep you, I buried you,
And thus putrefaction was your portion.
Fare thee well, past! Forgetfulness remains
The sole devotion worthy of being
Consecrated to you. The day is ours—
No, the moment. But isn't it the past
Already too, as soon as we've lived it?
The moment when Leonilda smiling
Handed me the slice of pear for dessert,—
Is it not now as distant and as little
Mine as childhood days or deceitfully
Close yesterdays? Only the future is mine,
Because the choice is mine. Thus—although
I'm tempted to stay—I've decided to go.—
The way is familiar, moonlit the night—
It will be a splendid walk—and the house
That is to be mine tomorrow will greet me
Before dawn,—my own field's dew will wet my feet,
And I'll step soft, over the bright threshold,
To the consecrated bed where, in blissful,
Anxious mother's dreams, the beloved waits.
He turns towards the left, as if to exit; the secretary, Andreas
Ungnad, suddenly comes up to him.

THORN, SECRETARY

SECRETARY My humblest wishes for a good evening.
THORN Who is it?
SECRETARY Andreas Ungnad, his Grace's Secretary.
THORN   What do
   you want? Were you
   Sent from the castle?
SECRETARY   I come on my own.
   I have a secret to reveal to you.
THORN To me, a secret? At such a late hour?

Why just to me?

SECRETARY   Because you're a poet.

THORN And hence you think it were best kept with me?
    You are mistaken. I reveal secrets.

SECRETARY Should you try to in this case—to the others
    It would remain a secret still.

THORN *impatiently*   Speak, then.

SECRETARY Do you believe that you exist, Herr Thorn—?

THORN You mean—?

SECRETARY   You do not. You exist no more
    Than anyone or anything. The Baron
    With his sister, daughter, servants, and guests,
    The castle, the park, the earth and its fruit,
    The sky in all its splendor, the river,
    Its whisper, day and night, human beings
    And nature, all are merely appearances.
    Even I, as you see me standing here.
    It's my spirit which created a world
    For itself and placed itself in its midst.

THORN Then you also created what, until
    Today, I thought I'd created myself?
    And my existence begins only now?

SECRETARY If I shut my eyes, the light goes out. No
    Flower is fragrant if I hold my breath.
    Should I slumber, the whole world sinks in sleep.
    And when I die, the world will die with me.
    And Herr Sylvester Thorn dissolves to nothing
    When I turn my face from him.

THORN   And since
    You created everything, then God as well?

SECRETARY Shuddering in awe at my own power,
    I stand the stronger against him, whom I
    Created deathless over the universe
    Of mere appearance—and whom, eternal
    As I created him, I will pull down
    With me into eternal nothingness.

THORN And you reveal all this to me, who does
    Not exist?

SECRETARY Don't try to confound with words

What needs must be conceived beyond all words.

THORN You, I, and God. The trinity's complete.

SECRETARY The oneness. For take but one from these three
  And, compute as you will, none will remain.
  So powerfully blows the wind of truth:
  It blows from three flames or from none at all.

THORN So, it is three?

SECRETARY   Indivisible—one!

He exits with a triumphant smile.

THORN *remaining alone, after a short pause.*
  Bewildered soul, what did you want of me?
  Did you appear before me in the guise
  Of my own distorted self?

LEONILDA, *coming from the castle,* THORN
                         This is where
  I find you?—

THORN *happy* You have been looking for me?

LEONILDA You stole from the table. Why? Is it true
  You want to leave before dawn?

THORN   I—meant to.

LEONILDA And without farewell?

THORN   It seemed simpler so.

LEONILDA You will come back to us soon?
  Since he remains silent   —Or never?

THORN Who knows before if he's to come again?

LEONILDA The person who wants to come.

THORN   I've tarried
  Many years in foreign lands. Home holds me
  Thrice fast now—as you know.

LEONILDA   And if it prove
  Foreign again, a mere mirage of home!?

THORN Not home—my own land, and my wife and child—?

LEONILDA It's longing that first gives these their purpose.

THORN It draws me with such might that you find me
  Here prepared to return before I've even
  Laid my head to rest. And you don't believe
  My longing?

LEONILDA I thought you rather—prepared

For flight.
In response to a movement on his part
        Oh, not from me, but from yourself,
From your being's deepest truth, which glitters
On you today not only from my eyes,
But from your own soul. Nonetheless, instead
Of taking the way into the open,
You go where all that luster—the signal,
Now first beaming forth, of your unfulfilled
Mission—will fade in duty's lukewarm mist,
Soon to go out in the dull, long since alien
Air of an unfortunate relationship.

THORN *more vehemently than before*
You must not say these things.

LEONILDA   What I must not,
I spoke for me. What I barely may, I
Spoke for you and your mortal part alone.
But your deathless part was made manifest
To me in an unforgettable hour.—
And thus—just as you did under the seals
Of those pages in which your past reposed,
Indestructible,—thus have I preserved
Your spirit's picture in me. I hold it
Out to you, so you will recognize it,
And so, before that oft clouded face hides
Itself again in fogs of dull routine,
You will allow it to shine to the world
At last, in pure unbroken beams of fire.

THORN And are you aware, what it is you are
Suggesting for the sake of this—perhaps
Deceitful—picture?

LEONILDA   Be it deceitful,
If only it keep you from worse deceit.

THORN And you don't consider what would befall her?

LEONILDA I'd not grudge even one, who loves you, grief,
If from her grief your happiness sprang up.

THORN You could be so cruel?

LEONILDA   That, too. But this time
I am not. She knows no grief.

THORN   If I did
  As you advise, she would learn to know it.
LEONILDA As if grief could be learned. Grief too is grace.
THORN Call it hate, then, despair, a curse;—all these—
  I would have to bear them like deserved guilt.
LEONILDA There's only one thing unforgivable:
  Selecting the wrong path with open eyes.
THORN Do you know the right one for me?
LEONILDA   You'll find it.
THORN At your side, perhaps—?
LEONILDA   Alone too, I'd say.
THORN Are you slipping away from me again?
LEONILDA We are still free. Let us ask the darkness.
  Perhaps the dawning day will answer us. *Exits.*
THORN *alone, with increasing excitement*
  Was this hour the purpose of my return?
  And did this wonderful child keep what I
  Never wished to keep with myself—did she
  Keep faith with me—beyond deceit and dream,
  Error and guilt? Are faith and youth rushing
  From her young heart into mine too, at last—?
  The Baron enters.

THORN, BARON

BARON Still awake, my friend?
THORN   Bright nights such as these
  Invite no sleep.
  Smiling   From you either, I see.
BARON Especially after so full a day.—
  Isn't it strange that on the very same one
  Two valued friends from past times should bring me,
  Here retired, news from the outside world,—
  One in person, the other through his son!—
  You said you liked him—?
THORN   Of noble bearing
  I found him, and semblance of his father.

BARON *speaking as if to himself*

How rare such a son! Yesterday he rides
Still upon his father's knee, on his head
A cardboard helmet, swings a wooden sword,
And of his games the gladdest is called war;
And tomorrow it will not be a game!
To his father and mother—still a child
Like yesterday (for not a thing is changed
By the soft down upon his baby face),
And he speaks—and acts—and fights, and, I dare
Say, also knows how to die like a man.
A blessing not unmixed to have such a son,
Whose childhood we've no sooner been allowed
To enjoy in peace of mind than he grows
Away from us in danger and distance—
And remains distant, although he return,
For he's become a man. Wish for a daughter,
Therefore, Sylvester, one as God kindly
Bestowed on me, who will remain ours
No matter what man carries her away,
And stay still near, however far removed.
THORN I'm very happy you feel that, my friend—
For both of us.
*The Baron looks at him in surprise, then Thorn adds,
suddenly*
You have a splendid child!
BARON What ails you?
THORN Let me receive from your hands,
Friend of my youth, the utmost happiness!
Give me Leonilda to wed.
BARON *alarmed* Sylvester!—
A jest, surely, but I don't grasp its meaning.
THORN I spoke in earnest.
BARON The pages you read—
The wine you drank—fatigue—have confused you.
Come to your senses. Have you forgotten—
THORN *quickly* I—am not married to that other one.
BARON To that other one!—
THORN I promised her nought—
She may very well hope for it. But she

Can hardly think that I owe it to her.
With forced lightness
One farewell more.—Is that so important?
You seem inclined to view it more seriously
Than she and I would—if it came to that.
BARON But this farewell would be different from
   Any you ever said before!
THORN   And here,
   In this area, my friend, lives there no child
   Of your blood who bears but its mother's name?
   And none complains that you abandoned her?
BARON I boast of no purer conduct than yours.
   Still, this case can't be compared to any
   That I, or someone else lived through. The house—
   Your own enclosed estate in your homeland—
   Did you not buy it for her, for your child—?
THORN For this child, first of all. For which reason
   I weigh whether for this child another
   Woman—
BARON No more!
THORN   —Whether Leonilda
   Might not make the better mother, whether
   She might not make your friend a better wife.
BARON *quickly and sharply*
   You spoke with her? She sent you to me? You've gone—
   How far?—
THORN   So far, that your unexpected
   Appearance here, on this spot which she left
   Not a moment ago, almost commands
   Me to press my suit for her. Not so far
   As to have become engaged.
BARON   I tell you—
   Because I would violate both friendship
   And a father's obligation were I
   To conceal it—that I am overcome
   With astonishment, indeed, with horror,
   When I see the man with whom, young together,
   I once roisted through many a wild feast
   Of pleasure—together unto ecstasy,

And to the bitterest dregs—can you still
Recall, Sylvester?—the man with whom, perhaps,—
And if it did not happen, it could have—
I shared the favors of a pretty wench,—
When I see the man who was the friend
Of my vanished youth desire my daughter.

THORN   And today, still as little old as you.

BARON   Far worse than old—we two—no longer young.

THORN   It can't be that bad. Forgive me, if for
The second time, in a most uncalled for—

BARON *interrupting him*
I know what they say of me hereabouts.
However—

THORN   They speak unasked. And there's none
Would begrudge you anything—or find you
No longer of an age to look out for
Maidens and women.

BARON   Still, they can hardly
Say that I am of a mind to court one.

THORN   And if you did, no one would consider
Dismissing as a fop the man for whom
Seventeen-year-olds pined.

BARON   And were he no fop—
A fool he would certainly be.
Gently   My friend,
Perhaps in our late-summer ripeness,
We may still be strong enough to conquer—
But to endure, never again—and were
She the youngest—or just because of that.

THORN   This disagreeable law is hardly
Applicable to all. For not every
Destiny is played out to the same measure
Of the stars;—and I sense most profoundly,
That he is ageless whom his mission calls.

BARON   Before God, perhaps, but not before maidens.
And if her green senses exult today
In the nearness of your gray head, which strikes
Her as being suffused in an aura
Of eternity;—let but a trifling

Moment pass, and all that was your magic
Will be gone—and a newer, stronger one
Will draw its circle around the awakened
Heart.
THORN   Then I would, without hesitation
And unbidden—grateful only for late
Happiness in which my being fulfilled
Itself for the first time—I would let her
Who had favored me so abundantly
Follow the road that tempts her to wander.
Indeed, lest shame or pity perplex her,
I would, at the farewell hour's first stroke,
Open the gate and show her the way myself.
BARON   And do you think you will hear the striking
Of that hour? Not at all! Human ears
Are deaf to unwanted sounds. Unwilling
To feel how the arms you still love embrace
You with caresses grown weary, you will
Seek imperiously to force her closer
The further off from you she tries to draw.
And you'll await the moment, long since missed,
As if it had not yet arrived.
THORN   If you
Mistrust my judgment so, perhaps my oath
Will suffice, that after a certain time—
Even if the joy of our first love days
Continued beyond all doubt—that before
Three years—before one has elapsed, I will
Vanish forever—and without a trace—
From Leonilda's nearness, from her life.
BARON   I must reject so blasphemous an oath.
THORN   Does this mean you're saying no to my suit?
BARON   Not no, not yes. It is too soon for either.
For even if I felt as close to you
As I felt distant just now—and as glad
Of my daughter's choice as I was at first
Still hesitant to be—I would never
Bless your bond so thoughtlessly and in such
Haste as you are willing to conclude it.

I request only time for reflection.
Not for me. For her—And for you.
THORN   How long?
BARON The time will determine itself. For, look
    How in a single day you've changed your mind.
    You scarce thought of abandoning the woman
    Who is to bear you a child tomorrow
    At such a time—one for which you made
    Provision. So, we will agree, that you,
    Before dawn, will set out on your way home.
    But this be my promise: If you return—
    Whether it be after months, weeks, or days,
    From the cradle of your newborn infant
    And from its mother's bed of pain, unchanged—
    And find her the same as you left today—
    And if the two of you are still determined
    Body and soul, to marry—then I shall,
    As happy and hopeful for the future,
    As I am doubtful now, with this my hand
    Place each of yours into the other's—and
    Prepare the wedding feast without delay.
THORN I'm satisfied.—Yet one more thing I ask,
    That Leonilda not learn anything,
    Of our conversation until I return.
BARON And I ask that you neither see nor speak
    To my child before your departure hence.
    And lest some accident frustrate my wish,
    I'll see to it at once that my carriage
    Stand ready in the yard before sunrise.
THORN Needless effort and caution. For I had
    Decided to leave secretly before
    My chance meeting here with Leonilda.
BARON At night?
THORN   Had I not met Leonilda,
    I would, at this moment, have long since been
    On the road back to whence I came; and now
    I've nought to do but carry out my purpose.
    Farewell, my friend.
BARON   Don't you want to rest first?

THORN There will be opportunities along
 The way. Good-bye!
 The Baron wishes to say something.
      Not another word for now. *He exits.*

BARON, *then* ANSELMA

BARON It may not be.—It must not be.
Anselma enters.
Anselma!
Still to himself
Does this night's specially temperate breath
Draw all these sleepers out of their beds?
ANSELMA Was it Sylvester Thorn who just left you?
BARON It was.
ANSELMA Not back to the house?
BARON   He set out
 On his way home.
ANSELMA   Were you so harsh to him?
BARON What inducement would I have?—
ANSELMA   That he asked
 For Leonilda's hand.
BARON   You know—?
ANSELMA   I sensed it.
BARON I did not throw him out. I only asked
 That he reflect a space, until his child
 Is born. I'm sure he will come to his senses.
 Anselma quietly pulls him into the darkness of the lane.
 Further back, Leonilda crosses and exits towards the right.
 It's she! Where to?
ANSELMA   On her way to the pond.
BARON Perhaps—to beg her God's advice.
ANSELMA   Take her
 Along to court—that's my advice to you.
BARON As if I had any business at court.
ANSELMA It won't be long before they summon you.
BARON Who—would do that?
ANSELMA   The only one who may.
 It will be lonesome, then, at Mayenau—

And in these parlous times—hardly as safe
As you might desire for your daughter.
BARON And even if I intended to heed
Such a call—an idea as far removed
From my mind today as ever—do you
Think the court is the proper place for her?
ANSELMA *as if to herself*
How long has it been now, since his wife died?
BARON The Empress?
ANSELMA   I think the year of mourning
Has just ended.
BARON   What's on your mind, Anselma?
ANSELMA *prophetically* I wonder if that princely destiny—
That hovered once over me so loftily—
Might not fulfill itself in Leonilda?

DOMINIK *comes from the castle, holding a torch, followed
shortly by* KONRAD. BARON, ANSELMA

BARON *at first noticing only the torchlight*
What is it? Who goes? Konrad von Ursenbeck?
KONRAD *very quickly*
Uncle—my gracious Miss—
BARON   You are welcome.
With intentional coolness
I'm pleased you have acceded to my wish
To stop for rest again at Mayenau.
KONRAD Thank you, Uncle. However, I can't stay
Here for rest and lodging this time either.
And if I begged admittance with a Marshal's
Letter in daylight, it is only right
That a more exalted commission serve
As my excuse at so advanced an hour.
Hands him a letter.
BARON Come closer, Dominik.
Dominik holds the light closer. A familiar
Seal—and fixed thrice the same, in his fashion.
ANSELMA Well, whatever secret lie beneath it,
The young warrior will be tired and hungry.

I'll go prepare him a snack and a bed. *Exits.*

DOMINIK *has placed the torch in a holder, and exits.*

BARON *has opened and read the letter in the meantime. Pause.*
How long were you—with him?

KONRAD   Three hours' ride
To the city—as many back—compute
Yourself what remains, Uncle.

BARON   Three whole hours
Alone with him?—

KONRAD   The Chancellor was present.
I mean the one who was, at that moment.

BARON And, I'd guess, still is at this one?

KONRAD   We may
Believe: not for long.

BARON   How did His Majesty
Receive your father's letter?

KONRAD   He read it
Once, and again—

BARON *continuing* Hands it to the Chancellor—

KONRAD The Emperor bid him leave us alone.
Then he had me inform him to the last
Detail how things stand along the border,
Interjecting a question here and there.

BARON A question only?

KONRAD   No more. But he knows
How to ask. And when I finished, he gave
Back my father's letter, without a word.

BARON What—?! In anger?

KONRAD   If he felt so, his glance
Hid it well. I have never seen a face
So wholly secretive from brow to lips.

BARON Oh noble mask of irresolution—
How well I know you.

KONRAD   Then he strode mutely
Up and down awhile. Suddenly, as if
Enlightened, he sat down and wrote.

BARON   First
An answer to your father, I suppose.

KONRAD Only this one letter to you.

BARON   You spoke
  To the Emperor about me—? He knows
  You brought me a message from your father
  Too? That you stayed with me?
KONRAD   The Emperor
  Knows nothing of all that, naturally.
BARON So, this letter—of his own accord, he—
KONRAD You can see, Uncle, we would have saved time
  Had you ridden with me straightway to court
  This morning, as I asked you. God forbid
  That we pay bitterly for the delay.
BARON This letter in my hand—are you so sure
  That it will change anything?
KONRAD   Just as sure
  As that it orders you to the Emperor.
BARON Were it an order, one could refuse it.
  Dominik and another servant bring wine and a snack, as well
  as a small table that has been set. As Dominik prepares to
  exit again, the Baron speaks to him
  Say, Dominik, get everything ready
  To depart for the city at daybreak.
DOMINIK *happy* For five years, now, at all hours of day
  And night, I have kept Your Grace's trunk packed.
  And—if it please you—a valise for me.
BARON Well, all the better, but don't be too glad.
  It will hardly be for long.
  Dominik exits. Konrad raises his eyes to the Baron with a
  look of surprise.   Do you know
  When the Marchese left the capital?
  In response to Konrad's questioning look
  I mean the enemy envoy.
KONRAD   Enemy—!
  You said it! May it be a fateful word.
BARON What—he was not gone yet?
KONRAD   I did not ask,
  And no one spoke of it.
BARON   So it's possible
  That he is still in town—that he has not
  Yet delivered his letter of recall—?

KONRAD What do such formalities matter now,
When things have come so far?
BARON   How far?—
Nothing
Beyond recall has happened yet, it seems.
KONRAD You yourself spoke of an enemy envoy.
BARON That still remains to be seen.
Calling back the already fairly distant Dominik
                    Dominik,
Have the black team harnessed to the lighter
Carriage. We leave—within this very hour.
Dominik exits hastily.
KONRAD Chancellor—
BARON   Do you know that I am?
KONRAD   You are,
If you wish it.
BARON   Did I say I wished it?
KONRAD I'm sorry, but why does the Marchese
Still concern you now?
BARON   In earlier days,
Better ones, we understood each other well.
It's not too late.
KONRAD *dismayed* You want to speak to him?
BARON Him first of all.
KONRAD   Chancellor—yes, you are that,
I beg of you, implore you—do not waste
A single irretrievable minute.
On a useless talk.
BARON   Useless—!
KONRAD   Degrading.
BARON Konrad!
KONRAD For, no matter how bold your words
Or clever, or how proud your expression,
The enemy's ambassador would hear
Just caution and worry—indeed—fear.
BARON   Would
They sounded so to him! Wicked the heart
That prior to a critical decision
Fails to tremble—oh, not for itself, but

For a thousand other, innocent hearts!
Paltry the mind that would not—at the risk
Of appearing cowardly—still dare do
The utmost to avert a threatening fate.

KONRAD What you call fate—you could not avert it
Anymore. Only postpone it for days,
Or months, perhaps, at the price of disgrace.
And still, no miracle could interfere
With the preordained course of history.

BARON What do you call preordained? What you deem
Likely to happen! And if it is ordained,
Why all the effort of persuading me?
Were I not aware that the storm of fate
Through which I am hurtling kindles in me
An equally determinant might—then
Truly, I could not live a single day
In this world, which knew nothing about blame
But knew expiation; knew action's wage,
But nothing of merit; where each today
Bore within the seed of its tomorrow—
A living-dead, completed construction;
Where the hunter would not espy his prey,
But where hunter and prey, arrow and heart,
Slayer and victim would have to be found,
Enslaved from their beginnings, hurled upon
Each other through space by a dark power.
Do you believe in such a world? I can't.
I do not feel a mysterious fate hang
Over me. The clouds above are so much
Fog and vapor, from human latitudes,
And my will is party to the shaping
Of my fate. So, it may well come to pass
That my decision to heed the King's call,
And a talk with the Marchese as well,
May cause some alterations in what seems
To you the preordained course of events. *Pause.*

KONRAD *more to himself*
We shall see.

BARON   And whatever it be, I hope

You'll await the decision here.
KONRAD   Uncle—
BARON *as if struck by an idea*
  Now you may call me Chancellor, actually.
  You were not wrong. The letter made me such.
  He holds the letter out to Konrad.
KONRAD *skimming it* With complete authority.
BARON *quite severely*   Yes. Instead
  Of expressing the hope that you will wait
  For the decision here, in the castle,
  I could have wished it, or commanded it.
KONRAD What for, Herr Chancellor? Waiting is my portion.
  And if one must wait,—better anywhere
  Other than near the foe.
BARON   Quite right. So, may
  The short rest in park and castle please you,
  Albeit in less warlike company.
  Drinks to him again. Pause.
  You do little honor to the dishes.
KONRAD Forgive me! The long ride. My blood burns yet
  From the fiery highway's white-hot glitter.
  And now, the sweltering night! *Drinks.*
BARON   Loosen, then,
  Your doublet. Your duty's done for today.
  They drink.
KONRAD I'd love to plunge into the ocean's depths
  Best of all, to cool both body and soul.
BARON Here, alas, must hospitality fail.
  If it's refreshment you desire, we have
  The stream below that rushes to the sea
  And a fresh water fountain in the courtyard.
KONRAD And a pond.
BARON   You're mistaken.
KONRAD   In the park,
  I still recall.
BARON   Where might it be? I thought
  I knew my garden.
KONRAD   And—I know—a ball
  Fell into that pond—it happened many

Years ago—it was Leonilda's ball,
Not mine.
BARON   But surely not in this park. Here
There is none.
KONRAD   Did I dream it?
BARON   Certainly.
Dominik enters and brings the Baron his coat.
Ready?
DOMINIK   At once, my Lord.
BARON *having thrown the coat around his shoulders, to*
Konrad   Well then, farewell;
Have a good rest.
To Dominik   Where will the young man sleep?
DOMINIK   In the tower, your gracious sister said. *Exits.*
BARON   Quite right. It's vacant now, again.
To Konrad   My friend,
Whom you saw this morning, Sylvester Thorn—
KONRAD   Oh, yes, that singular older gentleman—
BARON   Not exactly old, though singular—perhaps.
KONRAD   What about him?
BARON   He had to leave sooner
Than he thought. So, you will stay in the room,
Sleep in the bed I thought for him—but now
It turns out were by fate for you determined.
Turns to go; hesitating
Look here, it just occurred to me—the pond,
I do have an idea where you played ball
Back then. Not here in the park—in the wood,
There lies the pond you mean.
KONRAD   But close to here.
BARON   Not far. But not close either. I have not
Seen it in a long time. I think it more
Accurate to call it a swamp.
KONRAD   I'd swear
It was crystal clear back then, by green grass
Rimmed, transparent to its blue-pebbled bed.
BARON   Perhaps the eyes of children see more deeply.
KONRAD   Show me the way.
BARON   Even if I knew it—

I would hardly do it.
As if joking   It's said the pond
Is bewitched.
KONRAD *laughing* What?! Since when?
BARON *somewhat more seriously* Since mythic times.
KONRAD We noticed nothing then. And no one warned us.
BARON Well, yes, in daytime. But evil spirits
  Play their games there by night.
KONRAD   I fear ghostly
  Apparitions as little as you would.
BARON Call it fancy, if you will. But fancy
  Would not surface even in uneasy minds
  Without cause. And if people maintain that
  Water sprites float around that pond at night,
  They need not be precisely water sprites—
  But some other thing that one ought to fear.
KONRAD *recalling* A little gate leads out of this park. Then
  Deeper through the wood a narrow trail, and—
  Quickly Where is that little gate?
BARON   If there was one,
  It's long since been obscured by bush and thorn.
DOMINIK *returns, ready to travel.*
KONRAD I'll find it out—and trail and pond as well.
BARON *after a brief moment of thought*
  Perhaps, if you're destined to.
  Gives Konrad his hand   Farewell!
  Exits.
KONRAD *remains alone*   If
  I'm destined.—What did he mean? It sounded
  As if he mocked, almost. Accursed manner.
  When he stands before me I always feel
  Like a youth, a boy. Yet now that he's gone,
  I know I'm a man—and he is gray and old.
  I could leave now. And I could reach the army,
  Ahead of any news from court or city;
  Stand before my father. But what's the use—
  I bring him no response to the letter
  He wrote the Emperor.—But just that fact—
  Who knows—if I attempted—leapt to horse

At once, and flew down the road without rest?
What holds me here? Near paralyzes me?
Is it but my limbs' complete exhaustion
After all that furious, ceaseless riding?—
Is it not more likely the Baron's word,
Against which to rebel my courage breaks,
As it always fails in my father's presence,
So that I, against my better judgment,
Weakly give in to feeble second thoughts!
The world is poisoned by ancient men's breath!
They should be slain all together, so that
Sly inbred reverence, burrowing through
Youth's marrow, not be able to render
It as weak and cowardly as old men.
How I long for that refreshing water.
Right or left?—I must find that little gate.
Onward. Do I not feel the damp fragrance
Streaming towards me from this direction?
Rare fragrance! I think I recognize it.
What did he say? Bad ghosts first, then water sprites.
Although there are bad sprites too, still one does
Whatever he can to mollify them.
And, if I'm lucky, one will even help me
Find the ball that sank in the pond, that I
Might bring it to Leonilda tomorrow.
He exits to the right. The stage remains empty for a moment.

The curtain falls.

FOURTH ACT

Same scene as in the first act. Early morning. KONRAD, *at the door to the right, speaks with his* GROOM.

KONRAD Listen: wait for me where the highway bends
Sharply from the hillside's edge to run south
Along the stream. Should someone from the castle
Ask where you are leading the two horses,
Say—
He thinks for an instant, then adds quickly
     what you will. It's no one's business. Go!
The groom exits.
Two nights and a day since the Baron left.
Although he set no term for my stay, still,
Since he trusts me so little that he bound
Me here with spells, I'm free of every duty.—
Though he acted as if he were warning
Me about the path to the pond, he knew
Full well the warning was the very thing
To tempt me onto it. Was it of such
Great importance to him to hold me here?
Does he think my voice so influential
With the army that, rather than know me
To be out in the field, he would become
A pander in his own house? Well—however
It be—he has squandered his game. And I,
I am the winner in any event.
LEONILDA *enters slowly. At first they look at each other quietly, then she sinks in his arms; without releasing herself completely, she speaks*
    —All at once you were gone!
KONRAD   You lay so deep
Asleep—so I stole away.
LEONILDA   I can think
Of one who'd have waited till I awoke.
KONRAD You dearest—Loveliest—You water sprite!
LEONILDA *annoyed* I asked you not to call me that.

KONRAD   Pardon!
  But when I saw you step out of the pond,
  There surfaced in me a half-forgotten
  Fairy tale from childhood. Don't you recall
  It as well?
LEONILDA About water sprites?
KONRAD   Who bathe
  Beneath the full moon in the reed-ringed pond
  Of Mayenau, and—when morning approaches—
  Go among humans like normal women.
LEONILDA I do not know that tale.
KONRAD *hesitating*   And yet: when I
  Suddenly appeared to you at water's edge—*He stops.*
LEONILDA Why so surprised?
KONRAD   You—took no fright at all.
LEONILDA *smiling* I imagine you must not have appeared
  All that frightful.
KONRAD   Nevertheless—
LEONILDA   I know.
  I should—as befits children of mortal
  Birth—have fled from you through thorn and thicket.
KONRAD It would not have helped you.
  Draws her to him.
LEONILDA   I thought as much.
KONRAD And yet—
LEONILDA *since he hesitates*
                  Say it!
KONRAD   It's my manner to speak
  What's on my mind.
LEONILDA   And so you must, my dear.
KONRAD I felt as if you had been expecting—
  Not me, exactly—no, but somebody.
LEONILDA *seriously*
  That may well be so.
KONRAD   Well, then?—
LEONILDA   Him who came.
KONRAD You jest. But unjustly, Leonilda.
  The place is not that inaccessible,
  It is easily reached from the castle,

And I have scarce any doubt that a path
Leads to the pond from the village as well.

LEONILDA *teasing*

How comes it then you failed to notice the sign
Which reads, "To the pond of the water sprites"
As you rode past?

KONRAD *increasingly excited*

               Sign or no sign, path
Or no path; as I found it, lured and led
By its damp fragrance, so too could another—
And see you in the moonlight as I did—
Pledge to me no other man ever saw you
Brightly step out of the dark pond at night.

LEONILDA Or took me, as you did.

KONRAD   I didn't say that.
Nor believe it. If I did—you'd die, now,
And I with you.

LEONILDA *impenetrably*

            I want you to believe it.

KONRAD That is your answer?

LEONILDA   Do I owe you one?
Did I, at the moment we two, spellbound,
Floated into one another, set you
Above me as my master? Or surrender
To you, with my today, my yesterdays
And all my tomorrows? Indeed, can you
Even be sure I gave myself to you?

KONRAD I know it.

LEONILDA   No! Now you must first court me.
The sprite was yours. If you want the woman
Too, you'll not win her with youthful insolence.
And take note, how the sprite returns to her
Watery bed as quickly as she surfaced.

GROOM *enters hastily from the right.* LEONILDA, KONRAD

GROOM Sir—
Notices Leonilda and interrupts himself.

KONRAD   Go on—

GROOM   Your horse—the devil trifles
With it—an hour ago still sound—
KONRAD *impatiently*   What's
With my horse?
GROOM   It's lame.
LEONILDA   I would be surprised
If among the other apparitions
Hereabouts there did not live some witches
Who make horses lame before they can ride.
KONRAD *crossly, to the groom*
Rub it down thoroughly.
GROOM   I've used three pans
Of ointment, my Lord.
KONRAD   It works gradually.
There's no hurry. We have until evening.
LEONILDA *understanding*
Why the delay? From our stables choose
A steed. There are five, well rested, will take
You quickly wherever you want to go.
KONRAD Thanks. I ride only my own to battle.
*Noise and some disturbance outside which have already been
noticeable.*
SECRETARY *hurries through the room from the left, responds
to Konrad's and Leonilda's questioning glances*
The Baron is back.
Exits right. The groom has also exited.
LEONILDA *after a pause* You wanted to leave.
And if I am not mistaken, to leave
Prior to my father's arrival home.
What is it then, holds you here still?
She opens a hitherto unnoticed door left front
                     This door
Will lead you outside unnoticed.
KONRAD   Well, yes—
I wanted to leave. But do you also
Know why? *Close to her*
         If I spent yet a third night pressed
Close to you, your mouth, your heart, my being
Would be drawn into you so deeply that I

Would become your slave in body and soul.
It is that I feared and wished to escape.

The BARON *and* SECRETARY *enter, in conversation.*
LEONILDA, KONRAD

BARON   You'll find the entire correspondence
In the third drawer. Next to it loose pages
With the heading "Adjustments of the Border."
There are maps attached—bundle them up too.
The Secretary exits up to the gallery.
The Baron, after a hasty but observant glance at Leonilda,
kisses her on the forehead; then, after a barely noticeable
hesitation, extends his hand to Konrad, measuring him.
Ready so soon?
KONRAD   Awaiting your orders.
What message shall I bring my father?
BARON *simply*   Nothing
He would not have heard before you got there.
A messenger was sent to him last night.
KONRAD   Orders—to battle?—
BARON   *shaking his head slightly, matter-of-factly*
                          Our forward troops
Are to be withdrawn. Simultaneously,
The foe's forward sentries will be pulled back
From our border into their own country.

ANSELMA *has meanwhile come down the steps from the*
gallery.

KONRAD *controlling himself only with an effort*
Has this been confirmed, in writing, by both sides?
BARON   I have seen to it that it be done.
KONRAD *as above*   A pact concluded between two armies?
BARON *still calm*
One concluded man to man.
KONRAD   Prince to prince?
BARON   No draft will lack royal confirmation
Long when drawn up by Chancellor and envoy.

KONRAD The one you called enemy yesterday!
BARON And had I left but one hour later
   The name would have held true. His carriage stood
   Prepared to depart, its windows covered.
   I came in time.
KONRAD   And would have, in your view,
   Gotten there in time in any event.
   For had your carriages' paths crossed beyond
   The city gates, upon the King's highway,
   You would have halted his in full career—
   To beg for peace on our country's behalf. *Pause.*
BARON *calmly* Possibly. But, fortunately, I found
   The Marchese still at home, whom I thought
   Meet to visit—before my reporting
   To the King and taking up my office—
   As a friend from better days, who felt the urge
   To extend one final cordial greeting
   To his friend before he left the country.
   That is what I had in mind—nothing else.
   And he, as I have no cause to conceal,
   Who received me at first surprised, and cool,
   Soon felt the same. For just then, his carriage
   Standing ready to depart at his door,
   As I (—it was no ruse; I myself thought
   The decision had been irrevocably
   Made—) pressed his hand as for a long farewell,
   Our words flowed freer than ever before.
   Raising his voice
   In a way we'd often tried to achieve—
   In vain—when forced to hide under the robes
   Of our official dignities, we had
   Politely read cold calculated thoughts
   On each other's lips, equivocal ideas
   On each other's brow—well, since this was farewell
   Between two friends—and both of us feeling
   Released from all responsibility,
   We let our faded masks of office drop
   Without a care. And, as misconceptions
   Cleared up and old prejudices vanished

In the flow of give and take, unbroken
By muddy whirlpools of self-interest—
And we, two human beings, stood facing
Each other, without haughtiness, mistrust,
Or reserve—then the misunderstandings,
The grudges and the ill-will between princes,
And between peoples—which coalescing
To black storm clouds, must finally result
In thunderbolts hurtling down upon us—
Soon drifted lightly up and down before
Our now unclouded eyes like thin fog which—
As has happened to many another
Hellish exhalation—the mighty breath
Of heavenly reason saw fit to scatter.
And so, with a handshake far more hopeful
Than the one with which, on my arrival,
I greeted the ambassador, I left—
And could appear before the Emperor—
Even before taking the oath as Chancellor—
As the bringer of a message of peace.

KONRAD And you think these hellish exhalations,
As you call them, truly gone forever?
And that you were chosen to establish
A realm of love and goodness in this world?!—

BARON Of love—hardly. Still, one of coexistence,
In which a man, if he discount his neighbor's
Worth, may possibly allow him to live.
Of goodness?—No. Still, one in which evil
Does not rage around like a top gone berserk—
At others' cost, with no gain for itself.
And forever, of all things? Yesterday,
Today, and tomorrow is all the term
That I perceive to have been given us.
And it seems to me far wiser to build
A modest house on the secure, narrowly
Compassed ground of the present than dream up
A fanciful picture of elevated
Humanity in some distant future.
Much work lies ahead. My liege has until now

Granted me so much time to rest my mind,
In purer air, far from the court's intrigues,
That now I'll not cease before completing
What he required of me.
To Anselma

My former rooms
In the palace stand ready to receive
Me again, tonight. Three chancellors slept there
In the meantime. And tonight, I, again.

ANSELMA   You want to go back tonight?

BARON   Not so much
To sleep in the chancellor's bed. However,
I can't miss the council meeting I called
For tonight. For today I still belong
To you—and to me. I am going back
Before sundown.
Simply   And you, Squire Ursenbeck,
With me.

KONRAD *very much surprised*
You said—to court—I—go with you?

BARON   The Emperor wishes you to report
To the council, precisely as you did
To him, the condition of the army.

KONRAD   Is that what my father dispatched me for?
My orders were: to deliver the Marshal's
Letter to the Emperor, and bring him
His Lord's reply. I was a messenger
Only between these two. To be sure, since,
Counter to my duty, I did agree
To bring the Emperor's message to you,
Instead of rushing straight back to the army,
I feel how that first delay, like a noose
That lightly laid around an ankle grows
Gradually tighter, wants to hold me bound
To this ground. But I'm still able to tear
Myself from any snare, and I will ride
Not back to court, where I do not belong,—
But to the Marshal, and to the army.

BARON *calmly*
>Perhaps you will still meet your father there,—
>The Marshal not.
>*Konrad gives a start; the Baron continues, factually*
>   It seemed necessary,
>In order that not even the least doubt
>From any quarter disturb our peaceful
>Intent, in a period of decision
>So perilous, to wrest with respectful
>Gentleness the upraised staff of destiny
>From that noble but all too daring hand.

KONRAD You did that—his friend?
BARON   The Chancellor did it.
KONRAD My father—relieved of command!—You think—
>He would let himself—you think, his army—
>*In response to a look from the Baron*
>Yes, his—if he wishes—you think they'd suffer
>*Ever more passionately*
>Such an insult, such disgrace— or as long
>As he's alive, another commander—

BARON *interrupting him, calmly*
>No other's been appointed in his place.
>The Emperor retains supreme command
>Himself. The rank, naturally, remains
>Your father's, on whom, as on his issue,
>The title of Count is bestowed as well.

KONRAD *trembling* Count Ursenbeck!
BARON   The father and the son.
KONRAD Honorific as this is doubtless meant,
>Might not the—former Marshal have meantime
>Risen higher by force of his own might?

BARON I know him well. He never aspires
>To be more than his Lord's most faithful warrior.
>You're his heir, Konrad. Inherit this too.

KONRAD I am the Marshal's son and officer.
>I'll not go to court.

BARON   If the Emperor
>Doesn't make you expiate your willfulness,
>You may yet come to regret it yourself.

And, for my part, lest I bear any guilt
In it, I will force on you a period
Of reflection. Before I leave this house—
The first time in many years—and who knows
For how long—a number of things remain
To be done, which, with Anselma's sisterly
Advice, I'll see to at once,—you, meanwhile,
Strolling in the garden, may carefully
Weigh how best to proceed in this matter.
You, Leonilda, stay with him that long.

LEONILDA I—surety for him? Name another
To this office; for I'm almost afraid
I would not advise him to your liking.

BARON That is up to you. If I surrounded
Him with guards, however, he would escape.
But since I set a maiden to guard him,
He'll gallantly take it as close arrest.

KONRAD You said it: arrest. Whether close or mild
Is all the same. I am a prisoner—
In disregard of custom and justice.

BARON The safety of the realm takes precedence.
We will speak again in an hour.
Leonilda and Konrad exit left.

BARON, ANSELMA

ANSELMA   Brother,
I am glad.

BARON   Don't be too glad. In my heart
I am not as certain of my success
As with good cause I led this young noble
To believe. The messengers have not reached
Their destinations yet. They might arrive
Just in time to hear the opening shots.

ANSELMA Forgive me, if the fatherland's welfare,
The question whether we'll have peace or war,
Is not paramount in my mind right now.
What gladdens me is that the two of you,
You and the Emperor, have found each other

Again at last.

BARON   I confess: for me too,
Whatever the nation's fate proves to be—
Good or ill—what I have felt and lived through
These past days, will remain a deathless gift.

ANSELMA It sounded so when you spoke, and gleams yet
In your eyes.

BARON   And I have not yet told you
Of the greatest hour. The one I spent
Alone with him after the completion
Of our state business. How he opened up!
How his soul, now released from loneliness,
Gloom, and delusion, rushed out towards me;
And—years of alienation extinguished—
How fully we had each other again.
His life unrolled itself before my eyes,
Going back in time, day by day, it seemed;
And so, shining bright, his very essence,
The prince's as well as the man's, lay clearer
To my sight than it ever had before.
I saw how he'd failed others, others him,
And—I became aware of my own guilt.
He is silent. Anselma, moved, looks at him; he continues, as
if speaking to himself
I saw into his marriage, which the death
Of his wife only recently dissolved.
It was I, who, for reasons of policy—
Which I pled to him, the country, and myself—
Pressed him to make this most unhappy match.

ANSELMA *interrupting*
Unhappy, you say?—Has ever a princess
So lovely been seen?

BARON   Still, I had already
Recognized the bride to be unworthy
Of my noble friend. If I rushed to tie
Their knot, it was not loyalty to my
Hereditary lord that prompted me:
It was a brother's fancy of honor,—
It was anxiety for you, Anselma,

Who loved him and who, however equal
To him in heart and soul, and however
Worthy in my mind of a throne—could not
Have dared ever to raise your sights so high.
Indeed, I've long since come to understand
The folly of presuming to meddle
In another person's life; but today,
For the first time—my heart filled with his words,
In which, though he is barely conscious of it,
Your youthful picture blooms in memory's
Golden glow—I felt how I have sinned
Against you and him, and not just against
The two of you. Against this realm as well,
Which led by a happier prince, might now
Be standing at a more hopeful juncture.

ANSELMA   A foolish brother—yes! But guilty?—No!
Do you fancy that what happened, or not,
Lay within your power?—Do you believe
There was ever sufficient happiness
On this earth to release your noble friend's
Shuttered mind from its gloom and loneliness?
No more than there were ever woman's lips
Of such gentle breath as to be able
To cool Sylvester's restless heart. And had
I not been created just as I am,—
Do you think either a brother's strictness
Or a husband's loving tyranny ever
Threw into unbreakable chains a woman
Who was not fettered fast within herself
From the beginning. Dear brother, do not
Profane my fate with unasked-for pity.
If I had not kept myself for myself—
I would have then belonged to more than one—
And my knowing that—that protected me.

BARON   And even had it been a whorish fate,
Perhaps, you could have lived a woman's life.
He is at the window, in the bay.
Pause.

ANSELMA   I've lived it. And if it was not always

Happy, still, it was by choice. And was it
One of resignation, it was my own.
She follows his glance, which is going out to the garden
Of course, she whom your eyes are following
Now is of a different sort.
BARON *without turning around*

                              You think so?
ANSELMA You don't like to hear that?
BARON *at the window*   But is it not
The same in the end? I wonder. The one
Lives it, the other dreams it.
ANSELMA   For herself.
The sources of her dreams, however, stride
Unperturbed and free through a wakeful world.
BARON Not as freely as we may like to think.
Yearning that trails us secretly, hatred
That sneaks behind us, dreams which make us go—
Of which we have not the least inkling—
All these spin at our fate. And make certain
That none remain guiltless.
Pause. In a different tone

                              What do you think?
They do not look bad together. How long,
How short a time has passed since feather balls
Flew between them on the lawn down below!
And now—
Pause.   A pretty pair.
Pause.   You are silent?
ANSELMA *closer to him*
As you say, a pretty pair.
BARON *calmly*   But you know more!
ANSELMA No more than you. I did not follow her
To the pond a second time.
BARON   A welcome
Coincidence that they found each other
In good time. I'll not withold my blessing long.
ANSELMA It may not strike them as necessary.
SECRETARY *enters from the left.*
BARON Have you the papers?

SECRETARY   Here. But the pages
  To which Your Grace referred must be inside
  The secret drawer which no key will open.
BARON *remembering*
  Quite right. Anselma, come, I will entrust
  The most important papers to your care,
  So they'll be ready when the courier comes
  For them. You, Ungnad, prepare to travel.
  Exits, with Anselma.
SECRETARY *alone, aping the Baron*
  "Prepare to travel"—At your service, Lord,
  Only don't imagine it was you who
  Commanded me. I did it through your mouth.
  Yet, why did I—? Herein lies a puzzle.
  And a deeper one too: why does the Baron's
  Haughty tone, which is after all my own,
  Irk me so. I admit, it was not smart
  To entrust my secret to the poet.
  His doubts, even if they were but my own,
  Have confused me. What did I say? But my own?!
  Yes—All the worse then, if they were my own.

THORN *enters from the right.* SECRETARY

SECRETARY *bows.*
THORN *in a state of anxiety which he continuously endeavors
  to hide, at the same time seeming unable to hold still*
  It's you, Secretary? That's fortunate,
  Forgive my contradicting you recently.
  That was very arrogant. Certainly,
  I am nothing more than a dream of yours.
SECRETARY You're all too modest, Sir. I dreamt you not,
  You exist—if only through me.
THORN   Quite so.
  I your creature, my maker you. And thus
  Costumed, my face made up, a principal
  Actor, I step from the wings, play my part
  In the spotlight, bloated by a poet's
  Bombast—and feel fulfilled, as if I were

What I played. And soon, the role done, I crawl
To the cloakroom, an extinguished hero.
SECRETARY I will permit you to glow a while longer.
*He goes out, since the Baron appears at this moment up on
the gallery.*

Curtain, which goes up again at once.

FIFTH ACT

BARON, THORN

BARON *still on the stairs*
  Back—so soon?
  After a slight hesitation, extends his hand to him
                    Welcome!
THORN   Soon—but not before
  The stipulated time had passed. I've come
  To fetch Leonilda.
BARON   You're very terse.
THORN I wish to state the purpose of my coming
  Before all else. I return the same man
  As I left. That is what you required.
BARON Not only this. But also that you find
  Leonilda the same as you left her.
THORN If you please, I will ask her right away.
BARON Not so hastily—First, it seems to me,
  You must inform us what—happened at home.
  Are you released from all obligations?
THORN I am.
BARON Your bride?—Your child?
THORN   In its mother's
  Arms it lay with blank eye—nothing had been
  Neglected, midwife and doctor stood by—
  He was not destined to draw breath on earth.
  The umbilical cord had strangled him. *Pause.*
BARON And—she?
THORN   Knows nothing, and never will know.
  She greeted me with a smile, in blissful
  Delusion, showed me the dead child at her breast
  And softly placed her finger on her lips,
  As if I mustn't wake it from sound sleep.
  Then she offered me her brow to kiss, breathed
  An unintelligible word—and was gone.
BARON And you—the coffin barely shut—come here
  As a free man.

THORN   I was free when I left.
  And if I gave myself over to grief
  At their deathbed as fervent as ever
  Husband or father felt—to lose myself
  Therein would be weakness; to linger where
  Nothing more held me would be hypocrisy;
  But to give up the intended journey
  And everything waiting at journey's end,
  That would have signified a cowardly
  Misreading of the great awesome sign to which
  I bow in pain, in prayer—and in hope.
BARON *without sharpness* I fear your interpretation differs
  From what is intended for you where signs
  Originate. And if you believe in signs,
  Interpret that one, which seems no riddle.
  Points out into the garden.
THORN *calmly* A sign—where?
BARON   Look there.
THORN *ever calm*   I see a couple,
  Strolling leisurely beneath shady boughs,—
  I see the son of your friend, the Marshal,
  And—your daughter, my bride. Would you prefer
  For me to see something serious in this?
BARON If I were in your place, I would go back
  Where I came from.
THORN *after brief reflection*
                  It would be a sorry world
  If youth were all.—
BARON   Not all, but just enough—
  When the balance swings in a maiden's hand,—
  For fame, and power, and wisdom—all three,
  To weigh not so much as the blond down around
  A young man's lips;—and for their breath to blow
  From laurel wreaths and crowns on old gray heads
  And marble busts on pedestals. Look there.
THORN They walk in silence, distant—
BARON   Can't you hear
  Their hearts beating as one for each other?
  Or see the flames dancing about their brows?

For all your hurry, you have come too late.
THORN You seem hardly to know what's going on,
If you're all that eager to see me gone.
BARON I want to spare you from having to learn
The irrevocable truth from her lips.
THORN Are you speaking at her behest?
BARON   If I
Did so, it would be better for your cause.
For it would signify that she still thinks
Of you, that you are still alive for her.
THORN Not even that—? Become a ghost so soon?
BARON A ghost would have the strength to frighten her.
You are yesterday's newspaper, a name
On a gravestone.
THORN   Well, then I will ask her
At least, if it's written in gold letters.
BARON I did not want to hurt you, but keep you
From being hurt.
THORN   Did you have a solemn
Engagement? Is the wedding feast bespoken?
The guests already invited? The priest
Already waiting? And have I arrived
In time, the final, uninvited guest?
BARON No, but—
THORN *quickly* And if so! If he succeeded—
Which I do not yet believe—in turning
Her heart from me in the space of a day
And two nights—I'll wrest it back in an hour.
BARON In one hour—? Add to that days and years,
A lifetime add to it—a beggar's lap
Will sooner be flooded with great treasures
He never strove for from one day to the next;
Immortality will sooner cast bright
Beams on a forehead newly benighted
By death's dusk; blood-red roses will sooner
Bloom for you in ice fields—than you win back
A second time a heart that you have lost,
No matter what divine gifts you enjoy,
Nor how wholly yours it was at one time.

KONRAD *and* LEONILDA *enter from the left.* BARON,
THORN

Greetings without handshakes.
BARON *to Thorn, immediately on the others' entrance*
The rest, if you please, at table. Konrad
Has something to tell me now, I believe.
In response to a movement of Konrad's
Not here, quite right. Meanwhile I'll leave our friend
To you, Leonilda. See you later!
The Baron and Konrad exit left.

LEONILDA, THORN

LEONILDA *gives Thorn her hand*
Welcome.
THORN   —Am I?
LEONILDA   Yes, you are.—As a friend.
THORN A friend—? That too! But only as a friend,
That would be, as welcome from you, a word
To make me shudder.
LEONILDA   Is there a lovelier,
Then, than this: friendship—? One that promises
Permanence and purity as it does?
Friendship has seemed to me the nobler gift
Ever since I grasped how that other one—
Which sounds sweeter—burns not with heaven's heat
Alone, but with dark hellish flames as well.
Take it! Requite it! Let me not repent
That I perceived no sooner what drew me—
From childhood—drew me so strongly to you.
And—my error past, remain close to me.
THORN—And if you were wrong—are you quite certain
That you're not under a worse error now?
Should a feeling you've harbored since childhood
For me, faithfully, for over a decade,
Have been a dream? Is not the dream, rather,
The magic that creeps about you today,
And will drift away?

LEONILDA   It will. I know. Still,
   What you are to me, will be forever.
   My sole error—(who better to understand
   Than you!)—was how my dawning, unwakened
   Heart construed its troth to its distant friend.
THORN And now that it's awake, does its first beat
   Sound—betrayal?!
LEONILDA   Sylvester!
THORN   Could you forget,
   How when we parted last you adjured me
   Never to go back where I had come from?
LEONILDA I wanted it for your sake, not for mine.
   And if some grief inflicted by me drove
   You back now into that home's hollow fraud,
   Instead of into bright open spaces,
   It's that alone I could perceive as guilt.
THORN Rest easy. The way back is closed to me
   Without your admonition. The "hollow
   Fraud" of home is vanished. The woman is dead,
   And dead the child she bore me yesterday.
LEONILDA You—poor man!
THORN   No, you must not pity me.
   For even if I lay down in the crypt
   With both of them, I would still know: their death
   Was my fault. I wished for it in the depths
   Of my soul. And although in light of day
   Wish and fulfillment appear worlds apart—
   A chain, mysterious and invisible,
   Takes form, link by link, from one to the other.
LEONILDA So, it was your wish, then. It was not mine.
   And were your guilt greater than of conscience,
   Had you murdered them both with your own hands,
   Had I asked you to perform such a deed,
   Even then—an accomplice, guiltier
   Than you, and forfeit by rights to earthly
   Justice—beyond all earthly claims—I'd owe
   Myself to no one, and that includes you.
THORN Do you think I'd stand here asking payment?
   Forgive—although it seems excusable—

My daring to approach you not unlike
A devotee. If you mistook your feeling
For me—what you knew of me, that surely
Remained true. And thus, today, the same man
Stands before you who left two days ago;
He, to whom the fulfillment of his high
Mission was not vouchsafed until this day
Because he never enjoyed that peaceful
Happiness, the promise of which at last
Flows to him from your blessed understanding.

LEONILDA I can no longer give you that happiness.
You're still who you were. I no longer am.

THORN You are. I feel it. You're more than you were,
Since the pale shading veil of innocence
Last lay upon your cool maiden's brow. Now,
Since it's torn, you first stride as a woman—
Of experience—to the experienced man,
Worthy now of me as I am of you.

LEONILDA And if I came to you not from one single
Fateful night, but from a hundred adventures—
Do you think I would forego anything
Because I might feel unworthy of you?
And if you stood in front of me, as free
From stain of sin as I would be depraved—
Do you think my heart would fly to you then?—

THORN And were I bold enough to believe that,—
Would I presume to claim perpetual rights
Therefore? Pureness and sin, troth and betrayal,—
How I feel the sense of such wretched words
Fading before the breath of your free soul.
Truly, he wouldn't know and love you well,
Who coarsely insolent, like a bad husband—
Instead of receiving every new grace
As a new gift freely given each time,
Dared demand it of you as your master.
And I would strike myself as fool and wretch,
Could I ever call on an oath you swore
To me, call on a vow you offered me
Solemnly at the altar, to help me

Against a wandering, escaping heart.
And if you came, from heaven or from hell—
Aquiver with bliss that's barely died away,
Or shaken through with bitter torment—came
From splendor—from misery; came hallowed,
Elevated or disgraced and humbled
Back to me; yes, had you chosen my heart
Only as a patient pillow on which
You wished to rest one night between one pain
You fled the day before and happiness
That will blossom for you the next—I'd be
Blissful, Leonilda, to awaken
Over your sleeping form, and I would know
You belong to me as to none other.

LEONILDA   Oh, hush, Sylvester! Be still! Sully not
Your noble picture.

THORN   You've never seen it
More clearly. I'm not noble. I'm human.
A man who from earlier sorrows sends
His longing's call to the fields of your youth,
That he may recover, in their morning
Fragrance, from the evening curse of loneliness.

LEONILDA   Lonely, you—?! Who is surrounded by shapes,
Thousandfold, risen from your own bosom!
You lonely, to whom choirs of the yet
Unborn sing greetings from eternity—?!

THORN   Do you mock? Don't you know that only shades
Rise from my breast?—That immortality
Is but a myth which like all other myths
Brings joy only to the living?—And that
Whoever lies down to die unsated
By life would sell the blue infinity
Of heaven for one bright ray of sunshine;
The pallid potion of eternity
For one deep breath of sublunary air;
The blissful chant of a thousand choirs
Of angels for one lovely human sound—!
The handshake of a friend, a spring morning,
A cup of wine, a song, a flower's scent—

A faithful dog's eye—how often these trifles,
By us scarcely noticed while we wander,
Living, in the light—how often do they
Outweigh unquenchable tears of mourning
Oozing into a mute, unfeeling grave,
Or the gold inscriptions on marble stones
Beneath which a well-loved body decays,
And oh, how frequently this lie of lies—
This transitory immortality!
And the gratitude of a future world,
However deep it flow—the understanding
Of future races, however ardent,
The longing of audiences yet unborn,
So passionate that it might summon him,
Who has long since drifted up with the clouds,
To return to the world of the living—
Even if I believed that all this could
Ever reach up to my immortal soul—
How I would, laughing, sacrifice it all
For that single hour, that one among
All mortal hours bedewed with the scent
Of eternities, that hour in which—
My breast, though mortal, but filled with life's breath,
And my veins aglow with life's blood—I felt
A flaming heart beating next to my own.

LEONILDA If one such hour means so much, then you have
 Already had numerous eternities
 Allotted to you, and several more
 Await you.

THORN You know, oh young experienced,
 Young disappointed one, you, that I meant
 Other hours than those you, teasing, mean.
 And, desirable as you are—if I
 Court you with such fervor, it's not for that.
 Because you've divined my essence beyond
 The life I've lived and all the work I've done,
 And now, when you fancy me degraded,
 Still feel yourself uplifted by my love—
 I know—and you, in your shyness and doubt,

Know it as well as I do—that among
All women on earth you have been destined
For me from the beginning of all time.

LEONILDA I only know that you, with every word,
Move further away from me, and are grown
So distant now that your very voice sounds
As remote as that of one departed.

BARON *at the door to the right, turns back to speak to some-
one who is not visible*
Thanks for the news.
To Dominik, who is also standing behind the door
See to it, Dominik,
That the envoy is given food and drink.
Now Konrad enters as well.

THORN, LEONILDA, BARON, KONRAD

LEONILDA What has happened?
BARON   Not much. A mob made noise
In front of the Marchese's residence —
KONRAD But it's still not known if it was a mob,
In fact.
BARON The ringleaders were thrown in jail.
KONRAD Two who resisted were killed by the watch.
BARON It is the Emperor's will that every
Injury done to the ambassador's
Sacred person be punished without pity.
KONRAD Still, whether or not his people will thank
The Emperor when their brothers' blood flows
Here at home, instead of the enemy's
On the battlefield, and whether or not
The ambassador will continue to feel
Comfortable in our capital, what with
The popular scorn raging around him
Despite all royal protection—you are
As doubtful of that yourself as I am.
BARON We will yet manage to silence that scorn.
KONRAD Not for long. And whatever you force down—
Or think you force—will grow on in secret.

BARON Not so secretly as you think. We know
    The muddy springs from which the unknowing
    Masses get their scorn and hatred to drink.
    And we will light the corners from which stones
    Are hurled at the ambassador's windows.
KONRAD I don't know who it was cast the first stone;
    However, I shake his hand in spirit.
    Pause.
BARON *in a different tone*
    Konrad! Once more, take up your proper place
    While time permits. By tomorrow, perhaps,
    Your Prince may need your sword. But, for today,
    He has in council issued your orders.
KONRAD *with bitterness*
    And yesterday—he tore the Marshal's staff
    From my father's hand. You may, Herr Chancellor,
    Hold me longer in this house, as hostage
    Or as guest;—but if the roads are open,
    Then there is only one for me to take.
    Pause.
BARON There it lies.
KONRAD *astounded* For free passage?
BARON   I'll not hold
    You any longer. Make your way.
KONRAD *after an instant's thought* Farewell!
    Turns around.
BARON *highly surprised, quickly*
    No other parting word?
KONRAD   You mean of thanks?
    Forgive me, I thought you might interpret
    It as mockery, because what you showed
    Me as hospitality, all too soon
    Began to savor of captivity.
    Still, since you have granted me my freedom
    At last, thank you. And, dear cousin, to you—
    Hesitates.
BARON As one is wont to say to dear cousins:
    See you again soon.
KONRAD   Who knows, in such times—

BARON One knows what one wants. What will be, of course,
  Is written in the stars. Have a good trip,
  And give my best regards to your father.
  I still hope that brighter days are coming,
  And that you'll return with him to this house.
KONRAD *hard* That seems questionable.
  Turns to go again.
BARON *with some haste*   Or must I first,
  Formally, invite my valued old friend
  To the wedding of my only daughter
  To his only son—?
KONRAD   Do you mean to say—
LEONILDA That is quite a joke, father!
KONRAD   Ah, did both
  Our fathers secretly betroth us, then,
  While we were still in the cradle?
BARON   We never
  Discussed the matter. Still, whether engaged
  Or not, since you are married in God's eyes—
  Which surely you don't fear to acknowledge—
  A priest should consecrate this welcome bond,
  I think, in the traditional manner.
  And—come to think of it—I imagine
  The wedding should take place before the groom
  Leaves on a journey, the return from which
  May in these times be easily delayed.
LEONILDA Forgive me, my father, I do not wish
  To be married so soon, no matter to whom.
BARON You spoke first. Is it not astonishing
  That he keeps silent!
KONRAD   What Leonilda
  Said seems answer enough to anything
  I could possibly say. Hence my silence.
LEONILDA Let him depart a free man. I will remain
  Behind, a free woman. How—and whether
  We will find each other again, is known
  Only to that God in whose eyes we wed.
KONRAD You have spoken. I must accept your word.
  He bows his head, takes Leonilda's hand and kisses it, and

turns again as if to leave.

BARON *out of control*
  But before you go, bold lad, you must kneel
  Before her, who, standing at the outset
  Of your journey, has blessed it so richly
  As rarely befell unworthy sons of earth
  In mythic times from daughters of heaven.

KONRAD And as lovely daughters of earth may have,
  At times, experienced with sons of the gods.

BARON As long as they're not mere adventurers.

KONRAD There are those too. But none knows beforehand
  Whereto their path will lead—how low, how high.
  And it is just such adventurers' habit,
  Whether from whim or impatience, to take
  Along their way what good fortune bestows,
  Be she goddess, peasant, maiden, or sprite.

BARON But if they're too impatient or given
  To whim, such a dandy may encounter
  Trouble, too, in the midst of good fortune.
  Such as being haled to court, for instance,
  Charged with high treason.

KONRAD *ever calmer and more insolent the less able the
  Baron is to control himself* Tell me, Herr Chancellor,
  Why go to such lengths? You can hold court yourself!
  Because who knows whether other judges,
  Who, unlike you, don't have it in their heads
  To make me their son-in-law—I'm honored,
  Indeed, but you were too clever by half—
  Will see high treason there, where it appears
  To you.

BARON Not high treason that you, instead
  Of obeying your Emperor's call, plan
  To stir up the troops for the benefit
  Of the deposed Marshal? Not high treason
  That you—but I will not put into words
  The sort of mad plans raging in your mind.
  But since I know it, and since precaution
  Is this moment's duty, I wish, until
  You face your judges, to have you guarded

Better than heretofore. Hand me your sword,
At once!
KONRAD *after hesitating briefly, hands him the sword.*
LEONILDA   What are you doing, my father?
If you call what he committed treason,
Then you must pass the same sentence on me.
Ask him on his sword, or on his honor,
Who it was, with him wavering and set
To take the easier path you showed him,
Directed him to that alternate one,
Worthier of him. Traitor! I would name
Him one if he had done for me, for you,
For princely favor—even if later
It turned out a hundred times both clever
And right—what today he felt to be unjust;—
Unjust in three ways as it seems to me:
To himself, his father—and the nation.
BARON   And if it seems a threefold injustice
Right now—or a hundredfold—is he not
One of those men who, lusting for great deeds
At any price, no matter how senseless,
Desirous of fame, even at the cost
Of streams of strangers' blood, must bear the guilt
For the horror and chaos of such times—?!
LEONILDA   I don't know whether he bears as much guilt
In the current confusion as you think.
But I doubt anyone is strong enough
At this late hour to alter the course
Of events to his own mind. And I feel—
And however things turn out, you do too,
That this terrible period must find him
A free man, whether he's a fool and fresh,
Or a noble, and heroic. Therefore
I beg of you, return his sword to him.
Pause.
BARON *gives him the sword back*
Here—take it back without my good wishes.
KONRAD   As due to me, without thanks, I receive it.
BARON   And without any further farewell—go.

KONRAD *turns around to leave.*
THORN *who has been standing motionless in the bay*
  Only allow me, Squire Ursenbeck,
  To hurl a parting word after you. Boy!
KONRAD *remains standing at the door*
  If delay there must be, may it be short.
  Thorn reaches for his sword
  Not that way. Sheathe your sword. I can read it
  Written on your brow: you are less disposed
  To killing than to being killed. That would
  Make for an unequal game. Two pistols,
  Never fired, lie in my saddlebag.
  A cloth between us. The odds will be fairer.
THORN I am satisfied, come!
LEONILDA   Stay, I tell you.
THORN Here, Leonilda, must your power end.
  Just as Thorn and Konrad are about to leave, each offering
  to let the other precede him, Dominik enters, breathless
DOMINIK A troop of horsemen, Lord, in the village—
BARON And?
DOMINIK They come from the border—War! They are
  The same ones the Emperor sent down there
  To order the withdrawal of our troops.
  It was too late. The battle had begun.
BARON Which side fired the first shot?
DOMINIK   Galloping
  Wildly by, my Lord, they called out to us
  From their saddles what I have reported.
  More than that, Your Grace, I do not know.
BARON Why was
  One of them not detained? I want to see
  The next one. Give the order, Dominik.
DOMINIK *exits quickly.*
KONRAD Herr Chancellor, whichever side began it—
  And to which side victory will incline—
  The war is here—and the world is changed now.
  These eyes and this heart, my weapons and hands,
  Are no longer mine, but the nation's now,
  The Emperor's. And if I should return—

I'll settle every debt I left behind
With a mind much easier than today.
I gladly acknowledge them before departing.
You, Herr Sylvester Thorn, whatever happens,
May rest assured of your first claim on me.
And before the peace bells' ringing dies away,
I will appear at what place you determine.
To you, my cousin, I bow knee and head.
Whatever you decide, in my absence,
I declare myself solemnly engaged
To you. But, Uncle, before I dare sue
For Leonilda's hand, I beg of you,
Consider that the deed undone distracts
And bedevils the mind. And so forgive
The unseemly insolence of my speech.

BARON   If I were to speak words of forgiveness,
They would be lies—for all my annoyance
Aside, I was never angry with you.
The time opposed you, as you opposed it—
Now you are standing face to face, now both
May find fulfillment, each in the other.

KONRAD   Thanks for your noble words. And shall I hear
No parting ones from you, Leonilda?

LEONILDA   Go free from here. Yours be what you desire,
Yours be deeds and fame, yours heaven, earth, and hell.
You were made for attacking and seizing,
Not for looking behind and keeping safe.
And when memory clings, like a dark shade,
To other people's steps and holds them back,
May its wings bear you to new happiness.

KONRAD   This sounds like a blessing, but it's good-bye.

LEONILDA   A wish and a prophecy—take it thus.

KONRAD *bows again.*

LEONILDA *kisses him on the forehead.*

KONRAD *begins to go, then stops abruptly*
One answer is still wanting, Sylvester Thorn's.

BARON   He is gone.

KONRAD   He heard me. My word is good.

BARON   Farewell. And do not drive your horse to death,

Lest overhastiness delay you more
Than ever lingering might.
KONRAD   Have no fear,
I will ride into battle in good time,
To seek out for myself, among the crowd
Of foes, that one—do you still remember—
With whom, strolling leisurely along the brook
In conversation, I almost became friends.
I see him tower, strangely tall, and look
About, as if he sought just me, and longed
For a further meeting, of a fashion
More becoming to us.—He shall have it. *Exits.*

BARON, LEONILDA. *Pause.*

DOMINIK *appears at the door.*
BARON Look for Herr Thorn. I'd really like to have
A word with him prior to my leaving. *Dominik exits.*
Come, Leonilda!
LEONILDA *goes to him* Father!
BARON   To depart—
Much is weighing on you right now, my child.
LEONILDA Allow me to anticipate the question
I see in your glance. Do you know how fully
Your child understands you?
BARON   Yes, I know it.
And I go hence with lighter heart for it.
LEONILDA I'll not be far. If tomorrow morning
You want me, I'll be with you by evening.
BARON You would not find me. My useless office
Can be administered by another.
I will resign immediately, and march
Into the field with my old regiment
As I promised myself in the event.
LEONILDA Into the field—you too?
BARON   What choice remains?
Even senseless deeds are worthier now
Than words lacking power, however wise.
DOMINIK *enters* Herr Thorn is not in the garden or the

house.

But no one saw him leave.

The Baron and Leonilda look at each other.

The Secretary enters in haste.

BARON   Well, finally,
Ungnad, are you ready?

SECRETARY   I am, but first
Hear me. You had here a singular guest.
Sylvester Thorn—

BARON   What's the matter with him?

SECRETARY He leapt into the world out of my brain,
We were both on earth at the same moment.

BARON Millions of people are. Stop your nonsense.
Where is he?

SECRETARY I ran into him just now
At the small gate that opens to the wood.
I greeted him with all due deference.
But he looked past me. In that very instant—
I perceived it with horror—he escaped.
I called to him. He went. I followed him
Through the woods. He went.

BARON   Where?

SECRETARY   The enchanted pond.

BARON Who told you there's an enchanted pond here?

SECRETARY I smelled it in the breeze blowing from there.

LEONILDA Towards the pond—

SECRETARY   And no differently
Than if the forest trail he took went on
Invisibly beneath the mirrored surface,
He strode ever further into the flood—
And deeper, until it swallowed him up.

BARON You let it happen?

SECRETARY   Two of us on earth?
He or I! It had to be, I felt it
From the very first moment I saw him.

LEONILDA *has gone off.*

BARON *to the Secretary*
Out of my sight, madman!

SECRETARY   What do you want

From me? Everything will stay exactly
As it was, after all. You my creature,
I your secretary. And if you killed
Me,—the secretary would be done for,
Of course, but the Baron along with him. *Exits.*
BARON I fear there are men still madder than he.
*Anselma comes down from the gallery. The Baron, who was
about to follow Leonilda, speaks as if to himself*
Anselma!
ANSELMA *still on the steps*
       Here are the papers.
BARON   Thank you.
ANSELMA There are more than you asked for. I found some
You had yourself forgotten and which now
Will be priceless to you.
BARON   Give me!
Distracted   Let's see!
ANSELMA *surprised*
You are alone? Young Konrad is gone?
BARON   More
Has come to pass while you were rummaging
In my old papers than you may suspect.
Sylvester, too, was here.
ANSELMA   Is here—?
BARON   Was here.
He too is gone again.
ANSELMA *full of misgivings* What has happened?
BARON The war broke out. Konrad is in the field.
Sylvester Thorn—on a longer journey.
ANSELMA Where is Sylvester?—Brother—! Dead—?!
BARON   The mad
Secretary followed him and saw him
Do it: he has drowned himself in the pond.
ANSELMA For Leonilda—?
BARON   She bears no blame.
ANSELMA *reminding him of his own saying* Then
It has not been seen to that none is guiltless?
BARON If that's true, then I bear the blame with her,
Without regret. For—may God forgive me—

As painfully as his death has moved me,
My mind rests easier to know him dead
In the pond than in my child's marriage bed.
ANSELMA Words without pity! And if they are true,
It seems a truth of such deep presumption
That the courage to believe it, believe
In oneself at this hour, must shatter.
BARON Is it ever too soon to guess at law
And purpose, even there, where one may share
The guilt in so sad an event. Don't you
Feel yourself that our friend, so splendid
Once, opted in good time to take his leave,
While yet some dignity remained to him?
ANSELMA Oh, leave me my entire pain today.
There will be time enough to understand.
—Does Leonilda know?
BARON *suddenly remembering*
                    Come!
ANSELMA   She is there—?!
BARON I was about to follow when you came.
ANSELMA Surely you're not worried?
BARON   She took it hard.
ANSELMA Let her tears flow by the pond for today.
It won't last long, then she'll think as little
Of the corpse in the deep as does the wind
That blows careless over reed and surface,
And next year, her brightly colored rowboat
Will ride with merry strokes through the water.

LEONILDA *enters.* BARON, ANSELMA

LEONILDA Do not search for him. The water, stirred up,
Still circles where he glided to the bottom
And, bodiless, his picture breaks apart.
There let him repose. For no wave brings back
Whatever sank in the depths of the pond.
Neither thing nor man does the wave bring back.
The Secretary enters from the left, highly excited.
BARON Are you still here? What do you want?

SECRETARY   Your Grace—
  The most terrible things are happening!
  I'm going mad. It was Sylvester Thorn
  Who gave the signal, but now everything
  Is plunging in after him. Animals
  And men. And streams and woods. And peaks and sky.
  It was I—and behind this brow the world
  I created—which the monstrous shadows
  Hurled into nothingness for their pastime—
  Now it shines, roars, howls, it lives all around—
  And I stand opposing a world alone. *Rushes off, right.*

BARON, LEONILDA, ANSELMA

LEONILDA Father, take me with you. Old age, madness,
  And death creep thrice ghostly throughout this house.
  I don't want to spend another night here.
DOMINIK *enters in haste*
  Two riders have been detained, as ordered,
  They're bringing welcome news from the border.
BARON Where are they?
DOMINIK   They've just now reached the court-
  yard,
  But impatiently, well-nigh unruly,
  That without just cause, as they seem to think—
BARON *interrupting*
  Let them remain mounted then, and—riding
  At our side—on the road to the city,
  Give us the latest news. *Dominik exits.*
  To Anselma and Leonilda
                       You two, farewell.
  I must no longer tarry.
LEONILDA *almost imploring* My father!
BARON Very well. I'll take you along with me
  Right now. And you, Anselma, will follow
  Us as soon as you can.
ANSELMA   You can just leave
  Me here.
BARON   It won't be comfortable for you

Alone in the castle.

ANSELMA   I'm used to it.

BARON *as if feeling guilty* Anselma!

ANSELMA *quickly*   And tomorrow I will send
  Everything of Leonilda's that may
  Be useful at court—of dresses, jewels—

BARON Quite right, just so that all may be on hand
  When feasts begin again.

LEONILDA *comes down in her coat.*

ANSELMA   That could be sooner
  Than we think today.

LEONILDA *still on the steps*
                    What kind of feast—?

BARON   God
  Willing, one for peace.

LEONILDA   A victory feast!

ANSELMA Who knows—a wedding celebration—?!

LEONILDA *a few steps further down, as if surprised*
                              What do you mean?

ANSELMA That you may, perhaps, be fated to be
  The victor's prize.

BARON   Leonilda was meant
  To be not prize or booty but a gift,
  To the worthiest freely given.

LEONILDA   And
  As a gift, free also to keep herself.

DOMINIK *stands at the open door on the right.*
The BARON *and* LEONILDA *after a farewell glance and
greetings directed at* ANSELMA, *exit.*
ANSELMA *reciprocates glance and greeting, stands motionless; the door to the right closes; the curtain falls.*

The End

AFTERWORD

In the last ten to fifteen years of his life, Arthur Schnitzler's reputation rested on his prose. Such works as *Fräulein Else*, *Traumnovelle* (*Dream Novel*), and *Flucht in die Finsternis* (*Flight into Darkness*), published in the twenties, which explored the darker recesses of the human psyche, found critical acceptance. Schnitzler was not so fortunate with his late plays, especially those which appeared after the end of the First World War. These were perceived by most of their earliest critics (and many since then) as obsolete, as depicting a bygone world of no relevance to contemporary audiences. Indeed, most of the late plays are likelier than the prose of the period to touch upon what may be termed the conventional domestic situation—relationships between spouses, lovers, or parents and children, and to result in some sort of reconciliation.

In retrospect, we can see that the charge of obsolescence was the result more of form and approach than of actual content (as well, perhaps, of personal animosity, since Schnitzler made no secret of despising most critics). The fashion in drama was changing towards expressionism and a more direct discussion of social and political problems, as exemplified by Georg Kaiser and Bertolt Brecht, for example. But the three plays presented here in English for the first time touch upon themes of timeless application and relevance, such as growing up and growing old, war and peace, illusion and reality, truth and deception. True, their eighteenth-century and pre-1919 settings may be "old-fashioned" but their subject matter is no more obsolete than anything set in the Norwegian or Russian provinces by Ibsen or Chekhov.

I

The Sisters, or Casanova in Spa is the only one of Schnitzler's late plays that resembles a "comedy" in the sense familiar to the student of traditional English-language drama—i.e., in the sense of *The Comedy of Errors* or *School for Scandal*, for example. It is the only play he designated a *Lustspiel*, in contrast to a *Komödie*, the latter generic appellation appearing most congruent with what we have come to know as "dark" or "problem" comedies, such as *Professor Bernhardi, Fink and Fliederbusch*, or the *Seduction Comedy*. According to Klaus Kilian, one of the leading students of Schnitzler's comedic output, *Lustspiel* describes a drama of action, *Komödie* a drama of decision.[1]

A prior awareness of the play's genre is important to its resolution or, more precisely, to the audience's sense of how the action is likely to be resolved because the "obstacle" to be faced and overcome by the principal protagonists on their road to nuptial love is potentially far more threatening here than, say, in Shakespeare's *Much Ado about Nothing*, just as Santis is potentially more dangerous than any of Shakespeare's gulls. However, although Anina's encounter with Casanova, unwitting though it may have been, *could*, in a different context, lead to tragedy, it is not allowed to do so here. Instead, we are led to believe that Anina and Andrea will return home and marry.

Nevertheless, before the happy ending we expect in such a play can take place, that is, before the young lovers can be safely married off, Andrea (and to a far lesser extent, Anina) have to grow up. That is to say, the play contains a number of elements typical of the *Bildungsroman*. It depicts, primarily, a young man who has left home undergoing adventure, initiation, and disappointment, his subsequent acceptance of a less than perfect world, and his return home (here only predicted, by both Gudar and Casanova). It turns on Andrea's coming to terms with reality, unpleasant as it might be, and of his becoming reconciled to Anina, no matter how "flawed" she may appear to him after her encounter with Casanova. Anina has less to learn, in keeping with the tradition of romantic heroines' being superior to their male counterparts. She need only overcome her brief infatuation with Casanova and her feelings of injured vanity resulting from what is obviously her interchangeability with Flaminia in Casanova's eyes. But she knows that their encounter was meaningless, a notion seconded by Casanova when he declares the entire episode

---

[1]Klaus Kilian, *Die Komödien Arthur Schnitzlers. Sozialer Rollenzwang und kritische Ethik* (Düsseldorf: Bertelsmann, 1972), p. 23.

to have been invalid.

Within the bounds of the play, Andrea's initiation into the adult world begins, ironically, by means of *someone else's* (Anina's) sexual encounter with, of all people, history's most notorious seducer. Moreover, it is Casanova, a man living more for the impressions of the moment than any of Schnitzler's protagonists since Anatol, who teaches Andrea (or reminds him of) the values of bourgeois love amid the comforts of hearth and home. This interpenetration of values, the bourgeois, as represented by Anina and Andrea, and the impressionistic, as represented by Casanova, Gudar, Flaminia, Santis and Teresa, is instrumental to Andrea's successful transition to adulthood.

To be sure, he enjoys the important advantage of self-knowledge. Thus, he does not disagree with Casanova's assessment that "Your destination is peace, order, law,/As homecoming is the ultimate sense/Of your wandering," and he is absolutely right in telling Casanova, near the end, "This is not my world./It is yours." However, before he can achieve maturity, Andrea must also acquire moderation. He must overcome a number of childish traits, such as the foolish pride he displays when he insists that *all* his hunches are always right, the fragile male ego that causes him to attach excessive value to his (and Anina's) reputation, the insecurity that makes him immediately suspicious of Anina's having written to Casanova and causes him, in effect, to give up on their relationship even before he knows what transpired the previous night, and, finally, his view of women. The latter he shares with a number of Schnitzler's characters, with no middle ground between madonna and whore.

His inflexible, judgmental approach is best seen in contrast to Anina's. Andrea identifies Flaminia as one to whom love is a business or, at best, "a fleeting pleasure." He is pained that Anina can even keep company with her and Santis, whereas she, in response to Gudar's remarking that she is probably not accustomed to such company, says, "I am not that refined," and finds she has been treated politely even if Santis drinks and Flaminia talks a little too much. Similarly, Andrea, intolerant of and thus unable to understand the impressionistic point of view, interprets events the only way he can, from the vantage of bourgeois morality and male insecurity, and so carries on about Anina's body lingering in Casanova's memory, of the arch-seducer's taking her picture with him wherever he goes, and so on. The wiser Anina knows that she has been involved in an evanescent experience, a fleeting moment of abandon, a dream state in which she lost consciousness of past and future, but one from which she awoke free of guilt, essentially unchanged, and as worthy of Andrea's tenderness as she had been before.

That nothing and no one in the "real" world is perfect or untainted, a lesson all young people must learn, provides the basis for Flaminia's early reference to her and Anina's having been mistaken for sisters, which at first startles the younger woman, and for Casanova's observation of an essential sisterhood among all women, which is reflected in the title of the play. It also allows Casanova to identify Andrea as a fellow-student and friend. We may question Casanova's sincerity in this instance—he is, after all, primarily interested in convincing Andrea to lend him a good deal of money—but he does seem later to have Andrea's (and Anina's) best interests at heart, and refers to him as his "chosen brother" at play's end. Moreover, Andrea is linked to Casanova on two other occasions by Schnitzler's precise use of language. When he angrily accuses Anina of being a born deceiver and she replies she did it for him, he retorts, "Since I happened to be there." Soon after, Casanova, in countering Andrea's accusation, claims never to have been a seducer and states, "No, I was present,/Just when nature with its sweet sorcery/Began its work"; and when he describes Gudar as "An old man, and was once as young as I,/As you, even," in addition to touching upon aging in general, long a significant theme in Schnitzler's work, Casanova also equates all three men.

This does not mean, obviously, that all persons are similarly or equally flawed. Santis's and Flaminia's insistence or assumption that Andrea and Anina are like them as regards love of jewelry or a readiness to fleece others, for instance, shows only their desire to bring everyone down to their level. Still, for all that she represents an impressionistic outlook, as illustrated in her attitude regarding Andrea's newly acquired wealth ("And I hope/You'll be smart enough to seize the day's luck"), Flaminia is nonetheless capable of discoursing on the advantages of early marriages; and, not surprisingly given her relatively insecure lifestyle, she is also adept at accommodation and has something to teach the younger people about the compromises needful in the adult world:

> If every woman
> Acted that way after every quarrel—
> The half-packed suitcases would stand around
> In lodging-house bedrooms by the dozen.
> . . . .
> Why this obstinacy? You've had a fight—
> You'll make it up again. That's the custom.

Santis, like his wife a survivor, can teach Andrea something about discretion being the better part of valor in his readiness to give up the notion of fighting Casanova when a way out offers itself, in marked contrast to Andrea's silly insistence that he is fighting for a higher cause than Anina's "honor" alone.

It is with Teresa's arrival that Andrea can begin to learn the final, most important lessons. It was not enough for Casanova to claim that his encounter with Anina was invalid. It takes the dancer's making clear that beyond occasional mutual accusations, even of unfaithfulness, the past can not be undone, and that being together is the important thing: "I have him again—and so ask nothing. . . . And why the questions?/ Aren't I back?" If the claim that any lovers she may have had in the interim are more than dead, are forgotten, is a bit too impressionistic for Andrea, the forgiveness asked for and given implied in the return are worthy of attention.

But Andrea, insisting that he can not return to an unfaithful woman, while the surprised Casanova can, elicits the latter's final lecture. Ironically, the most cogent statement of the limits of human knowledge of another person's faithfulness, something the overly idealistic young man is obliged to hear, is itself the product of a limited, flawed mind and is, therefore, flawed as well. Casanova's deeply skeptical view that only a "coming back" is evidence of "faithfulness" (since vows can be faked) and that no one can be another's "home," argues that bourgeois certainties should not necessarily be seen as such. However, as one who lives only for the impressions of the moment, he is unable to conceive of any love as real in the absence of the physical presence of the object of that love.

Moreover, his attack on "homecoming" and "home" is as limited as the views espoused by Anina and Andrea, to whom

these values are so important. Even if the order resulting from
bourgeois concepts of "home and abroad" were as much a matter
of self-deception as Casanova claims, it would not therefore be
any less reliable or more a matter of self-deception than a per-
ception of universal chaos, since things of that sort are simply
not ascertainable. And while the bourgeois may attempt to see
things consistently, it does not follow that he or she always sees
them falsely, or that the sophist's vision is any truer.

Thus, in the end, for all the lessons available to him and all
the help he has received from unlikely sources, Andrea's
definitive acceptance of reality depends ultimately on his being
recalled to *his* world, on Anina's calling to him and, by
implication, forgiving him. It is only after she summons him to
join her outside that Casanova can simultaneously warn and
assure him:

> You're being called too. That was Anina's voice.
> And if you still hesitate now, you will
> Deserve nothing more than to be deceived.
> *In response to a gesture of Andrea's*
> For the first time.

In the end, Andrea leaves the room where an essentially insig-
nificant episode has been played out and steps into the "real"
world which, if populated by such individuals as Casanova,
Santis, and Flaminia, nevertheless also offers the possibility of
true, lasting, and reliable love as most "normal" people know it,
as well as of responsible behavior, which is beyond the capacity
of his and Anina's temporary companions.

II

In its multiplicity of elements and themes, Schnitzler's
Seduction Comedy enjoys a panoramic point of view. Like *The
Way to the Pond*, it combines conventional dramatic character
study, particularly of Aurelie and Falkenir, and political purpose,
the criticism of a world on the brink of collapse, a world represented here by a cross-section of pre-war Austrian society: the
nobility, the upper middle class, the middle class (including Max,

who serves as the link among all the classes), and the military.

In keeping with the psychological accuracy we associate with Schnitzler, no character is free of flaw. Even Ambros Doehl, the most positive of the men, misjudges Falkenir's passing his test in Act Three. By the same token, no major character is so negative as to be denied at least one redeeming quality, even if it is limited to a single insight. Even Gysar, a despicable individual, is allowed to respond to Skodny's remark about Arduin's condescending to keep company with a poet with, "Perhaps, Herr Captain, it is Ambros Doehl who is condescending in this case?"

The first theme is most evident in the name of the play and in its basic structure (especially of Act Two), in Max's interacting with his three partners. But there are many other seductions or sexual experiences as well, planned, wished for, or accomplished, including those between Julia and Arduin, Julia and Braunigl, Judith and Arduin, Gysar and his models, and Fenz and the Countess. There are also the love-hate relationship between Julia and Westerhaus and the unsatisfied desires cut short by circumstance or death: Doehl for Aurelie and Judith for Westerhaus. Judith's claim to have become an experienced woman during her vigil at her beloved Westerhaus's bier points also to the love-death connection so common in Schnitzler's work; it is most evident here in Aurelie's and Falkenir's suicide, but it is foreshadowed by references to Max's father having been Aurelie's mother's lover and shot by her father and to Falkenir's first wife's suicide, as well as by the exchange between Max and Aurelie at the end of Act One and in Aurelie's musing at the very end of the first scene of the second act:

> I'm shivering.—And yet, it's good to be alone. Alone once again. . . between one happiness and the other. Between one pleasure and the other. Between one death and the other. . . .

What we have is not exactly a new version of Schnitzler's 1897 *Reigen* (*La Ronde*), but something similar: portrayals of or allusions to multiple encounters, not always sexual in nature, leading to nothing wholesome or lasting. The one encounter that "should" have developed, between Aurelie and Falkenir, never gets off the ground at all. In general, the "love" situations lead not only to a "perversion of the erotic,"[2] but also, by extension, to a perversion of art (Gysar), law (Braunigl), and patriotism (Arduin). In contrast, there is the conventional, healthy relationship between Elisabeth and her Lieutenant leading to marriage. It is grounded on common sense, exemplified by her "Things will be settled wherever I am," and on basic values such as making each other happy, as Seraphine tells Leinsdorf.

A second, related theme concerns freedom: the desire for it, the extent to which it is achieved, and how it is handled. Most of the characters want sex and freedom, sex without commitment, often out of fear of commitment, which is one reason for the failure of their relationships. Arduin arranges to take Judith on his yacht without even knowing who she is; Gysar wants to enjoy any and every woman he can get his hands on; and Falkenir, although not sexually involved with Aurelie, obviously fears making a commitment to her. Curiously, among the men, it is Max, the "seducer," who wants a commitment, at least from Seraphine, but can not get it. This should not be surprising. Max is an upper-middle-class young man and it should come as no surprise if he embodies conventional, middle-class values, his "impressionistic" lifestyle notwithstanding.

Among the women, Julia wants freedom to humiliate her husband, and she will go to any lengths to achieve it, but she does not want to be tied to Braunigl either, or to fulfill the promises she seems to have made to him. Even so, her freedom remains limited and certainly amounts to no real autonomy. In her final appearance on stage she is confused, grasping after her pearls, and about to rush off to Braunigl, not for "love," but to hide her necklace. After her husband's suicide and Braunigl's arrest she remains alone, estranged from her sister, and beset by financial worries.

Judith, in response to her unhappy love for Westerhaus, not to mention her having witnessed what a marriage can deteriorate into, rejects any long-term involvement with a man and flees to a life of momentary pleasures. She wants no one to have control over her, but in her inability to give herself fully to another she

---

[2] Ernst L. Offermanns, *Arthur Schnitzler. Das Komödienwerk als Kritik des Impressionismus* (Munich: Wilhelm Fink, 1973), p. 129.

is no better than the self-centered Max. Following their rendez-vous, Judith does not care where he goes, and does not think it his business where she goes. She wants only happy memories of "happiness without compulsion, without torment" that will not deteriorate like other joys, and she rejects out of hand the male domination implied in Max's *wanting* to know what she will do next. Unable to go to England to pursue her studies because of the war, she sails with Arduin to an unknown destination, leaving her not exactly free but still uncommitted.

Seraphine, a stronger and more goal-oriented character than the others, is as free as anyone else in the play, though the child she expects will necessarily restrict her to some degree. Having weighed the facts, she resolves to pursue her career and refuses to marry Max. She knows that with the outbreak of war, Max's offer of a home for her and the child is meaningless. She also knows that no one can be protected forever in any event. When Elisabeth chides her and their father regarding his overcoat—"Oh, you two, one should never let you out of one's sight"—Seraphine replies, "And yet, one must occasionally," an attitude of some importance in *The Way to the Pond* as well. She is down to earth, whether she is urging her father to stop romanticizing her violin playing or assuring Max that there are people who simply go home after midnight.

The most important aspect of the freedom motif concerns Aurelie, the one character who does not want it but has it forced upon her by a foolish Falkenir, with tragic results. Aurelie sees Falkenir as a haven to which she can flee from the after-effects of her mother's affair. Forced by the man of her choice to live a life foreign to her temperament, Aurelie learns freedom quickly enough. In Act Two she tells Arduin that she owes an accounting to no one but herself and, later, that no man "will ever touch so much as the tip of my finger if I do not wish it." Shortly thereafter she asserts control over her life when she tells Falkenir that she does not require his protection. However, she does not achieve autonomy any more than Julia does. Having descended into self-alienation if not madness, and understanding that things cannot be made right again, she chooses death.

Who then is free? Gilda, perhaps, the "water sprite," a child still, and a citizen of a neutral nation—and the older Fenz, who, unfit for military service, maintains that life begins at sixty and that only a man of that age can truly sing Don Giovanni.

Falkenir, a former diplomat who withdrew from public life to take up archeology, is concerned with relics and does not seem to know what to do with a real live woman. Underlying his rejection of Aurelie is his attitude towards women (one of several embodied by the men in the play). In assuming Aurelie is governed by erotic desires, Falkenir shows his understanding of reality to be as problematic as hers. In practically forcing Aurelie to dance with Max and Gysar, he is forcing her to "enjoy" a freedom she does not want. His subsequent assertion, "I am giving you back your freedom—to become what you are, Aurelie," is a bit of presumption that demonstrates his low opinion of women and which, in fact, equates her with Gysar, who only two pages earlier, while nagging Aurelie to let him paint her portrait, maintains, "Only with yours, Aurelie, could I become the person I am."

By contrast, the other men's attitudes towards women are, if not necessarily worthy of imitation, more honest. Arduin, for instance, makes no effort to disguise either his libertinism or his double standard. Gysar is a thoroughly nasty individual who wants only to enjoy women's favors, and who uses his talent as a cover for his seductions. Westerhaus is either oblivious to Judith or condescending, neither of which is as crude as his attitude towards his wife. Max is a seducer but a kindly one who is actually used by the women with whom he has his brief affairs. Although his vocation is superficial, it is not without value. As Doehl, perhaps the most reliable character in the play, puts it, "Can there be a more useful occupation than to increase the total joy, to say nothing of happiness, in this earthly vale of tears?"

Clearly, Ambros Doehl is the best of the men. He obviously loves Aurelie, but he is a true friend to her, putting her interests and well-being above his own. His weakness, if it must be called such, is that he creates an idealized Aurelie, surely the most harmless of all the escapes from reality illustrated in the play, especially since he sees her clearly enough in Act Three.

Eligius Fenz represents not so much an attitude towards women as wishful thinking—that he can still be a Don Juan, another avoidance of reality, in this instance the inexorable passage of time. This is not to say that Fenz is unaware of the reality. When the Princess introduces him as a "member of the Imperial and Royal Court Opera," he quickly corrects her: "Past member. An honorary member for a long time now," even if he is still thinking about establishing new contacts or renewing old ones. Foolish as this may be, it represents something more positive than Falkenir's quitting on life and its possibilities.

Obviously, Don Giovanni was the great role of Fenz's career, and there is no problem with his displaying at home a photo of himself in the role nor in his having actually acted the part in his younger days, but the older man risks ridicule if he takes too seriously the two masked ladies' addressing him as "Count Almaviva" and "Don Juan." Fenz cannot prevail against the youth-inspired "myth about old age." Elisabeth, as usual, takes the sensible view: she finds it may be good for Fenz to become a grandfather so he could finally discover that he is no longer a young man. Although his singing the Champagne Aria and pursuing Gilda at the end may be humorous, or a bit ridiculous, even, it still serves as a healthy and harmless contrast to the attitude represented by Falkenir and Aurelie, who "didn't know that life becomes ever more precious the less of it remains."

Fenz's continuing to play Don Giovanni in the face of advancing age is but one of the instances where a blurring of the line between illusion and reality takes place, a thematic element that touches both the individual and political sides of the play.

The entire first act, with its dominos and masks, establishes the context, which is supported throughout: for instance, by Westerhaus's "Or do you mean to say that nakedness does not lie, Gysar?", by the first encounter between Max and Seraphine, or by Julia's suggesting that she and Judith might go see Verdi's *A Masked Ball.*

On the individual level, the crucial question growing out of the masking motif is the identity of the real Aurelie. Is she the one she thinks she is for Falkenir, the idealized one in Doehl's mind, or the almost demonic one of Falkenir's fears and/or supposed wisdom? Falkenir's failure to recognize her, together with what must be taken to be a certain predisposition on her part, causes her to lose her identity, in effect, to lose touch with reality, to the point of referring to her naked portrait as being the true Aurelie. Just as Judith tells Max he is just a dream to her, so too Aurelie begins to see people as in a dream, in part because it is "more convenient and merrier" to do so.

This sort of escapism is also the dominant feature of Schnitzler's retrospective of Austrian society on the eve of World War I. The threat of war is not taken seriously. The Princess reads most of the newspaper, but, as she says, never the political pages, and she plans, in blissful ignorance, to spend the summer on her estate on the Russian-Polish border. Leinsdorf dismisses the threat of war and the usually clearsighted Elisabeth attributes it to "Stock market maneuvers." The one time it threatens to become the topic of discussion in Act One, between Arduin and Westerhaus, it is allowed to surface just long enough for each man to make two very short speeches before the conversation turns to Arduin's yacht and the possibility of Gysar's painting a picture for it on commission.

People continue playing their games, light or corrupt, as if everything were all right, all the way up to the outbreak of war on August 14. Only Westerhaus has some inkling of what lies ahead and is actively involved, though not in a positive manner. There is an overall sense of drift. Arduin has no destination in mind for his yacht's maiden voyage; later he adds that the voyage will be a "voyage into the unknown," an idea he repeats three more times and one hardly complimentary to Judith on the one hand, but reflective of Aurelie's actual voyage into madness on the other.

One possible counter to the sort of drifting depicted here is the idea of a "return," a homecoming, hinted at by the security-seeking Aurelie when, after having danced with Max, she goes up to Falkenir and says, "Well, this feels like a homecoming." When Falkenir, having finally come to his senses, offers her "security, shelter, and my name" as well as a home, his words are reminiscent of a similar declaration in *The Sisters, or Casanova in Spa*, where Casanova defines love as a "coming back," even if no person "could/Flatter himself that he's 'home' to another." But Falkenir's words are emptier than Casanova's, even if the latter is not the most reliable authority on lasting love, and they come too late. The damage has been done.

A significant outgrowth of the interplay between illusion and reality is the fairy-tale aura surrounding the action, especially in Acts One and Three. The first obvious element is Aurelie's having three suitors among whom she makes her choice, but it finds many echoes elsewhere: in Arduin's description of Aurelie's unexpected arrival at carnival time or in her appearance precisely at midnight, immediately after Ambros Doehl's saying that he and his two competitors are taking part in a fairy tale. The lover's test, another common fairy-tale motif, occurs twice, when Aurelie thinks Falkenir is testing her and when Falkenir thinks he has to pass tests before he can take his princess home. When Aurelie asks Ambros, on August 14, 1914, to serve as judge, he replies that the time for such games has passed—"no fairy-tale wind blows in this world any more."

Significant too, in this regard, is the exchange between Aurelie and Max near the end of Act One:

> AURELIE . . . . It was such a beautiful party.
>
> MAX Yes, that it was. A strange, a fairy-tale-like party.
>
> AURELIE Do you think so, Herr von Reisenberg? I wonder how those fairy tales which do not end with a wedding come out.
>
> MAX They all end with a wedding. It only takes a while sometimes to get to that point. And there are adventures to be gone through along the way.
>
> AURELIE Dangerous adventures.
>
> MAX Harmless ones too. And merry ones. But in the end, without fail, comes the wedding.
>
> AURELIE Or death.
>
> MAX A fairy-tale death, not such a bad thing, I imagine.

The principal association between Arduin and the fairy-tale element, beyond his wanting, like Harun al-Rashid, to pick a woman out of the crowd, is his "fairy-tale yacht." The vessel is first mentioned in Act One but gains importance in Act Three, when it docks off Gilleleije, an appropriate locale given its reputed qualities. The initial reference to it, in Fenz's listing of Seraphine's concert dates, immediately ascribes something magical to the place: "Gilleleije! What melody in that word." It turns out to be Ambros's one-time secret retreat, his "enchanted beach." It features exotic birds, a tropical climate and palm trees (in Denmark!), and "delicious aromatic air" as well as Hansen's daughter, Gilda, who strikes Max as "somewhat exotic too. . . .

like a water-sprite," an assessment confirmed by Fenz and by Hansen himself. Into this scene, too, reality breaks in, even if Hansen can avoid facing the obvious fact of his wife's disappearing with another man. On August 14, 1914, the fairy tale, together with the closely related Austrian-Viennese world comes to an abrupt end.

That the ending would not be a happy one could have been predicted from Max's conversation with Aurelie at the end of Act One, if not from the moment that the chosen suitor refuses the lady's hand. The "hero's"—Falkenir's—unsuccessful return rounds out the action: things do not work out, the damsel is not rescued. Arduin, who would have liked to have been Aurelie's hero at one time, sails off into the sunset in what is at best an avoidance of responsibility or duty, and *not* with the woman he had hoped for, the one whose name glimmers so brilliantly on the bow, and of whose death he is not aware. We are left with a slightly ludicrous, Pan-like Fenz trilling the Champagne Aria from *Don Giovanni* in preparation to chasing the adolescent Gilda, but clearly too late even for wishful thinking. Gilda, in the last words of the play, has already voiced the epitaph for the world it depicts: "Now it has disappeared completely—the magic ship. Now I can't see it at all anymore."

III

The Way to the Pond is distinguished by multiple thematic elements—war and peace, youth and age, love and sexuality, reason and passion. Far from being excess baggage for just one play, as some critics have maintained, these comprise the different and timeless realities faced by the characters. That is, *The Way to the Pond* achieves unity in presenting a number of *faits accomplis* (such as Leonilda's sexual awakening, the passage of time, or war) and then examining the characters' reaction to them. These realities arise from apparently divergent issues or themes. However, seen *in toto*, they simply represent an overview of the real world as perceived by Schnitzler on the basis of a lifetime of thought and work.

The Baron, who has the clearest vision of reality, serves as the center of reference throughout. He consistently attempts to put an orderly, rational interpretation on events, as when he debunks Thorn's notion of signs, and to establish his control whenever possible, as when he manipulates Konrad in order to keep Leonilda from Thorn. As *paterfamilias* he is informed by Anselma of Leonilda's excursions to the pond; as former Chancellor and military leader he is consulted by Konrad, Konrad's father and, eventually, by the Emperor; as friend he is entrusted by Thorn with the safekeeping of his "past." At the same time, Leonilda is at the center of the private theme, the importance of which can not be overstated, since all the other principal characters have to come to terms with her, and which is acknowledged in the title of the play. It is *her* passage to the pond which is most important and the prerequisite for both Konrad's and Thorn's subsequent visits.

Almost every detail concerning the pond emphasizes the preternatural, mysterious process that takes place there. It lies hidden in the woods and is accessible by only one small path or, according to Anselma, by none; it is known to few; and the gate in the garden wall leading to the path is small, secret, and overgrown. Little wonder, then, that the pond serves to blur reality for those characters susceptible, by age or disposition, to romanticizing perfectly normal but not readily definable phenomena. Thus, Anselma *sees* (and Schnitzler incorporates numerous references to vision into her dialogue with the Baron) Leonilda's pondside activities as resembling a ritual not "altogether Christian." In reality, she is simply seeing a young woman on the threshold of sexual maturity discovering her own body and its loveliness. Konrad's vision, too, is blurred by the pond. Leonilda has to point out to him the difference between a water sprite and a woman. It may be tempting to see a kind of surrealism here, but everything that occurs falls comfortably within the parameters of ordinary human life, even if it cannot be defined or quantified. Schnitzler includes the apparently otherworldly element in recognition, from his dual vantage point as sensitive artist and man of science, that some human passages lie beyond the ken of human understanding or reason, and may therefore be seen in terms of some preternatural experience common to all humanity. Leonilda's nudity emphasizes the essential, basic nature of her passage to mature womanhood. In short, beyond the surreal, the occult, the otherworldly, what we have here is basic psychological and, indeed, biological realism.

The focus of the play is on coming to terms with reality, and Leonilda, a hard-headed young woman, comes to know (intuitively or otherwise) that there is a time for preternatural connections and a time for living in the real world; hence, she refuses Konrad as a permanent mate. She knows that no mystic union has taken place; and even if she admits that their sexual encounter signifies that she and Konrad are married before God, that notion necessitates no consequent permanent tie in the real world.

Of all the characters, none is more consistently aware of reality than the Baron. He is the center of reason and order in the play. One of the characteristics that helps define him and contributes to making him credible (and not only a paragon of virtue) is the way in which he deals with the past. He wants to recollect it without bias, "and not be lawyer, plaintiff, judge," and he generally faces it rationally. He interrupts Ungnad's inflated honorifics regarding his father, for example, preferring to deal with his first visit to court in a matter-of-fact way. Likewise, he has no difficulty accepting the inexorable passage of time. When Konrad offers to call him "Uncle," he responds, "Good, as befits my gray hair," in contrast to Thorn, who insists that not all individuals are subject to time's law.

The Baron is an Age of Reason character, which may have at least contributed to Schnitzler's decision to set the action in the mid-eighteenth century. His enlightened religious views are evident from his comments regarding Leonilda's piety and his assessment of her pondside experience. He ascribes no special meaning to the block of stone and rejects Anselma's view that it may be an idol. Nevertheless, he wants to protect his daughter, not from anything out of the ordinary, but merely out of conventional fatherly concern, although he is just anxious enough to ask Anselma to help protect her innocence as long as possible.

In the treatment of the public theme, the Baron represents the voice of reason, experience and *Realpolitik*, in contrast to Konrad, who represents a Hotspur, a rash young man with a lot to learn—in a variety of areas. He is realistic in his assessment of the Emperor and of what makes a ruler great, as well as in his understanding of what causes a chancellor to grow alienated from his emperor or a friend from a friend. The Baron's status is unmistakable. Not only was his house "the very center of the world" in the past, but at the time the play takes place, as Konrad acknowledges, he is the only one strong enough to save the country and the Emperor.

The Baron is always able to distinguish the fate that is inescapable from the fate that human beings appeal to in place of rational argument or as a convenient means of advancing their causes. When Konrad, speaking in favor of conquest, introduces God's will into the discussion, the Baron replies, "You'll fast reach the end of all questions thus." He knows from experience that military solutions are temporary. A lover of peace who knows that invading the neighboring country would have amounted to "a sneak attack, and theft," he knows too that the neighbor has been turned into an enemy by local militarists who manipulated the Emperor.

The Baron's principal responsibility, as he sees it, is to avoid war and save lives if at all possible, even at the risk of appearing cowardly—a concern of Konrad's—especially since he views the threatening conflict as one desired only by hotheads willing to pay for fame with streams of other people's blood. Unlike Konrad, he is not ready to assume that war is unavoidable. His reference to his decision to serve the Emperor emphasizes the element of free will. He feels that a talk with the Marchese may change some circumstances which appear fated to Konrad. It comes at the conclusion of the Baron's absolute rejection of Konrad's determinism in the brilliant "What do you call preordained?" speech that represents the principal statement of free will and human responsibility in the play.

When he returns from the capital after meeting with the Marchese and the Emperor, he raises no objection to Konrad's provocative remark about begging for peace and offers a realistic assessment in response to the younger man's skepticism regarding the establishment of "A realm of love and goodness in this world": "Of love—hardly. . . . Of goodness?—No. . . . And forever, of all things? Yesterday,/Today, and tomorrow is all the term/That I perceive to have been given us." After the war breaks out, the Baron retains his reason and his sense of right and wrong; but, together with all the other characters, he must face and accept a new reality. No matter his earlier position regarding the war, it has arrived, and who fired the first shot matters little, if at all.

The Baron displays the same pattern of behavior in the context of the private theme. When Thorn asks for Leonilda's hand, a request both unreasonable and offensive to the Baron's sense of responsibility, he characteristically takes the rational approach. Speaking both as a father and as a friend, he appeals to Thorn on the basis of their common experiences and their "vanished youth." At the same time, he gives clear expression to his sense of propriety. When the desperate Thorn threatens to make a mockery of the marriage vows by offering to stay with Leonilda for a limited period, he rejects the blasphemous oath out of hand. He appears to act evenhandedly when he asks Thorn for time to think over the proposal, but is only stalling until he can figure out something. He is resolved: "It may not be.—It must not be." He is in complete control, as he is again, if not to the extent he may wish, when he recognizes the solution to his problem in Konrad's timely return from the capital. The Baron has just seen Leonilda on her way to the pond. Now he need only get Konrad there.

Although he is at first simply interested in keeping Konrad away from Leonilda and hence denies the existence of any pond, the idea of using him as a counter to Thorn crystallizes in his mind a moment later. He turns to go, hesitates, and then tells Konrad:

> Look here, it just occurred to me—the pond,
> I do have an idea where you played ball
> Back then. Not here in the park—in the wood,
> There lies the pond you mean.

Still, when Konrad asks the way to the pond, the Baron says he would not tell even if he knew because it is said to be bewitched. Of course, the Baron *does* know where it is; and he certainly does not believe it to be bewitched. He is simply trying to tempt Konrad into going there. He presses his case in his next speech by raising the element of fear, which is sure to have the desired effect on the young hothead.

When the Baron returns after two nights' absence, he gathers in a glance what transpired and welcomes the young people's having found each other "in good time," adding, in terms of conventional order and a father's expectations, "I'll not withold my blessing long." Anselma, who is much more aware than her brother of the impossibility of protecting someone, responds that it may not strike them as necessary. The Baron's strategy has worked, but not in the way or to the extent he had hoped. The war and his daughter's independence seem to break out at about the same time. He needs to deal with both and, after overcoming some difficulties born of his concern for Leonilda, does so reasonably and gracefully. That is to say, reasonable individuals act according to the inescapable realities set before them by what they may designate as "fate" or "destiny" but which are actually a matter of biology, psychology, or pure chance.

On the public level, we have the Baron's unquestioning acceptance of the future emperor chosen for him by fate, representing the acceptance of what can not be changed anyway. Towards the end of the play, he resolves to take the field again, the Chancellorship having become a "useless office," and he faces the new political-military reality: "What choice remains?/Even senseless deeds are worthier now/Than words lacking power, however wise." On the private side, the Baron comes to realize that he can not determine other people's wishes. His sense of order and propriety and his reasonable view that the times are dangerous and unpredictable make him eager to see Leonilda and Konrad married. But he discovers that what *he* wants is not necessarily what the young people want. He has to accept that no one can protect another person in the long run (something Anselma, like Seraphine, already knows). Indeed, he keeps trying to protect Leonilda until he comes to terms with reality and demonstrates that he has understood and accepted his daughter, and has learned that "Leonilda was meant/To be not prize or booty but a gift,/To the worthiest freely given."

As noted earlier, Leonilda is the focus of the private theme in the play. It is *her* path to the pond which is the most important, and it is with the changes in her that the other characters must become reconciled. While her new maturity is presented primarily in terms of her changing views of and relationships to Thorn and Konrad, it is already hinted at when the rumors of war interrupt her usual games with her playmates.

When she is at the pond, Leonilda's eyes are (according to Anselma) sightless and vacant. This accords with her turning inward, her getting in touch with her unfolding womanhood, in a healthy, normal fashion, as opposed to Ungnad, who does very little in a healthy fashion but whose eyes are similarly described. She shows some traces of Ungnad too when she insists, to her protective father's alarm, that Thorn is not just a memory but actually lives in her, unchanged from what he was ten years earlier and beyond the grasp of time.

Leonilda's attitude illustrates Schnitzler's view that extreme subjectivity, or solipsism, is a sign of immaturity, of being unwilling or not yet able to face reality. Indeed, the point of Thorn's neglecting to tell her that he and Alberta are expecting a child is that he sees Leonilda still as a child herself, not one with whom one shares such information. However, although Leonilda has not been to the pond with Konrad yet, she *has* been there. Having set foot on her symbolic path, in the midst of her adolescent flirtation with her older, former hero, she mistakes him for a possible agent of her achieving mature womanhood. By Act Four she has come to know better.

During her second encounter with Thorn, in Act Three, Leonilda ignores the real world of adult responsibilities. At this point, she thinks everything can be controlled by will power. Her attempt to win Thorn for herself, in spite of everything he tells her about his feelings and obligations, shows her at her most self-centered and negative. The eventual result of her frivolous behavior—and it is an aspect of reality that immature people (and some not so immature) act frivolously at times—is tragedy for the now smitten Thorn. In her irresponsible temptation of Thorn, Leonilda acts in a manner analogous to Konrad's war-party views and tactics.

By Act Four, however, Leonilda has become a mature woman, which is clearly demonstrable in the way she handles Konrad and, later, Thorn. Konrad has misread the Baron's purpose as being purely political. Thinking along conventional male lines, he considers himself the winner of the Baron's game in having "had" Leonilda, a double misconception on his part. It turns out that his identity was of no consequence—she awaited "Him who came"—and that even if he had the "sprite," he did not have the woman.

Konrad's insecurity and his urge to exclusive possession, traits not unknown in young men, lead him to demand of Leonilda a pledge that no other man had ever seen her step out of the pond at night; she knows what he means of course, and states his real concern, "Or took me, as you did," and goes on, in the face of his hot-blooded response, to declare her independence of him. She may have given herself to Konrad, but she has not made him her lord. She knows the difference between sexual awakening and a mature committed relationship. By the end of the play, Konrad recognizes that Leonilda will grant him no power over her and that he has won nothing, and he accepts her decision to pursue an independent path. His "You have spoken. I must accept your word" shows a healthy difference between him and Thorn.

When the poet returns to claim Leonilda she tells him at once how things stand by telling him he is welcome as a friend. In the face of his negative reaction, she shows she has learned that friendship is a bond both purer and of longer duration than the other kind. She knows her relationship with Konrad will end soon and assures Thorn, "What you are to me, will be forever." She asks him to requite her feeling, demonstrates her understanding that her earlier attraction to him was confused, and states succinctly the difference between them: "You're still who you were. I no longer am."

In the scene immediately following she makes clear that she will not have Konrad either. She takes her father's suggestion that she marry Konrad as a jest, and asserts her emancipated will: "I do not wish/To be married so soon, no matter to whom." The play's ultimate reality, Leonilda's being in control of her own life and person, is emphasized by her having the last word: to Anselma's suggestion that she may be the victor's prize and to her father's hint that she would soon belong to someone, not as a prize, but as a gift of herself freely given, she adds, "And/As a gift, free also to keep herself."

It comes as no surprise that in a play focusing on reality Schnitzler should make use of one of his favorite topics, the confusion between reality and illusion, here embodied in the characters and interaction of Sylvester Thorn and Ungnad, whom the former recognizes as his "own distorted self" early on. Thorn displays a number of traits which appear in a more extreme form in the Secretary. His calling his diary not a record of his youth but youth itself blurs the distinction between the word and reality. Not unlike Ungnad in this regard, Thorn thinks he can destroy the past by burning the words. Anselma recognizes Thorn's compulsiveness and realizes that even after the diary is burned she and her brother will rise for him only as ghosts. The Baron's reply, "For him, yes. But we know that we exist," shows him once again to be a rationalist, as opposed to Ungnad, who happens to enter immediately after the Baron's remark.

In his extreme subjectivity, Ungnad goes well beyond Thorn:

If I shut my eyes, the light goes out. No
Flower is fragrant if I hold my breath.
Should I slumber, the whole world sinks in sleep.
And when I die, the world will die with me.
And Herr Sylvester Thorn dissolves to nothing
When I turn my face from him.

Thorn's "And you reveal all this to me, who does/Not exist?" threatens Ungnad's world view—"Don't try to confound with words/What needs must be conceived beyond all words." Thorn, a believer in the power of words (and here, of reason as well), recognizes the nature of Ungnad's fear and focuses immediately on the Secretary's "faith" ("You, I, and God") which Ungnad, in turn, insists on seeing as one, predicting prophetically, "For take but one from these three/And. . . none will remain": when Thorn drowns, Ungnad's world falls apart. Even the mad solipsist who thinks he can shape reality to suit his fancy whenever he wishes has to learn that there are things beyond his control.

However, Ungnad's function in the play is far more than to serve as a distortion of Thorn. He also represents the tendency of *all* the other principal characters to see reality in terms of their own subjective pictures, as Leonilda, for example, views Thorn early on, or as the Baron views the supposed bond between Leonilda and Konrad. His justification for making no effort to stop Thorn's suicide—"Two of us on earth?/He or I! It had to be, I felt it/From the very first moment I saw him"—is almost identical to the way Konrad feels about the enemy officer at the border. In his madness, he insists (like Thorn), that everything will stay as it was before, but it doesn't, as he soon learns; and he is forced to acknowledge, in one of the few truly humorous passages in the play, "I'm going mad."

When Ungnad reports witnessing Thorn's suicide, the Baron's incredulous "You let it happen?" speaks volumes for his (and Schnitzler's) view of free will and responsibility. It also focuses on an aspect of reality looming over everyone's concerns in *The Way to the Pond*, the inescapability of individual guilt.

The Baron and Leonilda both see the light eventually, but he is guilty of meddling in people's lives to the detriment not only of those people but of the nation as well, and she is at least partially responsible for Thorn's death. The Baron's attempt to excuse his daughter from any guilt may be understandable but it will not stand up under scrutiny, as Anselma points out when she reminds him of his earlier dictum. Anselma remains guiltless of meddling, but only because the Baron and Leonilda resist her attempts to marry her off, so to speak.

Konrad, or the attitude he represents, is at least partially responsible for the war, as is the Emperor. He is also guilty in a sense for acting counter to his better nature. He acknowledges the artificiality of borders and the humanity of his association with his counterpart on the other side but he insists on seeing both neighboring country and officer as the enemy.

Thorn may not be responsible for Alberta's and the child's death, but he is certainly guilty of planning to abandon them. He is also answerable for his folly in allowing himself to be misled by Leonilda and in refusing to accept either his age or the reality of Leonilda's having grown away from him. In short, even the best motives—fatherly concern, youthful enthusiasm, patriotism, fear of old age—may, with a slight change in perspective, appear as self-serving, foolish, or dangerous. In the real world, where free will is the determinant in most human affairs, they certainly do not guarantee freedom from guilt. In the end, everyone is responsible.

—*G.J. Weinberger*

ARIADNE PRESS

TRANSLATION SERIES:

February Shadows
By Elisabeth Reichart
Translated by Donna L. Hoffmeister
Afterword by Christa Wolf

Night Over Vienna
By Lili Körber
Translated by Viktoria Hertling
and Kay M. Stone. Commentary
by Viktoria Hertling

The Cool Million
By Erich Wolfgang Skwara
Translated by Harvey I. Dunkle
Preface by Martin Walser
Afterword by Richard Exner

Buried in the Sands of Time
Poetry by Janko Ferk
English/German/Slovenian
English Translation
by Herbert Kuhner

Puntigam or The Art of Forgetting
By Gerald Szyszkowitz
Translated by Adrian Del Caro
Preface by Simon Wiesenthal
Afterword by Jürgen Koppensteiner

Negatives of My Father
By Peter Henisch
Translated and with an Afterword
by Anne C. Ulmer

On the Other Side
By Gerald Szyszkowitz
Translated by Todd C. Hanlin
Afterword by Jürgen Koppensteiner

I Want to Speak
The Tragedy and Banality
of Survival in
Terezin and Auschwitz
By Margareta Glas-Larsson
Edited and with a Commentary
by Gerhard Botz
Translated by Lowell A. Bangerter

The Works of Solitude
By György Sebestyén
Translated and with an
Afterword by
Michael Mitchell

Remembering Gardens
By Kurt Klinger
Translated by Harvey I. Dunkle

Deserter
By Anton Fuchs
Translated and with an Afterword
by Todd C. Hanlin

From Here to There
By Peter Rosei
Translated and with an Afterword
by Kathleen Thorpe

The Angel of the West Window
By Gustav Meyrink
Translated by Michael Mitchell

Relationships
An Anthology of Contemporary
Austrian Literature
Selected and with an Introduction
by Adolf Opel

STUDIES IN AUSTRIAN LITERATURE, CULTURE AND THOUGHT

Major Figures of
Modern Austrian Literature
Edited by
Donald G. Daviau

Major Figures of
Turn-of-the-Century
Austrian Literature
Edited by Donald G. Daviau

Austrian Writers and the
Anschluss: Understanding the
Past—Overcoming the Past
Edited by Donald G. Daviau

Introducing Austria
A Short History
By Lonnie Johnson

Austrian Foreign Policy
Yearbook
Report of the Austrian Federal
Ministry for Foreign Affairs
for the Year 1990

The Verbal and Visual Art of
Alfred Kubin
By Phillip H. Rhein

Arthur Schnitzler and Politics
By Adrian Clive Roberts

Austria in the Thirties
Culture and Politics
Edited by Kenneth Segar
and John Warren

Stefan Zweig:
An International Bibliography
By Randolf J. Klawiter

"What People Call Pessimism":
Sigmund Freud, Arthur Schnitzler
and Nineteenth-Century
Controversy at the University
of Vienna Medical School
By Mark Luprecht

Quietude and Quest
Protagonists and Antagonists in
the Theater, on and off Stage
As seen through the Eyes of
Leon Askin
Leon Askin and C. Melvin Davidson

Coexistent Contradictions
Joseph Roth in Retrospect
Edited by
Helen Chambers

Kafka and Language
In the Stream of
Thoughts and Life
By G. von Natzmer Cooper

DEMCO